TOWARD A
TENDERER HUMANITY
AND A
NOBLER WOMANHOOD

TOWARD A TENDERER HUMANITY AND A NOBLER WOMANHOOD

*African American Women's Clubs
in Turn-of-the-Century Chicago*

ANNE MEIS KNUPFER

NEW YORK UNIVERSITY PRESS

NEW YORK AND LONDON

NEW YORK UNIVERSITY PRESS
New York and London

Library of Congress Cataloging-in-Publication Data
Knupfer, Anne Meis, 1951–
Toward a tenderer humanity and a nobler womanhood : African
American women's clubs in turn-of-the-century Chicago / Anne Meis
Knupfer.
p.   cm.
Includes bibliographical references (p.   ) and index.
ISBN 0-8147-4671-3 (cloth) : alk. paper).—ISBN 0-8147-4691-8
(pbk. : alk. paper)
1. Afro-American women—Illinois—Chicago—Societies and clubs.
2. Chicago (Ill.)—Social conditions.   3. Chicago (Ill.)—Social
life and customs.   1. Title.
F548.9.N4K58   1996
977.3'1100496073—dc20   96-25259
                                        CIP

New York University Press books are printed on acid-free paper,
and their binding materials are chosen for strength and durability.

Manufactured in the United States of America

10 9 8 7 6 5 4 3 2 1

To my grandparents, Alfonsus and Marcelinda Meis,
who taught me their language and culture,

and to my son, Franz Paul Knupfer

CONTENTS

All illustrations appear as a group after p. 84.

ACKNOWLEDGMENTS

THIS BOOK WOULD NOT HAVE BEEN COMPLETED WITH-out the assistance and friendship of many. I would like to thank the Spencer Foundation in Chicago for its financial support and the University of Memphis for a Faculty Research Grant and a one-year leave of absence. The grants provided me with the graduate assistance of Diane Taylor and Wei Ping, to whom I also wish to express my gratitude. In addition, I would like to thank the Educational Studies Department of Purdue University, with which I have been affiliated this past year, for their support.

The librarians and archivists at the University of Chicago, the Chicago Historical Society, the Harold Washington Library, National Louis University, the Evanston Historical Society, the Newberry Library, and the University of Illinois at Chicago were tremendously helpful in locating primary materials for the book. I would especially like to thank Mary Ann Bamberger of the University of Illinois at Chicago and Michael

Flug of the Carter Woodson Regional Library Branch of the Harold Washington Library. I also wish to thank the staff of the Microfiche Collection at Northwestern University for responding to my numerous requests for microfilms and copies. The Inter-Library Loan Department of the University of Memphis was helpful in providing secondary materials.

On another professional level, I wish to thank colleagues who have mentored and encouraged me, not only with this book but with other academic endeavors. To David Bills of the University of Iowa I owe my introduction to and study of Max Weber, as well as a further grounding in sociological theory. To Robert Kleinsasser, a former colleague now at the University of Queensland, who has continued our academic conversations through E-mail, thanks for your intellectual questions and musings. How I value your friendship and wish you were not so many thousands of miles away! To former colleague Anne Hassenflaug, your camaraderie and humor was much appreciated, especially when I was so far away from home and family. And to William Asher of Purdue, who constantly encouraged me during the last leg of the book editing, your positive words were much appreciated.

Working with the New York University Press editors has been a pleasure. I would like to especially thank Jennifer Hammer, Associate Editor; Despina Papazoglou Gimbel, Managing Editor; and the copy editors for their proficiency, cooperation, and professionalism.

Personally, I would like to thank several friends, including Rebecca Wasson and Sherman Perkins, for steadfastly engaging me with their community and intellectual perspectives. I am, however, most grateful to these family members: Sis Knupfer, thanks for keeping your door open. But even more, thanks for your humanity, your humor, and your sense of wonder about this world. And to my son, Franz, who accompanied me on many Chicago sojourns, bless you as you continue to challenge the boundaries that transgress your and our humanity.

TOWARD A
TENDERER HUMANITY
AND A
NOBLER WOMANHOOD

INTRODUCTION

ORIGINALLY I WAS GOING TO WRITE A BOOK ABOUT mothers' clubs in Chicago, comparing those of African American, native-born white, Jewish, and Italian women. Although I was able to locate many historical materials on native-born white mothers' clubs, there were few sources on African American mothers' clubs or the kindergartens with which most clubs were affiliated. However, when I turned to two Chicago African American newspapers published during the Progressive Era, the *Chicago Defender* and the *Broad Ax,* I found materials not only on kindergartens and mothers' clubs, but also about a multitude of women's clubs—more than 150. These clubs were involved not only in kindergarten and mothering, but also in suffrage, antilynching laws, literary contests, political debates, embroidery, sewing, municipal reform, philosophy, youth activities, child welfare, care for the elderly, drama study, safe lodging for working women, health care, orphanages, home life, and rotating economic credit.

In the tradition of Dewey and other Progressive educators, I have always held to a broad definition of education, looking to nonformal community institutions as learning sites that hold particular promise and value for study. This is especially true for the African American communities in Chicago from 1890 to 1920. Club women made tremendous contributions to their communities, contributions that have yet to be fully documented, chronicled, and analyzed. Such contributions included the founding and sustenance of nonformal community facilities, such as kindergartens, day nurseries, reading rooms, employment agencies, homes for the elderly and infirm, homes for working girls, youth clubs, settlements, and summer outings and camps for children. Working in conjunction with local churches, businesses, and urban chapters of national organizations, African American women participated in numerous educational and social uplift activities. Presentations through forums, debates, discussions, oratories, addresses, and lyceums not only gave voice to the club women's perspectives on community concerns, but also socialized young girls into a political and social consciousness. Through fund-raising activities as various as bazaars, raffles, picnics, dances, theater productions, and musical concerts, club women financially supported the institutions they created and provided in-kind gifts and moneys to poorer African Americans in Chicago. Furthermore, such occasions provided rich contexts for celebrating African American traditions and culture.

This is not to suggest that there was only one African American community in Chicago. There were *many* of them, in the neighborhoods of Woodlawn, Englewood, Hyde Park, Evanston, Morgan Park, and the Black Belt. These communities were stratified according to social class, educational attainment, and type of employment. Like many other cities, Chicago had its own African American "Elite 400," who attended exclusive social clubs, charity balls, dances, and promenades. Although this side of history is not always included in the club scholarship, it is critical to fully understanding the lives and deeds of the club women. For this reason, a social class stratification model, which examines notions of class, status, and prestige, is used. Such a model relies heavily on Weber's concepts of class, party, and status, as well as on his concern with multidimensionality.

However, social stratification is only one part of the history. A multi-layered analysis is necessary to portray the complexity and richness of the African American women's clubs. Therefore, I draw also from sociological, historical, and anthropological frameworks that examine the cultural expressions and practices of the women's clubs, particularly as they were grounded in community ways of knowing and doing. The central questions were these: What was culturally unique about African American women's clubs? How were they different from other ethnic women's clubs? The answers to these questions entailed a thorough examination of the economic, social, political, and cultural aspects of the many African American communities and their social institutions in Chicago. What I found was a web of various issues, agendas, practices, and ideologies not only within the communities, but within the women's clubs as well.

In addition to social stratification and an examination of a community ethos, the analysis relies upon feminist scholarship, particularly from an African American female perspective. In particular, I am partial to historical and sociological scholarship that insists on the interlocking of race, class, and gender. The historical work of club scholars Darlene Clark Hine, Deborah Gray White, Dorothy Salem, and many others come readily to mind. In terms of sociological studies, those by Bonnie Thornton Dill, Patricia Hill Collins, and Cheryl Townsend Gilkes have continually reminded me of how critical it is to ground scholarly interpretations in the daily experiences of people's lives.

I did not limit my study to the contemporary voices of feminist scholarship. Perhaps most importantly, I have drawn from the African American club women themselves. Indeed, many club women wrote their views on female suffrage, the importance of home life, motherhood, community uplift, and race progress in African American magazines, journals, and newspapers. Many delivered addresses and speeches, wrote editorials and letters, and kept club records. Such documentation has provided another layer of historical sources, with the momentous challenge of teasing out the rhetoric and ideology from the actual practices and activities of the club women. (This was especially problematic given the lack of archival materials on African American club women in Chicago.) Each issue revealed its own complexity, whether it was deliberating on an alderman candidate, discussing the merits of industrial education, or inspecting the vice areas in Chicago's Black Belt. Often there was no single view; when there was agreement, the reasons might be various. I discuss more fully below the three interlocking frameworks of social class stratification, community emics, and feminist scholarship.

A Weberian stratification model moves beyond that of Marx, in that social class and position are not simply related to an economic framework. Rather, it fleshes out social class positioning to include the concepts of privilege, status, and prestige, particularly in terms of group legitimacy. Weber found status groups particularly worthy of study, because they reflected practices, expressions, and lifestyles of particular social classes. His concept of parties or power groups is particularly useful for understanding the patterns of leadership in the African American communities, especially as they were expressed in the various institutions of church, clubs, and political organizations. These three interrelated concepts of class, status, and parties provide us with an analysis that is multidimensional and attempts to arrive at an understanding of the subjective meanings of individuals involved.[1]

A Weberian framework is critical for examining the African American women's clubs. As will become evident throughout the book, there were many types of African American women's clubs in Chicago. Although social uplift activities were expected and embedded in many of the clubs' functions, most African American club women were of middle- or upper-class status. Status was measured in various ways. For example, certain clubs reserved membership for those from the first African American families in Chicago. Some clubs proudly described themselves as "elite" and "exclusive." Matrimony clubs selected members from prominent families, thus ensuring that one's social class position would not be compromised in the future.

However, this framework, if used alone, would grossly distort the history of African American communities. Despite social class differences, African Americans in Chicago were united through the historical and persistent practices of racism. There were also cultural expressions that crossed over social class lines, uniting African American communities throughout Chicago. Such unity was critical in political campaigns, in advocating for antidiscriminatory legislation, in creating community facilities, and in fund-raising efforts. A model is needed, then, that also examines cultural and community practices, to provide an emic perspective. To arrive at such an understanding, I referred to African American newspapers, journals, magazines, addresses, and speeches as primary sources. In particular, the women's, church, and society columns of the Chicago newspapers contained contextually rich information on the women's clubs. Editorials and letters written for the newspapers reflected diverse perspectives on political, social, economic, and even moral issues. These voices represented various organizations within the Chicago communities: churches, settlements, women's and men's clubs, and local chapters of national organizations, such as the National Association for the Advancement of Colored People (NAACP) or the National Urban League.

In these multiple sources I found many cultural practices and expressions that were unique to the African American communities in Chicago. For example, lyceums for the youths continued the literate and oral traditions of oratory, elocution, and dramatic renditions that dated back to the all-day church meetings during slavery. African American jubilee quartets, choirs, and orchestras performed at charity balls and other fund-raising events. Paul Laurence Dunbar's poetry and Frederick Douglass's addresses were frequently read and recited at the club meetings. Certain annual celebrations, such as Emancipation Day on the first of January, Mothers' Day, and Frederick Douglass's and Abraham Lincoln's birthdays, held particular cultural significance for African Americans. In the tradition of "other mothering," club women set up kindergartens, nurseries, and homes for the aged. At their club meetings they gave testimonials and recitations and enjoyed spirituals and popular African American songs on the victrola. Even fund-raising efforts by the club women relied on the traditional handiwork of quilting, knitting, and embroidery. Such richness was documented and examined within these multiple conceptual frameworks.

Even economic matters became subject to multiple interpretations. For example, a Marxist analysis would interpret the elaborate evening gowns of club women or their expensive prizes in whist contests as examples of cultural capital. However, there are other interpretations to consider. First, supporting local dressmakers and hairdressers kept money circulating in the African American communities, an issue that received as much attention then as it does today. One could argue that a club woman was not simply buying a dress. Rather, she was helping to keep food on the table, to pay the rent, and to keep a dressmaker in business. Embedded in such business transactions, then, were social and community transactions. Second, these small businesses allowed women a livelihood, in addition to giving them an opportunity to work in their homes, where they could care for their children. Employment opportunities for African American women were severely restricted, most of them working as domestic servants, laundry workers, and cooks. Third, the aesthetic and technical skills of dressmakers, hairdressers, milliners, and beauty culturists deserve acknowledgment. Many of the club women's dresses were intricately designed and embellished with imported Irish lace and crocheted collars. Several African American milliner shops, located on State Street—the fashion hub of Chicago—were so renowned that a number of wealthy white women patronized them.

The third and last framework, that of feminist scholarship, attempts to portray the perspective of the club women and of African American female scholars. As mentioned, I have relied mostly upon scholarship that is grounded in the daily experiences of community members, as well as that which acknowledges how race, class, and gender are intricately connected. However, I would add a fourth dimension, that of regionalism, which was particularly significant because of the migration of Southern African Americans to Chicago. The club women's views ranged from traditional, even conservative at times, to what we might consider progressive and visionary. For example, some women were disinterested in the vote; some thought that women shouldn't meddle in what was a man's affair. Others protested and marched for it. These multiple views are presented in the book, as they portray the complex and rich textures of club life and community uplift.

In chapter 1 the discourses, ideologies, motifs, and images of the club women are examined. I argue that the club women conjoined the dominant ideologies of true womanhood, progressive maternalism, the Republican motherhood, and municipal housekeeping to their own culturally veritable beliefs. Although motherhood and home life were twin concerns of the women's club movement in general, the roles, practices, and images of African American women were quintessentially singular. Historically denied the opportunity of expressing their motherhood in culturally specific ways, the club women articulated their own vision—rooted in the community mores of "other mothering," a deep-seated Christianity, and an admixture of Du Boisian and Washingtonian tenets. Respectability, tucked within the prevailing concerns of race advancement and progress, assumed gendered and classed forms as club women constructed various layers of sisterhood and allegiances to poorer women while also maintaining class distinctions. Such positions were not contradictory. Rather, they pointed to a resilience in the club women's rhetoric, demonstrated by adapting their language to the multiple audiences of African American men, white club women, and poorer African American women.

Chapter 2 traces the histories of the various African American communities in Chicago, in particular examining class stratification through shifting residential patterns, church and club life, and the formation of Chicago's Black Belt. As Chicago's African American population increased during the 1890s, tensions between the African American elite and the middle class emerged, although as members of the "Elite 400," they mutually participated in charity events. Proceedings from their charity balls, dances, whist tournaments, and theater productions were collected for the newly created settlements, missions, kindergartens, day nurseries, and other facilities. Located primarily in the Black Belt, these institutions provided lodging, employment referrals, day care, manual and industrial training, and health services to the increasing number of Southern migrants. Again, social distinctions and concerns were intertwined, as the club women sustained these community institutions through exclusive philanthropic events.

The political activities of the club women are detailed in chapter 3. Because suffrage was one of the primary concerns, much of the discussion is devoted to the club women's involvement in political campaigns, voter registration, and suffrage debates and parades. The club women played a decidedly key role in the election of the first African American alderman in Chicago, Oscar de Priest. Nonetheless, I conclude that their potential for political leadership was limited, because it was primarily circumscribed around their traditional female roles as guardians of children and the family. This is not to suggest that the club women did not protest discrimination in employment or work toward antilynching legislation and legal redress. There are numerous examples of letter-writing campaigns, editorials, forums, and discussions on these matters. However, the club women's influence in these arenas was tenuous; they wielded little power in the larger business and political world.

Four social welfare institutions or "other homes" created and sustained by the African American women's clubs are examined in chapter 4: the Louise Juvenile Home and school for dependent boys; the Amanda Smith Home and school for dependent girls; the Phyllis Wheatley Home for young working girls; and the Home for the Aged and Infirm Colored People. The financial and administrative autonomy of the first two homes, and later schools, was complicated by their affiliation with the Cook County Juvenile Court. Facilities for African American dependent and delinquent children were limited, so the demands placed upon these two homes often exceeded their capacities. But the founders, Elizabeth McDonald and Amanda Smith, informed by their respective rescue and mission work, turned no children away. Although the club women assisted through fund-raising, donating clothing and Christmas gifts, and visiting the children, their efforts were more directed toward the Phyllis Wheatley Home and the Old Folks' Home (an alternative name for the Home for the Aged and Infirm Colored People). The clubs' networking and collaborative fund-raising activities ensured the latter two homes' financial security. The homes' annual reports indicated the deep involvement of many of the women's clubs, through in-kind gifts of food and clothing, contributions to the coal fund, monetary donations, and providing "good cheer" or counsel to the elderly and to the young working girls. Truly, the club women considered these community institutions, whereas the homes for dependent children, because of their court entanglements, were less so.

Five African American settlements and their programs for young children, youths, and working women are discussed in chapter 5. The chapter begins with an examination of the mainstream social settlement workers' ideologies as compared to African Americans' beliefs and practices. Although there were points of convergence, there were three essential differences. First, white settlement workers focused more on racialized differences between immigrants and African Americans, whereas African American reformers cited class and regional disparities, especially among African Americans. Second, white workers formulated African Americans' "maladjustment" to urban life as an inability to "assimilate"; conversely, African Americans framed the issues as ones of segregation, discrimination, and difficult urban conditions. Third, unlike white reformers who viewed African Americans as uprooted and disconnected from their traditions and customs, African American social workers and reformers spoke of the loss of dignity and family life during slavery.

Furthermore, many of the African American settlement workers discussed how their practices were informed by a deep-seated Christian faith. Their religious expressions were reflected in the range of social service institutions created within the African American communities: church missions, social centers, and settlements, which were often less secular than nondenominational. The settlement founders and workers especially nurtured these church affiliations, although not specific denominations, thereby creating collaborative webs of community institutions and support.

The club women's involvement was critical in the sustenance of the settlements. They supervised kindergartens and day nurseries; they taught domestic classes in sewing, crocheting, and embroidery; and they chaperoned dance clubs for youths. The various settlement activities were not merely social or educative but also had economic value. Sewing classes, according to Clotee Scott, provided another employment alternative to women, besides domestic and laundry work. Day nurseries and kindergartens provided child care for women who previously may have had to leave the younger children in the care of an older sibling. Employment referral agencies were organized to assist women in procuring respectable employment.

Chapter 6 begins with a discussion of the historical antecedents of the African American literary clubs: the literary societies, the lyceums, and the chautauqua movement. As pictured in the novels of Frances Ellen Watkins Harper and Pauline Elizabeth Hopkins, African American women formed literary societies and circles in which they spoke on political and social issues while developing their elocution and literary skills. The "literature" of the former societies, and of the Chicago literary clubs, embraced many topics and genres, as the written word was merged with the spoken, and social and political uplift with literary discussion. The African American female literary clubs in Chicago are examined alongside those of white women, reflecting how, once again, African American women persisted in the dual purpose of self-improvement and community uplift. To illustrate, the club women sponsored dramatic productions, musicals, and literary contests, which provided educative experiences and raised much-needed moneys for the poor. These twin roles were enacted through the church lyceums as well. Women not only spoke before the audiences on the "female" issues of children's welfare, probation work, and home life, but also formed lyceums for youths. Through participation in essay contests, debates, and oratory, the young were socialized into community forms of knowledge and activism and provided with "wholesome" forms of entertainment.

Whist clubs, dancing clubs, and matrimony clubs—which were often considered frivolous and self-indulgent—are explored in chapter 7. On the surface they seemed to be superficial because such clubs were primarily engaged in whist, progressive whist, and lawn tennis; six-course luncheons; masquerades; and dancing parties. Yet such activities were not always self-serving. Over teas and extravaganzas, charity cases were discussed and resolved; money for the poor was often collected during whist tournaments. Furthermore, there were multiple economic tiers embedded in these social extravaganzas. Such philanthropic events benefited both the poor and the many women engaged in the service businesses of dressmaking, millinery work, beauty culture, and chiropody who relied upon the club women's patronage.

As the following chapters document, the club women were instrumental in founding and sustaining a multitude of social welfare institutions. Their volunteer efforts in the Second Ward's political campaigns were crucial in terms of voter registration, coalition building, and the election of the first African American alderman. Through their clubs they not only engaged in literary, musical, and educational activities, but also sponsored various fund-raisers to support the community institutions they created. As Fannie Barrier Williams testified, the African American women of Chicago displayed a "passion" for clubs that promoted refinement as well as social uplift.[2] True to the motto of the National Association of Colored Women (NACW), the Chicago club women "lifted" others while they, indeed, "climbed."

ONE

AFRICAN AMERICAN
CLUB WOMEN'S IDEOLOGIES
AND DISCOURSES

THE AFRICAN AMERICAN CLUB WOMEN'S MOVEMENT evoked multiple ideologies, discourses, motifs, and images of womanhood, motherhood, and home life. Club members conjoined the dominant ideologies of the cult of true womanhood, progressive maternalism, the Republican motherhood, and municipal housekeeping with culturally specific ones: African American Christianity, Booker T. Washington's industrial education, and W. E. B. Du Bois's model of "talented tenth" leadership.[1] For example, the club women's allegiances to Booker T. Washington and W. E. B. Du Bois were not neatly cleaved, as they wedded self-help strategies to political protest.[2] Likewise, in promoting female suffrage, the African American club women not only espoused the tenets of the Republican motherhood, progressive maternalism, and municipal housekeeping but also emphasized their traditional community roles as "other mothers" and caretakers.[3] Such admixtures pointed to the complex ways in which African American club women mediated various ideologies and discourses to address the specific needs of their communities.

During the late nineteenth and early twentieth centuries, African American men and women were concerned with documenting race progress, in part through the exemplary lives of their leaders. Much of their literature refuted the retrogressionist portrayals of African Americans as savage, childlike, and immoral.[4] Drawing upon the discourses of Christianity and the cult of true womanhood, African American male writers particularly extolled the noble and virtuous qualities of African American women, thereby vindicating their moral integrity. Their images of motherhood and womanhood often resembled idealized, static, and even poetic versions of the dominant society.[5]

Club women, too, were concerned with aspersions cast upon their character. In response to a letter insulting their womanhood, a group of African American women convened in Boston in 1895 to form their own national organization, the National Association of Colored Women (NACW).[6] However, unlike the African American men, who persisted in images of true womanhood, the club women were more concerned with respectability, that is, a standard of behavior expected of all African Americans, especially of the women. Because these standards were based on "proper" home life and child care, the tremendous responsibility of race uplift was delegated to women. Club women conceived of their roles as not only teaching but also modeling respectable home life, child care, and social codes of deportment for poorer African American women. As Giddings noted, "they [club members] saw themselves not just as messengers but as living examples."[7] The club women's exemplary conduct was reflected in their subscription to Du Bois's "talented tenth" model of leadership, inscribed in the NACW's two-tiered motto "lifting as we climb."[8] In their discourse on raising the standards of home, family life, and motherhood, the NACW reinstated the sentiments of the Republican motherhood, insisting that the future of the race was moored to African American mothers' moral guardianship.

This is not to suggest that African American club women merely transplanted the templates of true womanhood or Republican motherhood onto their club activities. Rather, as many feminist club scholars have elaborated, the club women reshaped their language, rituals, and practices to correspond to historically and culturally veritable expressions of motherhood and womanhood.[9] As Yee has explicated, African American women envisioned true womanhood not in terms of submissiveness and passivity, conditions they associated with slavery. The images of domesticity carried different meanings for them than for plantation mistresses, as enslaved women had not been "confined" to the domestic sphere.[10] African American women consequently relished their *own* versions of domesticity, as they reinscribed the primacy of motherhood and home life. Mary Church Terrell affirmed this historical continuity in her declaration, "Nothing lies nearer the heart of colored women than the children."[11]

The discourses of African American motherhood that related the home to the larger community evoked another historical continuity. Since slavery, African American women had cared for and reared not only their own children but other slave children also. The club women rekindled this tradition of "other mothering" in their founding of "other homes" for children and youth, including kindergartens, day nurseries, settlements, orphanages, and homes for young working girls. In the spirit of "organized motherhood," the NACW's city, state, and regional affiliates established mothers' clubs to teach lessons in hygiene, health care, and household matters. As community activists and moral guardians, club women sponsored youth clubs, organized summer outings for children, and formed committees to canvass neighborhoods reputed for their saloons and dance halls. The twin images of motherhood and home, then, spoke of a community ethos nurtured through the individual and collaborative uplift activities of club women.

Despite their collective vision of race elevation, club women distinguished themselves from the recipients of their uplift activities through club and church memberships, as well as through the uplift activities themselves, which reflected selectivity, privilege, and cultural capital. This social class demarcation was not contradictory but rather illustrated the richness and complexity of the club movement. As I argue throughout, dual economic, social, and educative spheres were embedded within many uplift activities: one for the club women, and another for their beneficiaries, usually poorer women, the elderly, and children.

Thus far I have referred to the African American club women's ideologies and discourses within a community and ethnic context. However, the rhetoric and activities of these club women were not isolated but located within the mainstream women's club movement, as well as within larger sociopolitical structures. Although African American women were initially excluded from the white women's clubs, increasingly interracial clubs and coalitions with white club women were formed, especially in Chicago. Female suffrage was one specific issue around which many club women united. As more fully described in chapter 3, African American club women, like white club women, predicated their arguments for female suffrage upon the ideologies of Republican motherhood, municipal housekeeping, and progressive maternalism. Nonetheless, because the social and economic conditions in the African American communities, especially in Chicago's Black Belt, were markedly different from those in white middle-class communities, the African American club women's political platforms and strategies diverged. As detailed later, given the predominantly African American population in Chicago's Second Ward, the club women's role in educating and registering African American voters was critical. Their efforts were rewarded when they were largely credited with the election of the first African American alderman in the Second Ward, Oscar de Priest.

The club women were less successful, however, with their involvement in the Chicago juvenile courts. As more fully described in chapter 4, the court system was initially sustained through the volunteerism of club women, most of whom were white. However, beginning with Elizabeth McDonald in 1901, African American women served as probation officers and, later, as truant officers and social workers. What has yet to be fully explored is the degree of influence African American women wielded within the juvenile court system through their investigation of "neglectful" home conditions of dependent and delinquent African American children, their inspection of tenements and neighborhoods, their supervision of the lives of children and youths, and their intercession in court dispositions. Deliberately, the African American women's tenets of respectability underwent further transformation, as club women spoke out on the dilapidated and unsanitary living conditions wrought through segregation and racism, conditions that prohibited respectable living. African American club women were acutely aware of the contradictory positions they held as employees of a court system that segregated and underfunded facilities for African American children. Their resolve was evident in multiple-pronged strategies: political protest of segregated facilities, editorials decrying the lack of wholesome entertainment for youths, fund-raising activities for orphanages and homes, and club talks and reports on juvenile problems. Despite the club women's multiple roles as probation officers, founders of homes and orphanages, fund-raisers, teachers, and supervisors in Chicago, their social uplift and traditional roles in child welfare became increasingly compromised through state regulations, legal entanglements, and underfunded, segregated facilities.

This chapter, then, examines the club women's ideologies as reshaped from within the club movement, as well as by larger sociopolitical structures. I begin with the race literature of the late nineteenth century, arguing that African American women and men employed the rhetoric of true womanhood both to document and to advance their progress. Such documentation provided a foundation for the NACW, as club women associated their exemplary lives with notions of respectability for African American women and, ultimately, the race. Club women thereby created intricate layers of social uplift and social status; they emphasized not only their own but all women's responsibility in race elevation. Building upon the growth and success of the NACW, the club women furthered their political and social advancement by fusing the ideologies of municipal housekeeping, progressive maternalism, and a Du Boisian model of "talented tenth" leadership. Despite enormous political and social gains, African American women nonetheless remained subordinated to and less visible than their men in the political arena. Moreover, African American women lost ground as their child welfare traditions and social welfare practices were increasingly compromised through the juvenile court system.

GOOD HOMES: "THE VERY SALT OF SOCIETY"

The African American club women's ideologies of motherhood, home, and family issued from the historical denial of their womanhood during slavery. Josephine Silone Yates had pointed to how slavery had "blunted" African American women's "finer instincts" and "sensibilities."[12] Fannie Barrier Williams had ironically remarked, on the topic of sexual violence, how slavery had ensured that the African American woman was "the only woman in America for whom virtue was not an ornament and a necessity."[13] Whereas native-born white women bore the single historical burden of sexism, African American women wrestled with the double one of sexism and racism. As Anna Julia Cooper succinctly stated: "She [the African American woman] is confronted by both a woman question and a race problem."[14]

As African American men and women began the arduous task of reconstructing their lives after slavery, their images of womanhood diverged along gender lines. Before and during the early twentieth century, African American men more often emphasized the moral and domestic aspects of true womanhood, particularly the qualities of virtue, piety, and purity. This was particularly true of ministers, who fused Christian imagery with that of true womanhood. In William Alexander's estimation, the role of ministers was especially critical in inspiring women to be "angels of our household." [15] Although this image did not reflect the harsh reality of many African American women who worked as domestic workers and laundry women, such language exemplified the dignity African American men accorded to African American women. Long denied the opportunity of publicly praising their women, African American men embellished their language. Such images, as interpreted by scholars, may have been also an alternative strategy to protect African American women from the sexual violence of white Southern men. [16] As a matter of course, Fannie Barrier Williams encouraged African American men to display their "chivalry and protection" as demonstrations of respect. She further argued that men were granted a "high privilege" in helping to lift African American women from obscurity. [17]

Such idealized images not only positioned women as moral guardians, but often also restricted their roles to the domestic sphere. Many male leaders argued that family life and motherhood were paramount. They contended that, in order for women to fulfill their responsibilities, female education must be of a Christian and moral nature. Thomas Baker, writing for the *Alexanders Magazine* in 1906, argued that "she [the African American woman] must not be educated away from being a mother; slavery days degraded motherhood and made merchandise of it." [18] He accordingly promoted an education built upon Christian principles. Jack Thorne, too, advocated moral education for African American women. [19] Even higher education for women was to include "moral guides." [20]

Such moral and domestic dicta dovetailed not only with Christian beliefs but also with Washington's industrial education model. The Christian ideals of piety, purity, and virtue were, indeed, feminized ones, as women were considered the spiritual fonts of their race. In tandem, Washington's philosophy, in promoting the practical aspects of domesticity as well as race progress, stressed the importance of home care and domestic work. Toward this end the teaching of sewing, washing, broom making, cooking, gardening, and other household skills prepared women to be housewives, mothers, and, paradoxically, domestic workers.[21] Washington's industrial model gained additional momentum from the home economics movement, whose principles of scientific efficiency provided further justification for women's relegation to the domestic sphere.[22] Not only was housekeeping elevated to a vocation; it was purported to build character, edify moral integrity, and improve woman's health. Eunice Freeman, in *The Colored American Magazine,* argued that housework be thought of not as "drudgery" but as a business in which one was "trained." She further recommended housework for improving women's posture and carriage: "The home is a gymnasium; the broom, bedsteads, duster, dishes, etc., the apparatus by means of which the woman can make herself strong, erect, active and graceful."[23] In similar spirit, the stoopless dustpan was celebrated in one African American newspaper column for its healthful effects, as well as its influence in "cultivat[ing] the spirit of contentment."[24] Tucked beneath these touted advancements were prescriptions for restrictive female behavior and status.

The discourse of many African American male leaders reflected these prescriptions not only through their emphasis on moral education but also through their idealized imagery, which embellished the emotional and moral superiority of women. Consistent with true womanhood, female duties were extolled: "Tis her duty to uplift, purify and adorn." Occasionally, their language waxed poetic: "She [woman] is to mankind what the sun is to the universe."[25] Such attitudes no doubt prompted Anna Julia Cooper, in *A Voice from the South,* to conclude:

> *While our men seem thoroughly abreast of the times*
> *on almost every other subject, when they strike the*
> *woman question they drop back into sixteenth century logic.*
> *They actually do not seem sometimes to have outgrown that*
> *old contemporary of chivalry—the idea that women may stand*
> *on pedestals or live in doll houses.*[26]

Descriptions of such "chivalrous" attitudes proliferated well into the early twentieth century. Benjamin Brawley, professor of literature at Morehouse College and Howard University, heralded "the mother who chiefly bears the burden" and declared that "the story of love and patience and sacrifice is unending."[27] Henry Kletzing and William

Crogman detailed the characteristics of "good" mothers as "capable of being character builders, patient, loving, strong, and true, whose homes will be an uplifting power in the race." They also urged that women be enlightened so that "they may be able to bless their homes by the purity of their lives, the tenderness of their hearts, and the strength of their intellects."[28] In *History of the Colored Race in America,* William Alexander praised women who devoted their lives to others: "There is something more than intellect, and that is purity and virtue."[29] Dr. Kingsley, referencing his ideas to those of Dr. Edward Clark's, contrasted woman's intrinsic nature to that of man's: "Surely this is woman's calling—to teach man . . . to temper his fiercer, coarser, more self-assertive nature, by the contact of her gentleness, purity, self-sacrifice."[30] A frequent speaker to the Chicago African American women's clubs, Dr. Jefferson, concurred: "A virtuous woman is a crown to her husband. Her price is above rubies."[31]

Even though African American men elevated women, thereby circumscribing their roles, African American women were well aware of the egalitarian status they held with their men. Women even spoke of their superiority to men, subverting men's chivalrous portraits of them. For example, in her advocacy of female suffrage, Fannie Barrier Williams argued that African American women were better educated and prepared to vote than when their men had been granted the right.[32] Ione Gibbs insisted that African American women, who had been equal to men since slavery, now surpassed them.[33] Women often chose to promote their egalitarian status instead, arguing that the responsibility of upstanding moral behavior rested with both men and women. In her essay, "Enlightened Motherhood," presented to the Brooklyn Literary Society, Frances Harper advised mothers not to encourage double standards for sons but to hold them to the same Christian standards as their daughters.[34] Fannie Barrier Williams chided African American men for not protecting African American women's honor, as well as for failing to distinguish their physical beauty from character. She argued that if men treated their women respectfully, "it would help in their [African American women's] overall world-wide respect."[35] Such statements pointed to African American women's concern with respectability, not elevated stature. Nonetheless, as bell hooks noted, African American men and women often held "contradicting positions" on their roles.[36]

Unlike African American men who deemed women moral guardians because of their superior virtue, African American women considered themselves so because of their responsibilities as mothers and caregivers. Although the primacy of motherhood was an overarching theme of both African American and white women's clubs, African American women's articulation of motherhood differed immensely. Unlike the dyadic mother-child relationship in dominant society, African American expressions of motherhood extended to the care of others' children, the elderly, and those less fortunate. As Deborah Gray White articulated, the multiple roles of teachers, wives, and charity workers were expressions of mothering, not unlike Patricia Hill Collins's elaboration of "other mothers."[37] As mentioned previously, the NACW reflected this constellation of caregiving in their establishment of mothers' clubs, uplift activities, and "other homes."

In essence, African American club women wove these threads of motherhood into the very fabric of the race's destiny. The building up of home life was quintessential because all race reform and progress originated there. As Mary Church Terrell alliteratively stated: "Homes, more homes, better homes, purer homes is the text upon which sermons have been and will be preached."[38] The triad of mother, home, and child fittingly constituted one of the NACW's major departments. In their articulation of motherhood, the club women rekindled the spirit of the Republican motherhood. For example, in the spirit of what Josephine Silone Yates called a "new era," club women proclaimed that the future leadership of their race sprang from a firm foundation of home life.[39] Because mothers were their children's first teachers, Mary Church Terrell referred to home life as the "first step in nation building."[40] Mary Rice Phelps elaborated:

> In the home circle, and around the fireside, her teaching begins with the first dawn of intelligence. . . . She it is who teaches those qualities that are so essential to any race or tribe of beings — morality. . . . Christianity . . . economy.[41]

Reverting to the original Republican motherhood's preoccupation with male leadership, some women particularly encouraged the education of their sons. Mrs. Pettey, wife of Bishop Pettey, contended, "When our homes become intelligent, we shall have intelligent statesmen, ministers, and doctors; in fact, the whole regime that leads will be intelligent."[42]

In promoting home life, the club women re-echoed not only the Republican motherhood but also Booker T. Washington's maxims of thrift, industriousness, and self-reliance. This was particularly true for poorer African American women. The club women directed special efforts at women in the South, where the social and economic conditions had improved little since emancipation. Again, race uplift and respectability were imperative as club women employed their teaching and organizational skills to better the lives of poorer women and children. As Josephine St. Pierre Ruffin, national and state club organizer for the NACW, advanced, the lives of "fine cultured women" were inseparable from those less fortunate:

> Now for the sake of the thousand of self-sacrificing young women teaching and preaching in the lonely southern backwoods for the noble army of mothers who have given birth to these girls, mothers whose intelligence is limited only by their opportunity to get at books, for the sake of the fine cultured women who have carried off the honors in school here and often abroad, for the sake of our own dignity, the dignity of our race, and the future good name of our children.[43]

Although she and Fannie Barrier Williams encouraged Northern clubs to reach down and assist their Southern sisters, with increased migration to the Northern cities the club women refocused their efforts to assist African Americans new to the North. Again, industrial education, akin to Washington's model, was most often advocated for the poor. Sewing, cooking, and sundry domestic skills were taught not only to provide poorer women with improved homemaking skills; they also dovetailed with the "professionalization" of domestic service.[44] As described in chapter 5, the African American settlements in Chicago offered such classes, as well as employment referral services, so that poorer African American women could procure domestic work. Despite the denigration often associated with domestic service, African American club women accorded dignity to such work by acknowledging the efforts and sacrifices working women made to provide for their families. The club women, too, were acutely aware of the discriminatory practices that poorer African American women, as well as they themselves, faced in gainful employment opportunities.

SOCIAL CONCERNS AND SOCIAL DISTINCTIONS

As noted, respectability was an overriding concern in many of the club activities. Beginning with the organization of the NACW, club women demonstrated through their discourses and activities that their womanhood was beyond reproach. Respectability, however, was perceived and expressed as a collective strategy. It extended beyond the clubs because the African American club women's reputation, as well as the race's, was intricately connected to all African American women. A dialectic was formed, then, as club women conjoined rhetorically all African American women, yet in their social lives carefully chose their associations.

Although club women promoted a prescribed set of standards for home life and social life, which served as "badges of race respectability," they held themselves to higher ideals.[45] They followed Du Bois's prescription that "social distinctions be observed."[46] Because club women perceived themselves as "ambassadors" of the race, they took great care to ensure that their deportment was beyond reproach. In many cases this necessitated disassociating themselves from the behavior of poorer African Americans. Such stratification was evident in Mary Church Terrell's statement, "Even though we wish to shun them [less fortunate African American women], and hold ourselves entirely aloof from them, we cannot escape the consequences of their acts."[47] As Harley observed, African American club women occasionally expressed dismay when white persons failed to perceive class differences and judged all African American women collectively.[48] That such class differences were demonstrated and judged was evident in Du Bois's appraisal of African American club women's deportment at one women's convention: "Undoubtedly the women assembled at Chicago were rather above the average of their race and represented the aristocracy among the Negroes. Consequently their evident intelligence and air of good breeding served also to impress the onlookers."[49]

Accordingly, the club women split their Du Boisian-Washingtonian allegiances and ideologies along social class lines. More specifically, they most often prescribed Washingtonian remedies for poorer and less educated women, while adhering to a Du Boisian model in their own lives. To illustrate, the club women often engaged in educative practices—literary talks, political addresses, theater productions, victrola recitals, and lyceums—which marked, as well as preserved, their leadership roles. However, as the African American middle class mushroomed in the late nineteenth century in Chicago, club women further distinguished themselves from poorer women not only through their selective club memberships but also through exclusive social affairs and displays of cultural capital. Such rituals were not considered frivolous nor self-serving, as social uplift was usually embedded in such social occasions. For example, fees collected from a whist tournament were earmarked for a charity; concurrently, the circuit of cultural capital—whist prizes of Japanese vases, crystal dishes, and cut glassware—circulated within the club circles. In Chicago charity balls organized by the club women yielded thousands of dollars to support the Old Folks' Home, as club women begowned in lavish dresses of silk and imported lace promenaded in the ball's "Grand March." Clearly, some club women's lives moved beyond the exemplary or respectable in their conspicuous consumption. In the melding of their discourses and ideologies, as well as in their rituals and practices, African American club women mediated but did not always resolve the tensions of social class, regionalism, and gender.

Despite the visibility of social class distinctions, club women formed various layers of sisterhood and allegiances to poorer race women. Club women, as mentioned above, suffered discrimination in the North as well as in the South. Although the club women's language was replete with social class markers, it also reflected their acute awareness of the dilapidated tenements, inferior health facilities, and dearth of employment and educational opportunities that many poorer African Americans faced. Rather than placing blame upon the victims of such circumstances, African American club women, especially in Chicago, protested the roots of these conditions: persistent discrimination and racism. Club women knew how tenuous race progress and respectability were in light of the continued resurgence of Jim Crow practices.

African American club women not only mediated social class and gender tensions within their own communities but also dealt with tensions between white club women and themselves. The language African American club women used when speaking of motherhood, womanhood, and home life was remarkably complex and resilient; it served not only multiple purposes but multiple audiences, including white club women, African American club members, poorer African American women, and African American men. Building upon Hine's "culture of dissemblance," I argue that the club women's discourse created a "psychic space," through which they adapted their language and ideologies to multiple audiences, thereby maintaining their own autonomy and identity.[50] For example, the rhetoric of motherhood, home life, and children's welfare was common to both African American and white women's clubs. So, too, were the images of the cult of true womanhood and of Christianity, despite their culturally specific expressions, socially appropriate in the late nineteenth and early twentieth century for club women. Yet the subtext of the practices, rituals, and activities remained distinctly their own.

Indeed, the African American club women's "bicultural voice," to use Evelyn Higginbotham's phrase, acted as a bridge in educating "public opinion," or more specifically, in changing white club women's negative attitudes toward African American women.[51] The African American club women in Chicago were not immune from exclusion, evident in their denied participation in the Chicago World's Fair of 1893 and in Fannie Barrier Williams's rejected application for membership in the Chicago Woman's Club, a prominent native-born white women's club.[52] Williams noted that when African American club women founded their own national organization, white club women showed them greater respect.[53] Josephine St. Pierre Ruffin, too, observed that the NACW's success put African American women on an equal footing with white women: "It shows that we are truly American women, with all the adaptability, readiness to seize and possess our opportunities, willingness to do our part for good as other American women." [54]

Although African American club women spoke of the similarities between their clubs and white women's and used a common rhetoric, they also emphasized their differences. Fannie Barrier Williams noted how initially African American women had followed, not imitated, the example of white women's clubs. In the same breath she gave homage to the antecedents of the African American club movement—the churches and the secret societies—wherein African American women not only had engaged in social reform but also had become further informed on race issues.[55] As discussed more fully in chapter 6, African

American women historically had participated in antislavery societies, lyceums, literary societies, and chautauquas, testimony to their influence in these enduring African American literary traditions. Indeed, since the early 1800s, community uplift and self-uplift had been intertwined, as those more fortunate assisted those in need. This community ethos was restated by the club women who in studying the "sub-conditions" of the race proposed such resolutions as "better schools, homes, jobs." Fannie Barrier Williams observed that, unlike the white club movement, which uplifted the "already uplifted," the African American club movement consisted of "the few competent ones on behalf of the many incompetent."[56]

In distinguishing the two club movements, African American members especially solidified their sisterhood and networks with other African American club women. In her comparisons of African American and white club women's lives, Linda Gordon carefully noted the similar backgrounds of African American club women.[57] Most were college educated, of middle-class standing, and married to professional men. Likewise, many club members considered themselves members of the "talented tenth" and felt a combined sense of social commitment and superiority. Such portraits have been corroborated by Emma Thornbrough and Sharon Harley, who pointed out the prevalence of professionals, such as school teachers, in the women's clubs of Indiana and Washington, D.C., respectively.[58] In her enumeration of club women as teachers, authors, artists, musicians, and linguists, Fannie Barrier Williams praised the professionalism of club women: "The woman thus portrayed is the real new woman in American life."[59]

The backgrounds of many of the African American club women in Chicago were similar to those of Gordon's study. Through their multiple club memberships, the club women not only formed deep friendships and camaraderie but also created webs of collaborative fund-raising and uplift activities. My analysis of club memberships in Chicago has revealed that club women selectively joined clubs according to social class, neighborhoods, church affiliation, political persuasion, and common interests. For example, Fannie Barrier Williams and Eva Jenifer were members of the Frederick Douglass Center, as well as of the African American YWCA. These club women, as well as these two organizations, nurtured their affiliations with the leading white women's clubs and organizations. Club women Irene Goins, Joanna Snowden-Porter,

Sophia Boaz, and Dr. Mary Waring, all quite active in clubs noteworthy for child welfare, later worked closely with the juvenile courts. Members of the whist clubs, which proliferated, most curiously, during the war years, did not join many of the clubs involved in social uplift, and the club women most involved in social welfare did not usually join whist clubs. Generally, African American women's clubs in Chicago devoted a large part of their time and effort to supporting three "homes": the Phyllis Wheatley Home, for young working girls; the Amanda Smith Home, later the Amanda Smith Industrial School, for dependent and orphaned girls; and the Old Folks' Home. In focusing their efforts on these institutions, the club women ensured the homes' sustenance and at the same time created multiple social occasions in which they mutually participated, thus deepening their friendships and social ties. In essence, then, social status and uplift were enmeshed.

Despite these African American club women's *relatively* privileged lives, to use Gordon's phrase, they, like their poorer sisters, were subject to discriminatory practices.[60] The club women drew upon and synergized this collective identity, especially in the political arena. In the case of female suffrage, club women inverted the argument of respectability, providing irrefutable evidence that Jim Crow laws and practices prevented race women and men from improving the standards of their lives and their livelihood. The vote, they argued, would be one viable instrument for community representation and would improve the social and economic lives of African American citizens. In spite of their initial success with suffrage, the club women remained on the margins of the political arena. Although they worked alongside their men, women more often assumed subordinate and less visible political positions. They usually worked as volunteers, for example, in registering and educating voters on political platforms and issues.[61] Although most African American male leaders expected women to be involved in community uplift, they thought primarily in terms of the traditional female roles and concerns, especially social uplift and child welfare. Ironically, African American club women, in promoting their community roles as caretakers and "other mothers," had tacitly circumscribed their potential for political leadership (although Ida B. Wells was certainly one exception). This is not to suggest that club women did not engage in political activity, which is fully detailed in chapter 3. Rather, as Beverly Jones appraised the NACW's focus as largely "domestic," I would note, too, that the Chicago club women's agenda revolved mostly around the issues of home, family life, and children.[62]

Club women were deeply committed to social and child welfare, but their involvement was complicated by the juvenile court system. Like white women, African American women had initially served as volunteer probation officers, while males were accorded salaried positions. Although there were five African American female probation officers and one policewoman in Chicago by 1920, such representation in the county court was minimal, particularly given the increased numbers of African American children classified as dependent and delinquent children.[63] As more African American women became trained in social and settlement work, their ideologies and discourses assumed multiple perspectives. Like white social reformers Sophonisba Breckinridge, Jane Addams, and Louise de Koven Bowen, African American female reformers and social workers recommended environmental solutions, particularly more playgrounds, gymnasiums, and youth and physical culture classes. Such facilities, they argued, were sorely needed in Chicago's Black Belt, where with the surge of Southern migration, housing and neighborhood conditions had worsened.[64] African American social and settlement workers were also quite vocal about the exclusion of African Americans from the mainstream settlements and other social facilities. Although Breckinridge, Addams, and Bowen had also expressed strong disapproval of such segregative practices, their actual involvement in establishing and sustaining the African American settlements, missions, girls' homes, and orphanages was minimal. The brunt of this responsibility was placed on the African American club women's, and social and settlement workers', shoulders.

In addition to the mainstream humanistic and scientific discourse of settlement work, many African American female social workers drew from their Christian faith, as well as from a community-building ethos. Elizabeth McDonald, for example, combined her rescue work with probation work, as she distributed Bibles and prayer books and encouraged families to lead Christian lives. In her vision, Christian salvation was indistinguishable from a law-abiding life. Amanda Smith, founder of the Amanda Smith Home for dependent and orphaned girls, blended her missionary experience with Washington's industrial education model. Clotee Scott, founder of the Clotee Scott Settlement in Hyde

Park, although working closely with students from the University of Chicago's School of Civics and Philanthropy, emphasized that her work was "doing," not simply "acting religion." Relying heavily upon the churches and women's clubs for monetary and in-kind support, she frequently gave talks before congregations and clubs on the settlement's activities, thereby not only ensuring the settlement's future but also building community collaboration.[65]

However, as the African American population in Chicago expanded by more than 148 percent between 1910 and 1920, the club women found their social uplift efforts severely taxed.[66] Despite the creation of settlements, missions, nurseries, and other facilities, the African American club women were unable to provide resources for all migrants. Like other progressive maternalists, the club women continued their emphasis on motherhood, children, and home life. Lessons in respectability emerged once again, as many Southern migrants hearkened from rural settings. Robert Abbott, the editor of the *Chicago Defender* who had zealously recruited Southern African Americans to Chicago, now redirected his attention to teaching migrants, particularly women, proper modes of behavior and speech. Migrants were admonished not to walk barefoot, nor to wear bandanas on their heads, nor to hang their laundry on the front stoop, nor to use profane language in public.[67] Newspaper articles, many written by club women, chastised young women for their dress and deportment; they were described as "thinly clad," "loud," and "bold." Club women were particularly alarmed at the number of youths who frequented saloons, poolrooms, dance halls, and other places of ill repute. Clearly, they expected the youths to carry the banner of respectability, as is evident in one editorial's conclusions: "No permanent advance or progress can be made by the Afro-American race, until its boys and girls and its older members for that matter, drink in higher ideals, along the lines of decency, honesty, and morality."[68]

Despite their renewed appeal to respectability, the club women were well aware of the difficulties many families faced, particularly the mothers who often worked long hours as domestic servants or laundry women. Many left their young children alone or in the care of older siblings or neighbors because nurseries and kindergartens were often unavailable or unaffordable. They lived in crowded tenements with extended family or former neighbors; others took in male lodgers to help them pay high rents.[69] These living conditions were not peculiar to African Americans; many immigrant families too lived in over-crowded and dilapidated tenements. In any case the juvenile court system deemed such living conditions as "neglectful," thus necessitating the children's removal to orphanages or supervision by probation offi-cers. There were few orphanages, industrial schools, and "homes" for African American dependent and delinquent children, so many children were supervised by probation officers, settlement workers, and club women who volunteered their time.

The African American club women's ideologies and discourses were not only transformed by external and internal political, social, and economic factors. The ideologies and discourses were largely resilient and trans-formative, as the club women envisioned their identities, roles, and practices within a constellation of discourses. Their language was not mercurial but adaptive to audience, purpose, and sociopolitical con-straints, as they mediated their gendered, classed, and ethnic identities within their own communities and the larger mainstream society. Al-though there were points of convergence in all club women's social lives, the African American women's club movement was informed by unique historical conditions and culturally specific mores.

African American club women have been variously characterized as elite, conservative, radical, and traditional; they have been hailed as womanists, activists, sisters, and "other mothers."[70] Perhaps all of the above are true. The club women's rhetoric was often traditional and conservative; it rallied around issues of motherhood, children, and home life. In their actual lives, however, the club women drew from distinct African American community traditions, linking their roles as "other mothers" to the social welfare of communities and, ultimately, to the juvenile court system. Although their activism was often limited to social and child welfare issues, club women connected these issues to political ones, especially women's suffrage and political representation.

The next chapter examines the specific economic and social condi-tions in the African American communities of Chicago. There were various communities, demarcated by social class, institutions, club and church memberships, and ideologies. The Chicago club women's ideol-ogies reflected their positions within elite and middle-class communities.

As a matter of course, the burgeoning of the African American women's club movement in Chicago coincided with the emergence of an African American middle class. In accordance with their social status and sense of obligation, the club women were deeply implicated in political, social, and educative uplift activities, described in the subsequent chapters.

TWO

AFRICAN AMERICAN

COMMUNITIES IN CHICAGO

FROM 1890 TO 1920 THE ECONOMIC, POLITICAL, AND social lives of African Americans in Chicago underwent tremendous transformations. During this time period the city's African American population grew from 15,000 to more than 110,000, resulting in the establishment of a number of African American communities defined by social class, type of business, social institution, and political organization.[1] By the 1890s the influence of the African American elite had diminished as the middle class had burgeoned. While Chicago's Black Belt expanded to accommodate an influx of poor Southern migrants, it became increasingly segregated and impoverished. Despite social class and economic position, most African Americans faced increased discrimination, evident in higher rents, redlining tactics, bomb threats, and marginal employment. However, as Allan Spear surmised, racism was only one part of the calculus.[2] Social class distinctions, too, he argued, divided the African American communities, along lines of residential preference, club and church membership, and political allegiance.

This chapter examines the various African American communities in Chicago: the impoverished Black Belt as well as the wealthier neighborhoods of Hyde Park, Morgan Park, Englewood, and Woodlawn. In particular, social relations among the elite, the middle class, and the poor are examined through the communities' businesses, social institutions, churches, and clubs. The social interactions among these social strata were never simple or static but assumed a myriad of complex, varied, and often paradoxical patterns.

THE AFRICAN AMERICAN ELITE AND MIDDLE-CLASS COMMUNITIES

By 1843 there were nearly five hundred African American citizens in Chicago, many of whom were freed slaves. The community continued to expand through the churches' assistance to fugitive slaves. Four of Quinn Chapel's female members, the "Big Four," were reputed for their abolitionist activities, as was John Jones, founder of Olivet Baptist Church. So successful were their missions that by 1860 the African American population had grown to nearly one thousand. After emancipation the African American population more than tripled to thirty-five hundred, with most of its citizens residing in integrated neighborhoods on the South Side.[3] Until 1900 most African Americans lived in predominantly white neighborhoods.[4]

In addition to African American church societies, there were social clubs. By 1885 there were five exclusively male clubs; female auxiliaries were organized shortly thereafter, including the Sisters of the Mysterious Ten and the Grant Court Heroines of Jericho of Illinois.[5] By 1890, as the African American population expanded to fifteen thousand, social class distinction in church and club membership was evident. Olivet Baptist Church, for example, was considered "one of the largest and most flourishing of the colored congregations." The congregation of Bethesda Baptist Church was comprised of "many of the best of Chicago's colored citizens." St. Thomas Episcopal Church, however, was reputed as the most "fashionable" of the African American churches.[6] These churches demonstrated their status and prestige through literary societies, lecture series, forums, and debate teams, all of which contributed to the social and intellectual development of their members. They also reached down to poorer African Americans through their sponsorship of kindergartens, nurseries, and lodging services.

By 1890 Chicago became the second largest American city, because of the Southern migration, as well as the tremendous stream of immigrants.[7] The residential segregation of African Americans increased thereafter; it is evident in a comparison of the residential patterns of immigrants and African Americans. African Americans, constituting only 1.3 percent of Chicago's population then, lived predominantly in three adjacent southside wards, which stretched beltlike from downtown Chicago to Thirty-Fifth Street.[8] Despite social class stratification, many elite African Americans, too, lived there, with poorer African Americans mostly residing in the Fourth Ward.[9] Thus, these neighborhoods were not only economically diverse but largely integrated; the isolation index in 1890 for African Americans was only 8.1 percent. Spear has calculated that as late as 1910 in Chicago, African Americans were less segregated from native-born Whites than Italian-Americans were.[10] However, by 1910 the isolation index had risen to 15.1 percent; by 1920 it had more than doubled to 38.1 percent.[11]

Residential indices for immigrant groups also indicated an ethnic heterogeneity in 1890. Immigrants, who then constituted 77.9 percent of Chicago's population, lived mostly on the West Side, including the Eighteenth Ward near Hull House.[12] As Harvey Zorbaugh, a Chicago sociologist, documented, the Chicago immigrant neighborhoods, such as "Little Hell," were composed of many ethnic groups, including Italians, Slavs, Poles, Irish, African Americans, and Persians.[13] He noted, though, that discrimination, not toleration, was persistent, whether directed at European immigrants or African Americans: "On the school and public playgrounds are re-enacted the scenes of a generation ago when the Sicilian was forcing out the Swede. The Negro child is often mistreated and ostracized."[14] Unlike the immigrants who eventually moved to better neighborhoods, poorer African Americans more often remained in their southside communities or resettled in the ghettos vacated by immigrants. The isolation index for African Americans, which jumped to 70.4 percent by 1930, reflected this reality.[15]

From 1890 to 1915 the Chicago African American population mushroomed from fifteen thousand to more than fifty thousand. By 1910 African Americans constituted the tenth largest ethnic group in Chicago, even though immigrants (first- and second-generation Americans) made up 77 percent of the city's population.[16] As the African American population increased, ethnic and social class segregation ensued. Most poorer, Southern African Americans were directed to the Black Belt or nearby "vice areas," and wealthier African Americans resided in Hyde

Park, Kenwood, and Woodlawn. To illustrate, Ferdinand Barnett and his wife, Ida B. Wells, lived in a fourteen-room, four-bath mansion in a "posh" neighborhood on Rhodes Avenue; Laing and Fannie Barrier Williams's home was replete with a large library and a sizable art collection.[17] St. Thomas Episcopal Church, formerly situated in the Black Belt, moved with its elite congregation to a more affluent area. E. Franklin Frazier surmised that by 1920 Woodlawn's African American population consisted of mostly "upper occupational classes."[18]

In spite of their wealth and status, middle-class and elite African Americans were not always welcome in the predominantly white neighborhoods. In Hyde Park, white neighborhood improvement associations were purportedly established to protect the neighborhood, although their primary concern was depreciated property value. The Hyde Park Improvement Protective Club, formed in 1909 by Francis Harper, a wealthy white attorney, resorted to various maneuvers to hold the "color line" in Hyde Park. At one point the club threatened to hire "voodoo witch doctors" to cast spells on African American home owners.[19] Their later tactics became more virulent, including redlining, verbal threats, and bombings. Between 1917 and 1921 there were at least fifty-eight bombings of African American homes in Chicago, including the home of African American banker Jesse Binga, which was bombed seven times in one year.[20]

Most middle-class and elite African Americans expressed consternation at this blatant racism and at the fact that they had been collectively categorized with poorer African Americans. Some lifelong African American residents criticized the behavior of Southern migrants, blaming them for increased incidents of discrimination. As one citizen remarked: "The ones that were here had been here for years. They were just about civilized and didn't make apes out of themselves like the ones who came during 1917–1918. We all suffer for what one fool will do."[21] Another established resident remarked how formerly African Americans could dine at any restaurant without suffering nasty glares and comments. Most personal testimonies and newspaper accounts confirmed, however, that overt forms of racism had long existed. Numerous accounts of discriminatory practices in department stores, railroad cars, streetcars, women's clubs, trade unions, schools, restaurants, and other public facilities substantiated that the Southern migration had only exacerbated existing economic and social inequalities. Notwithstanding the occasional criticism and animosity directed at newcomers, many African Americans recognized the immense challenges that Southern African Americans faced in a new urban setting. Prominent club woman Fannie Barrier Williams contended that the migrants' adjustment demanded the collective, not individual, responsibility of all African Americans:

> *Prevented from mingling easily and generally with the rest of the city's population, according to their needs and deservings, but with no preparation made for segregation, their life in a great city has been irregular and shifting, with the result that they have been subject to more special ills than any other nationality amongst us.*[22]

She concluded that the primary obstacle most African Americans faced in the North was segregation.

Despite Williams's concern for improved race relations, she, like many others of the African American elite, approved of social class distinctions, not only between the elite and the poor but also between the elite and the newly formed middle class. Whereas the elite's identity was based upon ancestry, cultivated taste, and education, the identity of the new middle class rested on acquired wealth, education, and conspicuous consumption. The Williamses' social world, for example, was exclusive, consisting mostly of other professionals or "gentle folks," as Fannie preferred to call them. The Williamses and their friends attended the same church and the same social clubs and assumed leadership roles in community uplift. Fannie Barrier Williams was proud of this distinction, declaring that the African American elite to which she belonged were "better dressed, better housed, and better managed than almost anywhere else in the wide west."[23] She explained, "We are trying our best to be the real gentle folks in the highest and best sense of the term."[24]

Although middle-class African Americans frequently sought entry into this selective social world, not all were accepted. As Williams stated, "He [the Negro aristocrat] is very much needed and has good services to perform. The only hope is that he will not imitate the codfish variety so much in evidence on the other side of the color line. . . . This is not the kind we are developing in Chicago."[25] These distinctions between the elite and the "codfish variety" were captured by Julius Avendorph, a member of the elite, in his discussion of social etiquette. In an editorial he criticized the indiscreet dress and behavior of young women at dances and balls, as well as their faux pas of close dancing. Such indiscretions, he pointed out, would have never occurred among the elite, who intrinsically understood both proper deportment and socially distinct occasions: "The argument is often advanced that a lady can be a lady anywhere, or in any society. That is true. But a lady saves herself of the embarrassment of proving herself a lady when she shows class distinctions by not attending affairs where the distinction must be made."[26]

Such knowledge, he insisted, could not be bought nor imitated, but was cultivated. For some this knowledge proved difficult. For example, Dr. George Cleveland Hall, a graduate of what the elite considered a second-rate medical school, and his wife tried unsuccessfully to gain entry into the elite's social circle. They were refused, not only because Dr. Daniel Williams, founder of Provident Hospital, was unwilling to hire Hall at the Hospital, but because of Mrs. Hall's reported "loud" attire and behavior. At one social event Fannie Barrier Williams immediately exited upon Mrs. Hall's entry.[27] Despite their class differences, the Williamses and the Halls were members of Chicago's African American "Elite 400," a select group of patrons and patronesses invited to social and philanthropic activities. Members of this group, described as "the cream of society," were "elegantly costumed" for promenades, grand marches, and balls. Cultural capital and conspicuous consumption were quite visible, especially at annual charity dances, where club women's dresses were estimated to cost as much as five hundred dollars.[28] Members of the "Elite 400" were clearly those African Americans whom the governor of Mississippi would not have chosen to recruit to his state. In a letter to the Chicago mayor, that governor had asked if any of Chicago's "surplus" of African Americans might be returned to Mississippi, with the following stipulation: "We have all the room in the world for what we know as N-I-G-G-E-R-S, but none whatever for 'colored ladies and gentlemen.' "[29]

Class divisions were marked in clubs, especially the Old Settlers' Club, the Prudence Crandall Club, and the Lotus Club, all of which were reserved for the first African American families of Chicago.[30] Consequently, the middle class formed their own clubs, which reflected class stratification through selective membership and nomenclature with descriptions such as "Elite," "Exclusive," or "Elete."[31] In time, however, the elite and the middle class joined the same clubs, especially because the need for social uplift for the poor was great and was considered a collective responsibility. The Ida B. Wells Club (1893) and the Phyllis Wheatley Club (1896) were two such clubs, composed of elite members Mrs. Daniel Williams, Mrs. J. C. Stewart, and Fannie Barrier Williams and middle-class members Mrs. Julius Taylor and Mrs. George Hall. Because social uplift was expected, the clubs created nurseries, kindergartens, and homes for young working girls; they also dispensed charity to individual families. Indeed, the two African American newspapers, the *Chicago Defender* and the *Broad Ax,* not only reported these and other clubs' activities with the designation "race advancement" but also chastised club women and other individuals whose character or activities were less than exemplary. Julius Taylor, editor of the *Broad Ax,* was particularly scathing in his indictment of club women and ministers, both of whom he characterized as self-absorbed and socially ambitious. His newspaper, he claimed, would endorse only those women's clubs that did not "pander to cake walks and Jim-Crowism."[32]

As of 1915 there were more than 70 women's clubs listed under the Chicago Federation of Colored Women's Clubs. However, if youth clubs, church societies and lyceums, and unfederated women's clubs are included, there were well over 150.[33] Many of these clubs created educational and social organizations, whose sustenance was dependent upon the clubs' fund-raising network. Most of the nurseries, kindergartens, and "homes" the club women organized were segregated, not because immigrant and native-born white children were excluded but because the facilities were located in largely African American neighborhoods. Some members of the African American elite opposed such facilities, arguing that integration through white facilities was the better remedy. John Jones, for one, disapproved not only of the opening of the first African American YMCA in 1887, but also of Provident Hospital, the first hospital for African Americans in Chicago.[34] In 1893, when Ida B. Wells proposed the creation of a kindergarten to accommodate African American children in the neighborhood near the Institutional Church and Settlement, some of the elite accused her of "drawing the color line."[35] As a matter of fact, the "color line" had already been drawn; many kindergartens had closed their doors to African American children. The need for such facilities for African Americans demanded immediate solutions.

Kindergartens were not the only facilities denied to African Americans. Many settlements, day nurseries, homes for the elderly, and accommodations for working girls and women were organized along ethnic lines, evident in the Swedish, German, Jewish, and Polish communities. As elaborated in chapter 5, some of the leading mainstream settlements excluded African Americans by drawing boundaries, relocating their facilities, or establishing quotas. These practices further necessitated the creation, maintenance, and expansion of facilities for poorer African Americans by wealthier African Americans. Accordingly, Provident Hospital, which opened in 1891 with the assistance of Fannie Barrier Williams, expanded its services to include a dispensary, nurse visitations, and a milk station.[36] In 1898 a home for the elderly, the Home for the Aged and Infirm Colored People, was founded. Many club women donated their time and efforts to raise moneys for its provisions and to offer "good cheer" to the aged.[37] The Phyllis Wheatley Home, founded in 1907 by the Phyllis Wheatley Club, was created to provide a safe and homelike environment for young working girls new to the city. Many of the women's clubs contributed financially to the home's upkeep.[38] Other community institutions followed, including several homes for orphans and dependent children, settlements and missions, a YWCA in 1914, and city chapters of the Negro Business League, the National Association for the Advancement of Colored People (NAACP), and the National Urban League.[39]

In the creation of these facilities, wealthier African Americans' attitudes toward the poor varied from patronizing and maternal to "reaching across" to brothers and sisters. More often than not, however, social class distinctions were observed. Just as the elite had once excluded the "new elite" or middle class from their social functions and clubs, so, too, did the "Elite 400" exclude the poor from their social balls, club luncheons, teas, church lyceums, and summer resorts in Benton Harbor, Michigan.[40] Fannie Barrier Williams, in fact, recommended keeping social class and residential distinctions: "[The] huddling together of the good and the bad, compelling the decent element of the colored people to witness the brazen display of vice of all kinds in front of their children, are trying conditions under which to remain socially clean and respectable."[41]

As these social institutions expanded, so did African American businesses. A number of wealthier African Americans were professionals; there were at least sixty-five doctors (four of whom were females), as well as many lawyers, teachers, journalists, dentists, and pharmacists. Famous entrepreneurs included Jesse Binga of the Binga State Bank and

Anthony Overton, owner of the Overton Hygienic Manufacturing Company, which processed baking soda, skin powders, and other beauty items.[42] Many other businesses were service oriented, requiring low capital investment and little training or education. Of these, the most numerous were barber shops, beauty shops, dressmaking and millinery shops, restaurants, and hotels. Located within the Black Belt, they served a largely segregated clientele. Although businesses reportedly promoted and advanced the African American community economically, business-men and businesswomen were often accused of promoting themselves instead. Some historians and sociologists have concluded that individual African American businessmen and women had more to gain personally and professionally in developing segregated organizations and businesses than in promoting integration.[43] Such thoughts were, in fact, reflected in one doctor's comments: "They [poor southern African Americans] have been our best patrons. Of course, a lot of them were not properly adjusted because they had been used to rural life. I do not believe that this office building would have been here today if it had not been for those Negroes who came from the South."[44]

Certainly, the influx of migrants provided a ready-made clientele for budding African American businesses. However, the need for such businesses was great also because of exclusionary practices and segregated neighborhoods in which poorer African Americans lived. Again, estab-lished African Americans held conflicting ideas about the Southern migrants. Some complained about the newcomers, blaming them for increased incidences of racism and segregation. Their inappropriate behavior was referred to as "loud," "lewd," and "loose." In particular, the middle class criticized the "hollerin" and "shoutin" rituals at storefront churches, which they considered disrespectful and indecent.[45] Nonethe-less, those who criticized often relied upon the poor to support their businesses.

Although the middle class disapproved of poor Southern traditions, there were points of convergence. Historian Hine has astutely wondered whether migrants to the Northern cities were Northern Southerners or Southern Northeners.[46] The poor, though, were not the only ones to observe, even cherish, Southern traditions. Some of the club women's fund-raisers, for example, included the Southern traditions of teas, barbecues, buffalo fish fries, and testimonials. Many families in Chicago were visited by club women, friends, and relatives from Memphis,

Nashville, and New Orleans; news from these and other Southern cities was common fare in the *Chicago Defender*. Willard Gatewood's documentation of the African American elites' lifestyle in Southern and Northern cities at the turn of the century pointed to many similarities, because social class was the main criterion for social approval.[47]

In political affiliations, class distinctions were less clear. Chicago had many organizations affiliated with Booker T. Washington: a city chapter of the Business League, the Alumni Tuskegee Club, the Afro-American Council, and fraternal orders. Washington himself was a frequent speaker at meetings of these organizations and at the leading churches. His son, a student at Northwestern University, was a member of many Chicago clubs, including a matrimony club for eligible bachelors.[48] Dr. George Cleveland Hall and Laing Williams were two of many Chicago professionals who maintained their close ties to Washington's political machine. (Williams's position as district attorney was, in fact, secured through Washington's connections.)[49] Despite their support of Washington, Laing Williams and his wife, Fannie, shifted their alliances between Washington and Du Bois, as others did. Drake observed: "The Chicago middle and upper classes did not seem to be caught on the horns of the DuBois-Washington dilemma, and supported a National Association for the Advancement of Colored People branch as well as the National Business League, while the same people who entertained Mr. Washington when he visited entertained Du Bois."[50]

Regardless of political inclinations, wealthier African Americans recognized their obligations to those less fortunate. Furthermore, since most of their businesses were located in the Black Belt, their social responsibilities were webbed to economic development. Although social institutions in the Black Belt expanded, the poverty there was pronounced and its living conditions deplorable.

CHICAGO'S BLACK BELT

Historians and sociologists have written extensively about the formation and "ghettoization" of the Black Belt in Chicago.[51] Drake and Cayton traced the Black Belt's beginning to the Chicago fire of 1871, which destroyed the red light district. African Americans residing near the district thereafter moved to the Black Belt, then sandwiched between wealthy Whites and the "shanty Irish."[52] Between 1875 and 1893 most of the Black Belt's African Americans were employed as cooks, maids, and butlers in nearby white homes or in restaurants. By the late 1800s, however, the Black Belt had become stratified into three categories: "the refined," "the respectables," and "the sinners."[53] The last group, as noted, received the frequent attention of newspaper editors, who lectured them incessantly on "correct" living.

By the early 1900s the Black Belt stretched southward from downtown Chicago to Thirty-Ninth Street. As Southern migrants increasingly settled within its Second and Third Wards, white flight accelerated. As of 1906 more than 50 percent of African Americans in Chicago resided in the Black Belt; from 1906 to 1912 more than ten thousand African Americans settled there and in adjacent neighborhoods.[54] Accordingly, housing became difficult for all African Americans, regardless of social class, although it was especially problematic for the poor, who had few choices except to live in the Black Belt. As housing conditions deteriorated there, landlords continued to raise rents, making it necessary for families to take in lodgers. There were many single working women and men who needed accommodations, so finding lodgers was not difficult. One survey of the Chicago Commission on Race Relations estimated that of the 62 percent of African American households in the Black Belt, 35 percent accommodated lodgers. (This was in comparison to the lodger percentages of 13 percent of Slovaks in the Twentieth Ward, 13 percent of Greeks and Italians near Hull House, and 28 percent of Lithuanians in the Fourth Ward.)[55] Not only were more African Americans than immigrants lodgers; their residency in the Black Belt was more permanent than the immigrants' residencies in poor neighborhoods. Furthermore, their accommodations were in greater disrepair than the immigrants'. Only 26 percent of the buildings in the Black Belt were categorized as in "good" condition, in contrast to 71 percent in the immigrant sections of Chicago.[56]

From 1910 to 1920 the African American population in Chicago grew from 44,103 to 109,594, an increase of 148.5 percent.[57] From 1917 to 1918 alone, more than 50,000 African Americans moved to Chicago, a migration described by Zorbaugh as the "fourth invasion."[58] In his survey of nearly five hundred African American families in the Black Belt, Zorbaugh found that 89 percent were from the South and most were young wage earners.[59] Many had decided to migrate after reading in the *Chicago Defender* of better living conditions, wages, and schools. Most, upon their arrival in Chicago, had been directed to the Black Belt because they had relatives and former neighbors there.[60]

The living conditions in the Black Belt have been described by social workers and sociologists in terms of persistent poverty, unsanitary living conditions, and unhealthful tenant houses. Zorbaugh found the "poverty extreme and mortality high."[61] Breckinridge portrayed how the Black Belt was "conspicuously dilapidated," which, she concluded, greatly impeded "decent" family life.[62] Fannie Barrier Williams, referring to it as "the Darkest Africa," thought it "forbidding and demoralizing," a place where "there [wa]s scarcely a single ray of the light of decency."[63] Williams was undoubtedly referring to the Black Belt's red light district. As early as the 1890s, reformers and club women had taken the responsibility to clean up this district and other vice areas, with particular concern for the children who lived there:

> We are calling attention to the fact that a number of our girls and boys are on the road to ruin. The boys rioting in the Clark and 4th Avenue dives, laying the foundation for lives of thieves, thugs and murderers, and the girls walking the streets in gaudy attire. . . . How sad it is to see the girls we have known in their innocent childhood, change their lives, just when life's days should be the brightest, change from piety, virtue and happiness to vice, dissipation and woe. Mothers are you blind? Fathers are you deaf? Christians are you asleep? For the sake of God and Humanity, let some one rescue these young lives from dissipation's perpetual gloom.[64]

The population of children in the Black Belt in 1909 was estimated at 1,475, slightly less than one-tenth of its population. Despite this small population, Louise de Koven Bowen noted that one-third of the girls and one-eighth of the boys in Chicago's jails were African Americans, most of whom lived in the Black Belt.[65] Although Bowen did not directly account for the higher number of girls, other reports revealed that young women and girls were placed by employment agents as maids in prostitute houses in the vice areas and then arrested on prostitution charges.[66] As discussed later, the club women circumvented the unscrupulous efforts of these employment agents by founding safe homes and employment referrals for girls and women; they also met them at the train station. In conjunction with the juvenile and adult courts, club women insisted that raising the standards of the home and family life were the solutions, not the police courts or reformatories. Club women did not, however, specifically address the issue of lodgers, a practice deemed "neglectful" and "immoral" by the juvenile court. Louise de Koven Bowen of the Juvenile Protective Association contended, "While this practice is always found dangerous to family life, it is particularly so to the boys and girls of colored families, who are often obliged to live near the vice districts."[67]

To compound the family issue, many African American mothers worked long hours away from their children and for little pay. As of 1900 42.5 percent of African American women in Chicago were breadwinners, slightly less than the national rate of 43.2 percent. (As a point of comparison, 20.6 percent of white women, .04 percent of whom were married, worked.)[68] In 1910 this pattern remained essentially unchanged; more than 80 percent of African American working women were employed as domestic workers and servants. During World War I nonunion industry jobs became available to African American women who then did embroidery, needlework, and garment work on segregated factory lines. Although the pay was higher, long hours were still spent away from their children.[69]

Not only were housing and employment conditions dire in the Black Belt; health and sanitary conditions were also substandard. Dr. George Cleveland Hall, in a 1904 article in the *Chicago Defender*, placed the blame on Chicago landlords' lack of upkeep of "damp, insanitary [sic] and overcrowded dwellings." Hall pointed out how smallpox, tuberculosis, and pulmonary consumption were associated with the stagnant water in the streets, the rubbish in the alleys, and the "herded" conditions in apartments.[70] Hall's correlations were, unfortunately, accurate. When compared with statistics for other ethnic groups in Chicago, the stillbirth rate among African Americans was twice as high, and the likelihood of tuberculosis and syphilis was six times greater; pneumonia was three times as prevalent. One scholar likened the Black Belt's death rate to that of Bombay, India.[71]

Hall blamed not only the landlords but also the lodgers, who, he argued, kept their apartments unkempt and unsanitary. He called them "shiftless, dissolute, and immoral" and offered them lessons in hygiene and sanitation that were reminiscent of advice given to newly arrived immigrants by settlement and social workers.[72] Hall was not alone in dispensing such advice. Dr. Wilberforce Williams, in his weekly health columns in the *Chicago Defender,* lectured on ventilation, bathing, and food preparation. Other articles frequently appeared in the newspaper, urging home owners or lodgers to mow their grass or tidy their yards. L. W. Washington, in his newspaper column, "The Sayings and Doings of the People in Hyde Park," devoted one article to the proper way to clean house, giving minute details on washing bed linen, rugs, and other household items.[73] Another 1917 article admonished newcomers on their social behavior with the following list of "don'ts": "don't use vile language, don't be a public nuisance, don't be a 'beer can rusher,' don't get intoxicated, don't let children 'run in the streets,' and don't appear on the streets with 'old dust caps, dirty aprons, and ragged clothes.' "[74]

To further educate and assist newcomers, social institutions were founded. As St. Clair Drake noted, one had only to walk through the Black Belt or read the *Chicago Defender* to gain a sense of the number of African American uplift organizations in Chicago.[75] Facilities included nurseries, kindergartens, employment agencies, reading rooms, homes for the aged, homes for young working girls, a YMCA, a YWCA, settlements, missions, youth clubs, women's clubs, community centers, and city chapters of national organizations.[76] As of 1902 the Chicago Federation of Colored Women's Clubs had organized nine kindergartens in the African American churches in several different sections of the city. By 1903 that number had increased to twelve church kindergartens.[77] The Institutional Church and Social Settlement, founded in 1900 by Reverend Ransom, consisted of an auditorium, community rooms, a dining room, a gymnasium, a kitchen, clubs for women and children, a men's forum, and a nursery. Classes in sewing, cooking, and music were offered, as well as concerts and lectures. The facilities at Trinity Mission and Burning Bush Mission were more modest. Trinity provided bathing facilities, an employment agency, and a medicine dispensary; the Burning Bush offered lodging for homeless and destitute women and training in sewing, cooking, stenography, and typing.[78]

The secular settlements' services were more extensive because they employed professional social and settlement workers, in addition to relying upon the volunteerism of club women. Facilities at the Wendell Phillips Settlement, located on Chicago's West Side, consisted of a day nursery, a center for twenty-five groups, a Boy Scout division, and a division for women and girls. Two African American social workers,

Sophia Boaz and Birdye Haynes, who had studied at the University of Chicago's School of Civics and Philanthropy, were head residents there. At the Clotee Scott Settlement in Hyde Park, nearby University of Chicago students volunteered as playground supervisors, and club women taught music and sewing skills.[79]

The Negro Fellowship League and the Frederick Douglass Center, two other settlements, not only offered social services but also educated the African American community on political issues. Founded by Ida B. Wells in 1910, the Negro Fellowship League consisted of a reading room, an employment agency, political forums, and lodging rooms for men. The League also provided legal representation to prisoners and protested discrimination in public facilities and employment. The most controversial settlement was the Frederick Douglass Center. Cofounded by Celia Parker Woolley, a white Unitarian minister, and Ida B. Wells, the center's original intention was to promote a "just and amicable relationship" between the white and African American races.[80] Accordingly, the center's foremost clientele were not the poor, but middle-class and wealthy African Americans and Whites, who enrolled in fiction and sociology classes and joined the women's club. Although the Frederick Douglass Woman's Club indulged in the finest literature, art, and music, it also was quite active in promoting women's suffrage and in integrating public facilities.

Despite the commitment of many club women, church members, and community leaders to these institutions, Spear concluded that their services were far inferior to mainstream ones.[81] Not only did the African American facilities not receive the amount of financial support from wealthy patrons as did, say, Hull House, but they also were located in older, dilapidated buildings. Later chapters of this volume reveal that, except for the Phyllis Wheatley Home and the Old Folks' Home, most of these community institutions were short-lived because funding was problematic. As Fannie Barrier Williams concluded, uplift organizations generally could not be sustained through the African American community alone but relied heavily upon the "dominant race."[82]

In 1917 a city chapter of the Urban League was established in Chicago. Some of the settlements and missions were subsumed under the league's auspices, as prominent city reformers and businessmen placed their support there. A number of the club women, too, shifted their allegiances in working with the league, especially in activities that "touch[ed] the heart of the careless, indifferent and troublesome man and woman."[83] The league's traveler's aid, along with the women's clubs, dispensed information to newcomers on lodging, employment, and churches. Ida B. Wells suspected the league's motivations, thinking its intent was to undermine the more grassroots, community-based organizations.[84] Nevertheless, the organization grew in membership and services, establishing community neighborhood centers, clubs, employment agencies, classes, and gymnasiums. But, like the women's clubs, the Chicago Urban League still could not assist all of the African American migrants.

This chapter has examined the growth of the African American communities in Chicago, as well as their economic, political and social conditions. Attendant with the influx of African American migrants was increased class stratification, portrayed in club and church memberships, neighborhood residencies, and economic privilege. The club women assisted others through their sponsorship of kindergartens, settlements, day nurseries, and other facilities. Because the club women were members of the "talented tenth," the clubs' social uplift was tied to social privilege: charity balls, theater performances, and musical concerts were exclusive to those within the clubs' social circles. However, the clubs certainly performed "good deeds," since admission fees were earmarked for a coal fund, a charity case, or Christmas toys for poor children. Thus, as the club women's friendships, social networks, and class distinctions deepened, so did their responsibility to those less fortunate.

In chapter 3 the club women's involvement in political issues, particularly female suffrage, discrimination in public facilities, and economic self-determination, are examined. Suffrage and political representation were arenas in which club women cooperated both with political organizations and with all other African Americans, because voter turnout was imperative. The women were clearly influential in the ward politics of Chicago, especially when they were first granted the right to vote in municipal elections. They experienced less success, however, from their protests of discriminatory employment practices.

THREE

THE WOMEN'S

CLUBS AND POLITICAL REFORM

THERE WERE MANY POLITICAL ISSUES AROUND WHICH
Chicago African American club women rallied. Faced
with discrimination in schools, businesses, and public facilities, women held forums and discussions, conducted letter-writing campaigns, and wrote editorial and speeches.
In some cases the women's clubs assisted in providing legal representation
and counsel to political prisoners and others who could not afford it.
However, female suffrage was one of the more pressing issues and the
one in which the club women most demonstrated their political clout.

Before World War I African American and white club women had
formed fledgling coalitions, at least in Chicago. These coalitions paralleled the formation of the interracial national organizations the NAACP
and the Urban League. Jane Addams, Louise de Koven Bowen, and
Mary McDowell, to name only a few white female reformers, worked
in conjunction with African American women in Chicago on issues of
discrimination in housing, juvenile facilities for African American chil-

dren, and female suffrage. Despite African American and white women's agreement on female suffrage, their specific political agendas and strategies differed. African American club women, like white women, often used the issues of child welfare and home life to foreground community concerns, but they drew from their womanist identity, an identity that demanded and ensured community collectivity.[1] The mandate for such collectivity was decidedly effective in the Second Ward's alderman elections in 1914: the more African American votes, the greater the likelihood of electing an African American politician.

Although African American women were acknowledged for effecting political change within their communities, there were nonetheless gender tensions resulting from their involvement. Undaunted, the club women, when granted the right to vote in municipal elections, registered voters en masse, thereby forming a formidable voting block. Such strategies ensured political representation, evident in Oscar de Priest's aldermanic victory. However, as with much Progressive reform, their female volunteerism formed a dialectic relationship: it expanded, as well as diminished, the possibilities for female political leadership. For one thing, women campaigned tirelessly as volunteers but were not accorded *visible* leadership positions. Furthermore, in predicating their political agency on the issues of children's welfare and family, the club women limited the extent of their political influence. Conversely, though, the women conflated their *voluntary space* to achieve what no other African American organization in Chicago had done: elect an African American official.[2]

THE PERSUASION OF POLITICS, THE POLITICS OF PERSUASION:
FEMALE SUFFRAGE

Nationally, there was no consensus among African Americans, nor among the club women, on the issue of women's suffrage. Some thought suffrage imperative; others found it extraneous and inconsequential because much progress had already been achieved without it. Even when there was agreement, it was often for varying reasons. Some African Americans, both male and female, articulated arguments for the moral superiority of women, reminiscent of true womanhood ideology. Fiction writer Charles Chestnutt, for one, praised women's "fine intuitions" and "sympathies," qualities he believed would make women a "valuable factor in government."[3] Even Du Bois, although considering female suffrage a matter of human rights, thought women would not seek suffrage for "private gain," because they were morally superior to men.[4] Some African American women, predicating their arguments on the Republican motherhood, emphasized their maternal responsibilities. Mrs. Carrie W. Clifford, honorary president of the Federation of Colored Women's Clubs of Ohio, argued that because the family was a miniature state and the mothers' influence profound, women should be granted the vote.[5]

In grounding their arguments on motherhood and domestic duties, the club women both expanded their political sphere of activity and circumscribed it. African American club women, like their white counterparts, often appealed to matters of domestic affairs and home life, to persuade not only male legislatures but also reluctant women. Again, the club women's language was adaptive as they attempted to recruit other African American women to their side. Anna H. Jones, chair of the Department of Education of the NACW, dismissed the separation of the domestic and public spheres as she elevated women's domestic role in her statement, "All the questions touch in a very direct way the home—woman's kingdom."[6] In the spirit of municipal housekeeping, Adella Hunt Logan of the YWCA contended that just as women had always been competent housekeepers, so too could they become competent inspectors of buildings, sanitation, and food. All of this, she argued, followed the "course" of motherhood.[7] Such ideas dovetailed with the male perspective. Rev. Francis J. Grimke of Washington, D.C., arguing that social issues were, indeed, moral issues, surmised that women needed to participate in passing laws that would protect "the peace and happiness of the home."[8] Mr. Z. Withers, in a Chicago editorial, baldly summed up the situation: because women could not vote, they were still held in slavery. In underscoring how women's role as protector of the family and home was undermined, he dramatically juxtaposed women's moral guardianship to images of brazen sexuality: "Social diseases like a river of poison is [sic] carrying death to all. While women are enslaved, syphilitic plague, the modern leprosy, is striking death everywhere. While women are without the ballot the infamies of prostitution are increased. While women are without the ballot the foundation of home is crumbling."[9]

Despite the persuasion of such rhetoric and arguments, not everyone was convinced. Some dissuaders countered that women were simply not "trained" to vote. Club women responded with a ready solution: education. After all, as Dr. Mary F. Waring of Chicago pointed out, training was necessary in any field or subject that demanded decision making; voting was no exception.[10] Club woman Adella Hunt Logan pointed to precedents in Colorado, Idaho, and Wyoming, where women's interest in suffrage was so great that books on government were often sold out. Furthermore, she added, the female influence there was beneficial: schools and prisons were in much better condition than in states where women had not secured the vote.[11]

As a corollary to the argument of training, some club women thought that women had already undergone a rite of passage simply by virtue of their record of activism. When Mrs. Blanche K. Bruce, editor for the NACW, tallied women's club activities in terms of numbers of members and dollars, she found overwhelming proof of women's ability to vote.[12] Even in the home, in churches, and in schools, Nannie Burroughs noted, African American women had assumed much of the economic burden. She concluded that voting would simply be another avenue for women to exercise their responsibility.[13]

Even before women were granted the right to vote in municipal or state elections in Illinois, African American club women in Chicago influenced campaign results. In 1900 Dr. Carrie Golden read a paper before the Phyllis Wheatley Club on "The Sanitary Condition of the City and Its Relation to the Homes." After inspecting more than six hundred tenements of African Americans and Whites on the South Side, she and her committee had concluded that African American homes were "less sanitary." She not only stressed the importance of keeping a home "clean and attractive," but especially directed her attention to the owners, whose tenement houses were not fit for living, and who, furthermore, charged African Americans higher rents than Whites. She urged her club members to influence their husbands to vote for aldermen who would improve this situation. Thus, women wielded influence through their husbands' votes.[14]

Like national views on suffrage, Chicago club women's opinions varied. At one 1910 meeting of the Cornell Charity Club, most members were not in the affirmative. Mrs. Cordelia Yarbrough had argued that since women paid taxes, they should be given the vote. Another club member disagreed, submitting that all women should "stay at home and care for their children." Another member added that she would vote "when the time came." The last speaker and guest, Mr. J. H. Roberts, advised that mothers should give more care and attention to their boys so they would become better men. His refrain, "the hand that rocked the cradle is the hand that rules the world" was received with loud applause.[15]

Some Chicago club women argued that suffrage was not as pressing an issue as education and employment. Speaking before a church congregation on "Some Problems of the Colored Race" in 1903, Fannie Barrier Williams proposed that the right of suffrage was not as urgent as the right to be educated. Moreover, she pointed out, one could not vote in an intelligent manner unless he or she was educated.[16] Because of her position, as well as her affiliation with Booker T. Washington, she was often the target of editorial criticism. In one 1904 article in the *Broad Ax,* titled "Mrs. Fannie Barrier Booker T. Washington Williams Slops Over on the Negro Question," editor Julius Taylor harshly assailed Williams's character. According to the editor's version, Williams had argued that "disenfranchising" African Americans in the South had been "a blessing in disguise" because land ownership was a greater priority than political power.[17] In remarks that typified his strong anti–Washingtonian sentiments, Taylor conjectured: "Possibly we may be mistaken, but we are of the opinion that Mrs. Williams needed a new fall dress and some other finery and that Booker Washington was willing to give her several hundred dollars of the money he begs from the public to enable her to obtain the new traps."[18] Mrs. Williams's husband, the president of the Hyde Park Colored Republican Club, retaliated by speaking out on the "disgraceful acts" of editors who "boost[ed] up" politicians who were considered enemies of African Americans.[19]

Williams, however, became increasingly supportive of women's suffrage. In 1914 she proclaimed before the Progressive Negro League that African American women were handicapped "on all sides." After pointing to women's extensive education and training through the schools, churches, and clubs, she suggested that "they [we]re much better qualified for suffrage than were the Colored men when they were first enfranchised."[20] At another 1914 meeting, she declared that the power to vote in the state of Illinois would "lift Colored women to new importance as citizens." They would finally have an "effective weapon" to fight discrimination.[21]

One of the first women's clubs in Chicago to promote women's suffrage was the Frederick Douglass Woman's Club. Founded in 1906 and made up of middle-class white and African American women, the club met weekly to discuss mutual concerns, including suffrage. That year a discussion slated for one meeting was "Shall the New Charter Grant Municipal Suffrage to Women?" Speakers included Elia W. Peatrie, literary editor of the *Chicago Tribune;* Mrs. G. M. Faulkner of Liberia College in Africa; and Mrs. Elmira Springer, one of the most "liberal financiers" of the Frederick Douglass Center.[22] Unfortunately, as usual, their comments were not recorded. The same year a paper on the "Ideals of Citizenship" was read, followed by discussion on "improvement work," the "clean" ballot, and affirmation of woman's suffrage.[23] In 1912 neighborhood meetings were occasionally held at the center, which, again, focused on the need for a "good" government and a "clean" vote. One candidate for alderman in the First Ward visited the club to give "valuable hints" on good citizenship; at another meeting, African American author Dr. M. A. Majors, spoke on "The Woman Suffrage Question." Also in 1912 the Woman's Club held an open house for the neighborhood to receive ward and precinct leaders in the election.[24] Granted the municipal vote in 1913, the club women observed the 1914 election day with an afternoon "at-home," during which they listened to reports from the various precincts in the Second Ward. Their mood was jubilant because "the movement of a colored alderman in this ward [was] well under way."[25]

The Frederick Douglass Center broadened its political agenda to fight discrimination against African American women in other female political organizations. In 1912 the club women protested the Chicago Political League's rejection of three membership applications of African American women. President Woolley encouraged a letter-writing campaign against their exclusion, and nearly one hundred letters were sent. The league responded by promising to take up the matter after the biennial meeting of the national General Federation of Women's Clubs. At the next federation meeting the matter was resolved. Fannie Barrier Williams, Elizabeth Lindsay Davis, and Mrs. George Hall were granted membership in the league. The center declared victory: "The League by that action has evidently decided that the color line has no place in a suffrage organization."[26]

One of the best known suffragists in the Chicago African American community was Ida B. Wells, who organized several suffrage clubs. Not content to wait for the female vote, Wells founded the Women's Second Ward Republican Club in 1910 "to assist the men in getting better laws for the race and having representation in everything which tends to the uplift of the city and its government."[27] That the club was timely was evident in the attendance of nearly two hundred women. Moreover, the club continued to press for female suffrage, inviting both white and African American women to speak. At one meeting in 1910, a white suffragist, Minora Jones, insisted that it was "just as important that the black woman be as free as her 'fairer sister.' "[28] The Ideal Woman's Club, with which Ida B. Wells was closely associated, likewise took an active interest in suffrage. At one 1911 meeting, Wells herself read a paper on "Woman's Suffrage," followed by "general discussion."[29]

The Alpha Suffrage Club, organized by Wells in 1913, was the only African American suffrage club in Chicago and Illinois during that time. It was also the only suffrage club to hold its meetings in a prison, the Bridewell Penitentiary. There, Wells attempted to interest the women inmates in suffrage, encouraging them to "so deport themselves that they might be proven worthy of the gift bestowed."[30] The location also provided valuable lessons to the club women and opportunity for activism. During one of their meetings a young man interrupted, "his face all swollen and head bandaged up." He reported that he had been beaten by sixty white prisoners there at Bridewell Penitentiary. The club immediately gathered a collection for his food and lodging, then set up a committee to investigate the situation.[31]

One of the club's first activities was to raise funds to pay for Ida B. Well's travel expenses to the National Association of Equal Suffrage League's parade in 1913. It was at this national parade that Ida B. Wells was ordered to march in the "colored section" but refused and walked alongside other Illinois women, including Belle Squire and Virginia Brooks, "who stood so loyally by Mrs. Barnett in her fight for colored representation." Thirty-five members of the Alpha Suffrage Club also participated, although it was not clear in what section they marched.[32]

The Alpha Suffrage Club met weekly to "study political and civic questions for themselves" in hopes of becoming "strong enough to help elect some conscientious race man as alderman."[33] They insisted that African American men and women work together toward this goal.

There were several reasons for this. First, racial solidarity was absolutely essential for the election of an African American politician. Since the majority constituency in the Second Ward was African American, it was especially critical for the club women to concentrate their political efforts there. Second, because many African American businesses, including those of women (millinery and dressmaking shops, chiropodist and manicure parlors), were located in the Second Ward, as well as in the larger Black Belt, more than political representation was at stake.

Accordingly, weekly instructions were given on voting, with the argument that a large number of foreign women, many of whom did not know English, were already learning how to vote. Within six months of its founding, the club had more than one hundred members. Club members canvassed various African American wards, encouraging residents to register. The club's influence was evident when a white representative from the Republican Party visited, promising that if the club worked for a Republican candidate, at the next election the Republicans would nominate an African American candidate. Both parties agreed and the promise was kept by both.[34] Credit for the election success of Oscar de Priest was given to the "newly enfranchised women" who worked vigorously for this election.[35]

In 1914 the Alpha Suffrage Club celebrated its first anniversary. The club continued its work of teaching women "their duties as good citizens" by distributing lists of candidates, recommending candidates, providing a directory of voting locations in each ward, compiling reports on national suffragists, and sponsoring speakers. Nina T. Curtis, assistant to county judge Owens, gave a talk on the voting laws and demonstrated how to use the voting machine installed at the Progressive Club. Election commissioner Czarnecki attended a club meeting, giving final instructions on voting. When Judge Owen decided that women could vote for city commissioner, the club encouraged women to vote for the two women and African American candidates. All of the candidates visited the club to outline their platforms. In order to arrive at a consensus, the club women decided in 1915 to hold a primary of their own. The candidate who received the highest number of votes would be the one for whom they would all cast their ballots.[36] Through this collective strategy the club women ensured the election of their candidate. Even when women could not vote for a position, as was the case then with circuit court judges, they still felt it was their duty to "use their influence to aid in selecting good judges," most likely through their husbands' votes.[37]

The women had a choice not only in candidates, but occasionally in political parties also. Although most African Americans were Republicans, many joined third parties. One such party was the People's Movement, founded by Oscar de Priest in the Second Ward in 1918. According to de Priest, the movement represented those of the African American Republican Party in the Second Ward "who [could] not be bought at any price." De Priest had astutely noted that 75 percent of the Second Ward's population was African American, of which 85 percent were Republican. Yet only 15 percent of the Republicans in the ward received seventy-three thousand dollars in combined salary while the remaining 85 percent received only ninety-five hundred dollars.[38] The People's Movement, de Priest promised, would "purify" the Republican Party by respecting the majority. Consequently, many of the club women in the Second Ward supported de Priest and the People's Movement.

Although the club focused mostly on ward politics, it also kept increasing the momentum on female suffrage at the national level. The club continued to worked with white women on this issue; suffragists Jane Addams and Mrs. Grace Wilbur Trout were regular speakers. Dr. Anna Blount of Oak Park, who had protested barring African American women from white clubs, also addressed the club. At another program Mrs. L. S. Bishop, a white suffragist leader, gave a presentation, which was followed by a poetry reading by local African American poets Bettiola Forston and Fenton Johnson. (Bettiola Forston was not only considered a fine young poet and orator but was also the second vice president of the Alpha Suffrage Club and one of the city organizers of the Chicago Federation of Women's Clubs.)[39]

Other African American women's clubs, too, were dedicated to the suffrage issue, but to a lesser extent than the Alpha Suffrage Club and the Frederick Douglass Woman's Club. In 1913 the Phyllis Wheatley Club held suffrage classes and invited various candidates to speak at their meetings.[40] The Alloha Suffragist Club, formed in 1913, participated mostly in national suffrage parades. The Ideal Woman's Club sponsored a speaker series that included Mrs. Booth of Glencoe, a leader in women's suffrage, and Ida B. Wells. The Billiken Hoop and Needle Club hosted Dr. Schulz, an African American female medical doctor, who spoke on women's suffrage; Mrs. Ella S. Stewart, one of Chicago's foremost suffrage leaders, spoke before the Clotee Scott Settlement's Sunday Club. The West Side Women's Club organized a bazaar, where each night a different political party was represented. In 1915 the Negro Fellowship League featured a number of discussions on the pertinent topics of the circuit court elections, bond issues, Oscar de Priest's campaign, and cooperative work with auxiliary suffrage clubs in Hyde Park and the West Side.[41]

Despite women's savvy in political campaigns, some newspapermen and male leaders held tenaciously to their true womanhood beliefs. Stovall noted how after state-wide suffrage was granted to women in Illinois, Robert Abbott returned to his previous descriptions of women as "noble" and "virtuous." One *Chicago Defender* writer proposed that if women voted, they would purify politics because of their natural goodness and purity. He described the "noble women" of the Second Ward, who "loyally stood by their race and showed that they were actuated by principle in politics just as they are in everything else." He further praised the women for their "sense of duty" and stated that "through them the second ward [wa]s to be purified."[42] One prominent African American woman wryly remarked that it was strange to be praised for simply doing her duty.[43]

During the period 1916 to 1920, the suffrage fervor on the local, regional, and national scene continued. At the Alba Rose Club and the Negro Fellowship League Reading Room, the Second Ward's alderman elections were discussed. The Chicago Women's Amateur Minstrel Club in 1916 performed a "screaming farce" entitled "Woman's Suffrage." Mrs. George Cleveland Hall, "acknowledged to be the world's greatest interlocutor" was the star performer for that event.[44] Another national suffrage parade was held in 1916, and the Chicago clubs participated. The Phyllis Wheatley Club placed a notice in the newspaper for "all women desiring to march in the big suffrage parade" to meet at the Phyllis Wheatley Home, where "hats and sashes [could] be secured."[45] In October of 1916 the women in Illinois were given their first opportunity to register to vote for president of the United States. Many took up this challenge, including one Chicago woman who claimed to have been born a slave in 1803 and was 113 years old when she registered.[46]

Although Dorothy Salem noted that most women's clubs were not involved in the suffrage issue until after 1910, this was not the case with the Chicago club women.[47] As early as 1900, even though club women could not vote, they persuaded their husbands to vote wisely. At their club meetings they discussed political issues, arrived at a consensus, then campaigned vigorously. Once they were granted the right to vote, whether in city, state, or national elections, they educated other women and encouraged them to register. That club women were influential in their political base was evident in de Priest's admission that he owed much of his campaign success to them. The vote, however, was not an isolated victory or challenge for African American club women. Club women also fought discriminatory legislation and practices.

"THE VITAL AGENCY OF WOMANHOOD": FIGHTING DISCRIMINATION IN EDUCATION, EMPLOYMENT, AND PUBLIC INSTITUTIONS

The club women's political efforts, like many of their other activities, focused primarily on child welfare. As they had done in the issue of female suffrage, club women positioned themselves as community caretakers, especially for children and youth. They directed their protests to schools and educational facilities that discriminated against African American children, they urged African American businessmen to hire youths from within their communities, and they formed rotating credit associations and clubs to ensure the financial security of their children. Although club women were involved in fighting legal and legislative discrimination, especially by promoting the passage of antilynching laws, they realized that such issues required the concerted efforts of all African Americans. Accordingly, the NACW wedded its efforts to those of other national organizations, most notably the NAACP and the Urban League.

In Chicago the Negro Fellowship League and its founder, Ida B. Wells, were most active in advocating antilynching laws; they also worked to redress legal discrimination in the jails and penitentiaries. Wells was joined by several women's clubs who engaged in letter-writing campaigns and editorials. In one editorial published in the *Chicago Defender* in 1910, the president of the Coterie Club inquired:

> *Would it not have been wiser and far better had we sought to reach our white friends from a humanitarian point of view? Rather than through racial agitation? We have been agitating and agitating year after year, and what has the Negro accomplished? We have not stopped the lynching of the Black man for every real or imaginary crime; we have not succeeded in*

either tearing down or creaking through the wall of prejudice that rears up
so gloomily ahead and cast [sic] its shadows over us; we have listened to
the most eloquent speakers, the most gifted orators, intellectual women tell
of the great wrongs done the African American race of people.[48]

The club president concluded with the following advice: "One cannot think it is time to recall those missionaries from foreign shores, as we have abundant work at our own doors."[49] Members of the Giles Charity Club expressed their concern differently, sending letters to Congressman Martin Madden to protest the lynchings in East St. Louis in 1918. The same year Ida B. Wells urged the Negro Fellowship League to draw up resolutions concerning the lynching of six men in Texas.[50]

Of all the Chicago organizations, the Negro Fellowship League was the most active in legal redress and representation, especially of political prisoners. The league had publicized the inhumane treatment of Joseph Campbell, a prisoner who had been confined to a solitary cell for more than fifty hours. In representing the league, Ida B. Wells not only promised him a lawyer but also assured him that she would continue putting pressure on the courts through newspaper coverage. Several other inmates also requested and received assistance from the league. One was Dr. Bundy, who had been confined to a convent at Belleville, Illinois, and had been charged with conspiracy in the East St. Louis trials. Wells and the league provided him with legal counsel, as well as keeping the public informed of his case. In addition to securing legal representation, mostly through her husband-lawyer, Wells occasionally obtained reprieves for prisoners. She also made jail visits on behalf of the prisoners' families.[51]

Wells directed her attention not only to individual cases but also to the larger legal arena. This was especially true with regard to the East St. Louis riots, which preceded the riots in Chicago by two years. In 1918 the league sponsored a symposium on the East St. Louis race riots, at which Wells urged that a thorough investigation of the riots be conducted and that all facts be published. She promised that the league would "keep up an agitation on this matter until something [wa]s done." Consequently, the league adopted a resolution to print the testimony and photographs of the riots in entirety. Copies of the resolution were sent to Congressmen Martin Madden and James Mann and Senator J. Hamilton Lewis. One Kentucky congressman strongly discouraged such printing, arguing that it would be too costly. However, Wells asserted that the cost of publication, which she estimated at five thousand dollars, was far less than the cost of committee appointments, which she estimated at fifteen thousand dollars.[52]

The Negro Fellowship League and the Progressive Negro League worked closely with other organizations on issues of discrimination, including the Chicago branch of the National Equal Rights League. In 1915 the Equal Rights League of Chicago held a meeting to consider a Jim Crow bill before the Illinois House. That same year the Chicago branch had expressed concern over a law that made it a felony for African Americans and Whites to marry in the Washington, D.C., area. This law, they declared, was "an insult to and an official stigma upon the colored people of the country, depriving colored women of the protection all other women have."[53] The Negro Fellowship League wrote a letter of protest. Delegates from Chicago, including Wells, were sent to the National Congress.

The Negro Fellowship League, along with the Frederick Douglass Center, confronted discrimination in employment, schooling, and public facilities on a local level. Although various strategies were employed, such as letter-writing campaigns, conferences, and forums, the Negro Fellowship League frequently acted directly and on an individual basis. Despite the league's dwindling financial support, Wells persisted in her efforts, evident in an 1915 report that recorded assistance to a young woman who was "despondent and almost frantic" because she had no money, and to a woman who had worked as a domestic servant for a white family for a dollar a week for fifteen years.[54] In the latter case the woman was prevented from attending an African American church or otherwise associating with other African Americans. Wells responded swiftly to her situation: "The president of the League got her clothes and money from the white people to whom she had been in slavery all that time and saw that she had a good home with a excellent Colored family, who will pay her good wages."[55]

Nonetheless, letter writing, editorials, speeches, and conferences were more usual forms of protesting discrimination. As early as 1901, Alberta Moore-Smith had reported to the National Negro Business League in Chicago that for every "five avenues of employment" available to white women, only two were open to African American women. This was especially true in department stores and business firms, where African

American women were rarely hired as saleswomen or secretaries, respectively.[56] That such discrimination existed in Chicago was evident at a 1915 Paul Laurence Dunbar Celebration, where the audience passed a resolution protesting Marshall Field and Company's refusal to hire African American women: "Whereas, it has been unquestionably established by careful investigation and proof that Marshall Field & Co., in the matter of public accommodation, shows deliberate discrimination."[57] The following year the Negro Fellowship League sponsored a conference on the company's discriminatory practices. Not only were African American women not hired but they were also often refused service. The league encouraged every club and organization to send delegates to the conference because "something must be done, and that something must be done in union."[58] However, Marshall Field and Company was not alone in discriminatory hiring. A motion was also forwarded by the Negro Fellowship League to send a letter to Libby, McNeil and Company, inquiring why African American women were not employed there. The women sought both economic advancement and respectful treatment, as the league also protested the misrepresentation of "Negro mammies in corn-meal advertisements."[59]

Discrimination in the schools, recreational facilities, and movie theaters was also confronted. The Frederick Douglass Center, which was particularly active in these efforts, scored two victories in 1910 for "race justice and race equality." In the first situation, the center secured membership for African American residents at the Hyde Park Center, which had been recently opened by the Juvenile Protective League. Following joint discussions with the Frederick Douglass Center, the board of the newly opened center voted against its exclusionary practices.[60] Second, the Frederick Douglass Center assisted in rescinding a rule that drew the color line in Gad's Hill Summer Encampment at Lake Bluff, a popular location for summer camps for children.[61]

Schools were another contested site. Wendell Phillips High School was a frequent target because of its continued racial segregation and tensions. In 1915 the dean and principal had organized segregated social evenings for white and African American students, because many parents did not wish to encourage interracial dancing and dating. Fannie E. Smith, dean of girls for Wendell Phillips School, who "was responsible for drawing the color line in the social room," was invited to speak before the Progressive Negro League. After her talk, a committee was organized, with Ida B. Wells as chair, to visit the school.[62] Segregation and unfair treatment nonetheless persisted in the high school, as well as in the Wendell Phillips night school. The league issued a 1918 report, based on an investigation of the night school, and adopted a resolution that condemned the school's "separation propaganda." Instead of segregation, the league recommended "co-operated action, allied activities, earnest efforts, and social service agencies as a cure for the alleged evil."[63]

Wendell Phillips High School was not the only school fraught with racial tensions. The Frederick Douglass Center's president, Celia Parker Woolley, sent a letter to the Illinois Technical School at Park Ridge, inquiring about "the exact status of the colored girls in your school." In particular, Woolley asked if the cottages were segregated according to race: "What is the principle of classification in the use or occupancy of the cottages: age, standing in school, character or racial descent? And if race is a principle, is it applied to races other than colored children?"[64] The center was also concerned about the segregation of African American girls sent from the juvenile court. Because Protestant schools refused their admittance, the girls had little choice except to enroll in a segregated Catholic school. The center and the women's clubs argued that if segregation was the principle, then African Americans should be responsible for their own institutions.[65] This controversy, examined in greater detail in the following chapter, resulted in the creation of an industrial school for African American girls, founded and administered by an African American woman.

Movie theaters, too, were segregated, especially in Evanston, where African Americans were led through a separate entrance and seated in a separate gallery. Several editorials had been written by club women and others, demanding immediate action.[66] It was not clear how the theaters responded. The African American community was more adamant about banning the racist movie *Birth of a Nation*. In 1912 Celia Parker Woolley had been assured by the wife of the newly elected mayor, William Thompson, that the film would be permanently withdrawn from the movie theaters in Chicago. Thompson's wife had spoken of her gratitude toward the African American community for its support of her husband as mayor. Her promise was not long-lived, however: the film was shown in Chicago in 1915. Shortly thereafter, the Negro Fellowship League held a discussion, led by Irene McCoy-Gaines, titled "What Can the Negro Do about the Birth of a Nation?"[67]

Although such incidents often ended in small victories, they also poignantly revealed the persistent and systematic levels of discrimination faced by African American women, men, and children. The club women confronted each incident individually, but they were well aware that the events were not isolated and singular but part of a larger racist tide. Clearly, the success of their efforts in fighting discrimination in the business world was dubious, as there were no responses recorded from Marshall Fields or Libby, McNeil and Company. However, the protests regarding child welfare and educational facilities more often resulted in improved conditions, new facilities, and integration. There were undoubtedly several reasons for this. First, issues of child welfare were perceived to be a female domain; thus, women, as municipal housekeepers and moral guardians, were perhaps considered best suited to deliberate on such matters. Second, most of these protests involved the mutual efforts of white and African American club women. In many of the examples above, Woolley's influence, as well as Wells's, was decisive. Third, because the African American business community was largely segregated, it was unlikely that African American women would wield much influence in a commercial and business world that was predominantly white and male. Interestingly, Woolley did not choose to join African American club women in their protests of discrimination in employment, perhaps because she did not want to alienate philanthropists and social reformers with whom she was closely affiliated. Thus, African American club women created their own forms of economic self-determination.

"OUR SHIP IS MANNED BY WOMEN": ECONOMIC CLUBS

Economic self-determination in the African American communities was another measure taken by women to ensure political autonomy. In 1911 the University Society Club noted that there were at least one hundred African Americans in Chicago who were "worth well over ten thousand dollars." They recommended that these individuals establish businesses to employ African American youths, thereby "put[ting] them on a footing which would make them more respected by other races than they are at the present time."[68] By employing this intergenerational approach, the club argued that younger people who lacked capital would get a head start: "The young Negro has the education, the older ones have the money and experience; why not begin enterprizes [sic]?"[69] The Negro Fellowship League in 1916 recommended a similar strategy at the annual Abraham Lincoln–Frederick Douglass celebration at Olivet Church. There Anthony Overton of the Overton Company presented a speech on "Developing the Overton Company into a Million-Dollar Corporation." The league promised to help procure African American patronage of his company's products if he would hire young African Americans. This, Ida B. Wells insisted, was one of the most effective ways for young people to secure jobs, as well as to build up African American businesses.[70]

Club women promoted not only community businesses but also their own economic independence. In the tradition of rotating credit associations, and following the living example of Maggie Lena Walker, several women's clubs were formed, to which members paid dues and were guaranteed, in turn, sick benefits and money for burial.[71] The first such women's club in Chicago was the Twentieth Century Penny Club, founded by Fanny Ralston in 1902. By 1904 forty members had joined the club, which not only provided economic insurance but hoped also to raise enough money to build a home for members who could not afford rent. In addition, the club functioned as an employment agency or "exchange," which provided the "housewife a chance to dispose of any kind of work" that she performed at home.[72] As other women's clubs did, the members met weekly to discuss topics "of practical benefit to the race."[73]

The president of this club stressed individual thrift, as well as a collective economic determination. Ralston, like Booker T. Washington, encouraged African Americans to develop the characteristics of punctuality, discipline, and orderliness, which she considered crucial for business success, and she criticized the African American communities' "short-sightedness." She—like other club women Ida B. Wells, Joanna Snowden, and Alberta Moore—recommended community collectivity. She pointed out that if each African American in Chicago gave a penny to the club, the total would be thirty thousand pennies.[74] Targeting the wealthier African American businessmen, she chastised them for not hiring younger persons from their own communities. Unlike these businesses, the Twentieth Century Penny Club ensured by its savings plan the financial security of both its members and their children. As Ralston noted: "We all work and make our money, then let us organize financial clubs instead of so many pleasure clubs. Then we, as mothers and father, will be able when our children come to maturity to start them out in life with some prospects before them."[75]

Two other economic clubs were organized for and by women during the war years. The Easter Lily Club was founded in 1914 by Emma Smith, who described herself as a "country woman who didn't know what a mailbox was when she first saw one."[76] Despite her self-deprecation, Smith's organizational savvy was evident in the club's growth. Beginning with five members, in two years' time the club had grown to more than 1,250 members; by 1917 membership had increased to more than 3,000.[77] The Easter Lily Club was designed as "an organization controlled and governed exclusively by women for their protection and benefit."[78] In exchange for monthly dues of thirty cents, women received sick benefits amounting to four dollars a week. Such benefits were especially important to its members, who were often the sole wage earners in their households, particularly during the war period. The club assured members that it would permit "no case of sickness, distress or death to occur without immediate attention."[79] The women prided themselves on their club's success: "They have made all the progress by themselves never accepting the aid of the other sex and are very proud of their record."[80] Not only did the club function as a rotating credit association, but it also organized a singing club, which performed regularly at Olivet Baptist Church. (The director, Mme. Hawkins, a graduate of the St. Louis Conservatory of Music and the Northwestern Conservatory of Music in Ohio, was publicly known for her singing.)[81]

Because of the limited accommodations for the club, as well as its growing membership, Emma Smith organized another economic club in 1916, the Mayflower Club. On April 19 of that year she invited a few club women to her home, where they discussed and prayed over the decision. As if inspired, Emma Smith "sprang to her feet and said: 'We'll organize and save the balance of our women.' "[82] Although the club was named after the Pilgrims' ship, Smith described its mission in distinctly gendered terms: "Unlike the good old Mayflower of Pilgrim days, which did not stop until it reached its journey's end—all of its officers being men—our ship is manned from stern to stern by women. We pull into port the first and third Mondays of each month and take on new passengers."[83] The club began with nine members and the same number of dollars. Within two years, membership had increased to 560 women, who had accumulated almost $1,700. In exchange for monthly dues of $1.30, members received $4.00 a week for sick pay for twenty-four weeks. For an extra $2.00 a year, members received an endowment of $100 for burial expenses. Clearly, the club provided for many women's sick pay and burials, as the total amount of dues far exceeded the club's accumulated savings. But the club's transactions were not only economic. In the spirit of Smith's faith, she hoped that the club would teach women "to be broader, kinder and forgiving in [their] thoughts and actions toward each other."[84] Members probably visited one another when ill or provided food or other in-kind donations to families, as was the custom in women's clubs.

Although suffrage seemed to be one of the most pressing political concerns for the African American women's clubs in Chicago, discrimination in employment, education, and public facilities were also addressed. Discussion and speeches were linked to letter writing, protests, marches, and, infrequently, boycotts. Women's clubs collaborated on local and national levels through speakers, marches, and legislative action. The Frederick Douglass Center and the Negro Fellowship League, in particular, were exemplary organizations in their attempts to politicize the African American communities.

In many cases political action was moored to the social welfare of children and youths, as women fought discrimination and segregation in schools and in other state and city facilities for children. Although scholars have argued that African Americans promoted their own segregated institutions, this chapter has documented the extent to which club women fought segregation and discrimination. When such practices continued in spite of their efforts, African Americans had little choice except to create social institutions to meet the growing demands of their own communities.

FOUR

HOMES FOR

DEPENDENT CHILDREN,

YOUNG WORKING GIRLS,

AND THE ELDERLY

THERE WERE MANY FACILITIES FOUNDED BY THE African American club women for African American children, young working girls, and the elderly. This chapter focuses on four such homes: the Louise Juvenile Home, for dependent and orphaned boys; the Amanda Smith Home, for dependent and orphaned girls; the Phyllis Wheatley Home, for single working girls; and the Home for the Aged and Infirm Colored People, for the elderly. Although social and economic tiers were created through charity balls, theater productions, victrola recitals, and other exclusive philanthropic endeavors, which supported these homes, there were also numerous activities that did not necessarily accord the club women status. For example, the women provided in-kind donations such as food; they offered "good cheer" to the elderly and encouragement to the young. The club women often spoke of providing and caring for "their own," in large part because of the discriminatory practices of mainstream orphanages, industrial schools, and homes for young working girls and the elderly.

African Americans were not alone in their exclusion from mainstream facilities: many homes, charities, and settlements were demarcated by ethnic and denominational affiliation. However, the sustenance of African American community facilities for children and youth was complicated by the *parens patriae* of the state, particularly the juvenile court system. The African American women's administration and financial support of the homes for dependent and delinquent children were intricately webbed to the Cook County Juvenile Court. Because African American women served as probation and truant officers, they further implicated themselves in a court system that paradoxically permitted and rationalized inferior and segregated facilities for African American dependent children.[1] Such ironies were evident, for example, in Elizabeth McDonald's probation and rescue work. As the first African American female probation officer in the United States, McDonald combined her rescue work with home and jail visitations required by the court. Seeing the need for a home for African American orphaned and dependent children, McDonald took in several children voluntarily. This was the beginning of the Louise Juvenile Home, which she later incorporated into the Louise Juvenile Industrial School in order to receive county funds through the juvenile court.

This singular example corroborates contemporary scholarship, which demonstrates the prominence of a maternalistic rather than a paternalistic influence in the juvenile court system.[2] The roots of this maternal influence ran deep in the Cook County Juvenile Court, beginning with the Chicago Woman's Club's advocacy of the first juvenile law and court in 1899.[3] Indeed, even the language of the first juvenile law intimated a maternal influence. Words such as "neglected," "disreputable," "depravity," and "unfit" carried images, interpretations, and recommendations largely culled from ideologies that reflected middle-class maternalism. As Eileen Boris has astutely assessed, the very language and ideas that female reformers used to guide them in their activism promulgated women's subordinate economic and social position.[4] For poor African American women and children, the consequences were especially dire.

The conditions of crowded and dilapidated tenements, unsanitary living conditions, and poverty in the Black Belt were what court officials considered especially "neglectful," "unfit," and even "immoral." Such conditions were certainly not conducive to what they considered "proper" home life. Nevertheless, child welfare reformers argued that keeping home life intact was of utmost importance in preventing delinquency and truancy. The nagging question before the court was whether poverty itself constituted "neglect"; if so, many children, especially African Americans and immigrants, would by necessity be removed from their homes. Social reformers sympathized with their impoverished conditions, arguing that reform should encompass family life, not atomize it.[5] Despite this cloaking of reform in terms of the family unit, the intervention of probation officers, as well as the creation of mothers' pensions, pointed to ways in which motherhood was carved into prescriptive, and thus restrictive, roles through the juvenile courts and the welfare laws. For example, inscribed within the restrictions for mothers' pensions were the criteria of morality, economic dependency, and citizenship.[6] One unwritten restriction was race: court records in Chicago and the rest of the nation indicate that African American women and their children received few mothers' pensions. In 1920 mothers' pensions were granted to 24 African Americans out of the 573 applications in Chicago.[7]

Thus, African American women—as club members, juvenile court officers, and founders of homes—faced not only immense challenges but also contradictions. This held particularly true for African American probation officers, many of whom were also members of women's clubs. For one thing, they had to deliberate on home conditions in communities where the city government had not yet provided any infrastructure through laws or inspection agencies. As of 1905 the city of Chicago had no tenement house department; instead, the inspection of tenements rested with the Building Department and the Department of Health. Furthermore, no chief sanitary inspector had been legally appointed.[8] Paradoxically, then, even though there were few mechanisms in place to inspect the unsanitary conditions of tenements, garbage disposal, and vacant lots, parents were held accountable for "neglectful" conditions within their own homes.

Second, African American women received little training or remuneration for their efforts as probation officers. In the early years of the juvenile court, there were sporadic and unsystematic efforts at "standardizing" education for probation work.[9] Curiously, this allowed women further influence in their clients' homes. Consistent with the true womanhood and municipal housekeeping ideologies, women thought themselves morally superior in domestic and household affairs; most male officers and judges concurred. Although their visits were termed "inspections," replete with case study reports and evaluations, the probation officer was encouraged to form personal relationships with the family: to be a friend, a confidant, a teacher, and even a member of the family. Female probation officers performed a multitude of roles and duties, ranging from instruction in child care and household chores to visiting children's schools and canvassing the neighborhood for unwholesome pasttimes.[10] As Eli Zaretsky has epigrammatically noted: "The form in which the welfare state expanded was public, the content private." This "private" instruction, under the moral guardianship of probation officers, dovetailed conveniently with volunteerism, as early court officials argued that salaries would lead to political corruption.[11]

The third constraint faced by African American women concerned the placement of dependent and delinquent children. Despite the fact that probation officers in many cases intimately knew the conditions of family life, they served only in an advisory capacity to the juvenile court judge who made the final decision. Although court deliberations were not recorded, it is likely that probation officers exerted some influence, particularly because they were matched as "cultural brokers" to the families, based on their similarity in race, ethnicity, religion, and first language.[12] Nonetheless, there were few facilities in which African American children could be placed. According to Crawley, by 1926 there were only three African American facilities that accepted dependent children.[13] In the case of African American delinquent children, they most often remained at home under the supervision of probation officers or were sent to state institutions.

Despite much evidence of progressive maternalism, we still know little about the specific contexts of the probation officers' home visits and interactions. How, for example, did the women mediate, interpret, and make recommendations concerning family conditions and court laws? On the other hand, how did their court work influence their ideologies and community practices? The activities of club women, many of whom were appointed probation and truant officers, have provided us with glimpses of such contexts. African American club women employed multiple strategies for child welfare issues. They formed committees and canvassed the streets, with an eye to keeping the young away from harmful influences. They inspected tenement conditions. Numerous newspaper articles were written on the need for playground and recreational facilities; they wrote prescriptive lists on the elements of an upright home life. Mothers' clubs were formed to study various aspects of child culture. The Children's Aid Society and the Giles Charity Club, affiliated with probation officers Ezella Carter, Alberta Moore-Smith, and Joanna Snowden-Porter (see appendix 2), were especially active in studying issues related to social service, as well as in sponsoring events for poorer children.[14]

To alleviate delinquency, wholesome recreational activities, such as youth clubs, dances, lyceums, and picnics were organized and chaperoned by the club women to lure adolescents away from neighborhood saloons, dance halls, and pool rooms. In particular, the club women were concerned about young girls' protection. The Chicago Afro-American Mothers' Council accordingly directed mothers to:

> instruct their girls in all matters pertaining to their future welfare; not to let them roam the streets by day or by night, but they must keep close to their daughter and make constant companions of them, and wield such a refining influence over them for good that there will be no danger of them ever wandering from the path of rectitude.[15]

Club women also spoke of "rescuing" and "protecting" young women, as the YWCAs and other predominantly white organizations did. Many other African American women's clubs, however, including the Giles Charity Club, the K. D. Tillman Club, the Cornell Charity Club, the Necessity Club, and the Volunteer Workers' Club, to name only a few, directly acknowledged and confronted the economic and social ills facing many parents. They established day nurseries for working mothers, health care facilities for school children, industrial education classes, and homes for dependent and orphaned children and for young working girls.

Underneath the concern of African American girls' protection were the tensions and implications of sexual misbehavior. This was not unique to African American girls: immorality and incorrigibility were the two primary causes for all young girls' delinquency in Chicago. However, the historical and persistent sexual violation of African American women made the issue of morality an especially troubling one. Hine has unfolded the argument that many Southern African American women migrated to the North to escape the sexual aggression of men.[16] But many young women were prey to the very same behavior in the North. Most young migrants from the Chicago train station were directed to the Black Belt for lodging, where, according to Grossman, they roamed past brightly lit saloons, cabarets, and pool halls in search of lodging. Often men were given preference over women as lodgers, in part because they were perceived as less demanding.[17] This left many young women without accommodations.

The club women were alarmed at such vulnerabilities. Elizabeth Lindsay Davis warned that "many of [these] girls were going astray by being led unawares into disreputable homes, entertainment and employment."[18] Much press coverage was given to "disorderly" and "good time" houses, one purportedly managed by "a sporting Colored lady and low white women or female cats."[19] Other club women, such as Mrs. Gaten of the African American YWCA, voiced alarm at the apparel and dance steps of some women.[20] What remained unacknowledged, at least publicly, by both white and African American club women, was the possibility that young women might prefer such life styles. Joanne Meyerowitz's study of "women adrift" in Chicago has documented an underside of young women's lives, revealing increased independence, sexual curiosity, and frequenting of public dance halls, cabarets, and movie theaters.[21] Such independence, of course, ran contrary to the Young Women's Christian Association, the church-sponsored homes, and the juvenile court.

Suffice it to say that African American club women realized that their children and youths were particularly at risk. As will be evident in the following sections on the Louise Juvenile Home and the Amanda Smith Home, discrimination for dependent children was double-edged. On the front end, many African American children and youth resided in impoverished neighborhoods, making them more vulnerable to the judgment of "neglected." On the back end, they were placed in segregated institutions that had inadequate facilities and in which they were trained through manual and industrial curricula for future menial occupations. In the Phyllis Wheatley Home young girls were also trained and encouraged in domestic work. The chapter concludes with one "other home" that was not mired in court dispositions, inspections, nor moral imperatives: the Home for the Aged and Infirm Colored People.

Even before Elizabeth McDonald founded the Louise Juvenile Home, she was deeply involved in rescue work. Much of this work stemmed from her desire to perform missionary work, an ambition that had been delayed because of little schooling, as well as by the untimely death of her first husband. Shortly thereafter, in 1886, she and her young daughter moved to Chicago, where she met and married James McDonald from Louisville, Kentucky. It was not until 1895, however, that she was "anointed" by God to "go into the highways and hedges and compel men and women to come in."[22] Although there are no records of her rescue work prior to 1903, it is likely that her volunteer work as a probation officer to the juvenile court gave her further access to dependent children and their families. The first annual report of the Cook County Juvenile Court in 1900, in its enumeration of probation officers, noted six probation officers paid from private sources, in particular the Chicago Woman's Club, as well as "one colored woman who devotes her entire time to the work, free of charge, and whose services are invaluable to the court as she takes charge of all colored children."[23] There is little doubt that the "one colored woman" was Elizabeth McDonald. Indeed, McDonald epitomized what a later annual report considered essential for successful probation work: "the spirit of a missionary."[24]

Such a missionary spirit was evident in her report from 1903 submitted to the *Broad Ax,* in which she rendered a brief sketch of her life and her recent work. She described there her rescue of eighteen persons from "shameful lives." Similarly, although her recorded activities as probation officer included removing children and mothers from "disreputable" homes to less "criminal surroundings," she also spoke of her efforts to deter young girls from frequenting the "dens" and "traps" of the Black Belt.[25] Although McDonald occasionally attempted to divide her "official duties" as probation officer from those of rescue worker, her solutions were often informed by her deeply felt religious beliefs. In one home visitation, she found the family in abject poverty and the parents subject to much drinking. Upon discovering that the parents had "wandered" from their faith, she urged them to attend church, as well as to "leave off strong drink." Her efforts were successful: not only were the children baptized, but the family also returned to church.[26] In another case a young girl was removed from a "house of immorality" and sent to an industrial school. Shortly thereafter the house was torn down so that other young girls would not fall prey to such temptations.[27] Efforts like these, which merged reform with rescue, were in fact consistent with the juvenile court law of 1899, which defined "dependent" not only in terms of neglect, homelessness, or improper parental care, but also as holding residency in "any house of ill fame or with any vicious or disreputable person."[28]

In reference to her probation work, McDonald stated that she did not receive "one cent of salary." This was in accordance with the earlier juvenile court law that stipulated that the court could appoint "discreet persons of good character" as probation officer but that they would receive "no compensation from the public treasury." However, McDonald did receive donations, particularly clothing, which she distributed to needy families. She also received financial assistance in 1903, especially from the Chicago Woman's Club and private donors. When her expenses far exceeded the donations, her husband contributed.[29] Despite the lack of funding in 1905, McDonald continued to receive clothing and shoes from donors, which she distributed to the needy. Because her funds were limited, she decided to take an examination necessary to procure a salary as a probation officer. Although McDonald did not pass the examination, due in her account to her lack of formal schooling, she nonetheless continued to draw young girls away from the saloons and cabarets and to visit inmates in the jails and asylums; in one case she convinced a young couple to marry before the Juvenile Court.[30]

In 1907 the Louise Juvenile Home officially opened at 6130 Ada Street. McDonald's private home had always been open "to receive the suffering of any nationality," and she continued this nondiscriminatory policy. Located west of Morgan and Hyde Park, in a ward where the population was no more than 20 percent African American, the home provided care for fifty-six white and African American children and two mothers. Two nonsalaried staff members, McDonald herself and Elizabeth Scott, a student of Walden University, taught the children industrial education, consisting mostly of washing, ironing, cooking, sewing, and needlework. During the day the children attended a school several blocks from the home.[31]

No information is available on the early administration of the home. Although no names are listed for the board of trustees for the first year, the list of speakers at the home's opening indicated McDonald's continued affiliation with the juvenile court. Probation officers Henry

Thurston and J. H. Witter contributed to a discussion on "The Necessity of Homes for Neglected and Dependent Children," as did Reverend Stewart of the Institutional Church and Rev. C. J. Quille, Superintendent of the Catholic Charities.[32]

At the home's first anniversary in 1908 its accomplishments were highlighted, especially the purchase of an eleven-room house. The upper level was rented, providing revenue for the home, which occupied the lower flat. McDonald indicated that although most of the funding was to have come from charitable organizations, she "had failed absolutely along that line."[33] McDonald's deep involvement in rescue work must have certainly consumed much of her time, time that might have been spent on fund-raising. She argued, however, that there would not have been as many jail and penitentiary inmates to rescue if she had been able to reach them as younger children through home visitations, preaching, and prayers. Like Du Bois, she insisted that rescue work was "greatly needed."[34] Since her rescue work did not contribute financially to the home, McDonald relied upon income from the rental property, her lectures, and the slight tuition fees of one to two dollars per student.

It should come as no surprise that the 1909 annual report continued to detail the number of religious conversions and prayer meetings alongside her home efforts. She enumerated: "49 conversions, 250 home visits that included prayer meetings. 40 visits to the jail, paroled 3 prisoners. Cared for 89 children and 1 mother. Got employment for 7 persons."[35] Although it is not clear how all eighty-nine children were cared for, through short-term residencies at the home, home visitations, or referrals, the yearly amount of nearly $450 from room and board exceeded the tuition fees. In fact, money from room and board was sufficient to cover the home's monthly payments, interests, and taxes. Despite the revenue from property rental and several fund-raisers, the home was already in debt in 1909 by nearly $1,000. Even though donations of clothing and groceries had been received, mostly from churches and private donors, the cost of caring for eighty-nine children must have been considerable. Fortunately, McDonald could rely upon the volunteerism of Ethel Simpson as teacher, Agatha Williams (McDonald's niece) as assistant matron, and Dr. William Tyler as the house physician and surgeon.[36]

Perhaps because of the mounting debt, some of the African American women's clubs began to contribute, albeit mostly through in-kind donations. The Volunteer Workers' Club often met at the home, visiting with the children, mending and sewing their clothes, and chaperoning them on picnics and outings. McDonald continued to plumb her previous connections, turning to white settlement workers and clubs to solicit their support. In 1911 Miss Henderson of the Chicago University Settlement spoke to several white clubs on behalf of the home, whereby a donation of aprons and nightgowns was soon received. The Woolleys from the Frederick Douglass Center sent the young children twelve baby dolls.[37]

Although the later annual reports were not as detailed as earlier ones, they clearly indicated a rising debt, as well as conflicting accounts. For example, although expenses for 1910 were less than those for 1909, more children were taken in; yet financial or in-kind donations did not seem to increase. Amanda Smith had taken in six of the children, but that did not fully explain the incongruity. By 1913 the debt had grown to over fourteen hundred dollars, despite the increase in individual donations. Such donations were too small to be of much significance.[38]

Relying again upon her affiliation with the juvenile court system, McDonald found a solution. In July of 1913 the home was incorporated and became the Louise Juvenile Industrial School for Colored Boys, which "provide[d] home and proper training for such boys as may be committed to its charge."[39] The school officers were mostly legal and court representatives, including President Will Davies, jailer of Cook County; Treasurer John Whitman, superintendent of the John Worthy School; and Secretary William Lamonte, a probation officer. The board of trustees was multiracial; it included jailers and probation officers, as well as African American editor Julius Taylor, McDonald's husband, and Alice Caldwell of the Volunteer Workers' Club.

Thereafter, the reports were no longer signed by McDonald as "Yours in His name," but as superintendent. The previous annual reports of prayers and conversions were replaced with descriptions of anniversary celebrations, where state inspections were followed by military drills, choir singing, plantation songs, and uplifting reports and talks. The school grounds were decorated with flags and Japanese lanterns. Long-stemmed red roses were strewn throughout the interior of the school. Reports stressed exercises and activities reminiscent of Washington's industrial education, the YMCA's character-building lessons, and the patriotic fervor of the Eighth Regiment recitations and marching.[40]

According to the 1914 report, covering its first year as a state institution, boys age five through age twelve were taught vocational skills such as shoemaking, fixing window screens, and other handiwork.[41] The curriculum paralleled that offered at John Worthy School, the Juvenile Detention Home, and other homes for dependent and delinquent boys. The Juvenile Detention Home's course of study steadfastly directed the boys' future as industrial workers and helped them "readjust mentally and morally" through wood work, basket making, and folksong and patriotic singing.[42] However, such training for African American boys was considered by many court personnel to be futile, given the youths' lack of opportunity and discrimination in employment. Bowen concluded, in fact, that these problems were the major causes of delinquency among African American boys.[43]

Unlike the Juvenile Detention Home, which strictly separated children according to the classifications of dependent and delinquent, the Louise Juvenile Industrial School took in both dependent and delinquent African American boys. In the case of delinquents, however, the juvenile court most often sent first-time offenders to homes and industrial schools; second- and third-time offenders were sent to the John Worthy School. Most of the children at the Louise Juvenile Industrial School were dependents who would be later released to relatives or placed under the supervision of probation officers.[44]

Concurrent with the incorporation was increased financial support from Cook County. The "Training School for Boys" Act stipulated a payment of ten dollars per dependent boy committed to training schools. The Cook County Juvenile Court Reports from 1914 through 1919 indicate that not only was this obligation met but that the county often provided additional funds of up to five thousand dollars.[45] The African American community also lent its support. Alice Caldwell's newly appointed position on the school's board guaranteed further commitment from the Volunteer Workers' Club, of which she was president. Records from the club indicated increased involvement and its members' approval of McDonald's efforts: "She deserves much credit for the way the house is kept and the excellent training of the children."[46]

There were few newspaper accounts of the school from 1915 until 1920, when it officially closed. McDonald's dream of moving the school to a farm was partially met in 1917, when the school relocated to a thirty-acre plot adjacent to the Glenwood Manual Training School, twenty-five miles outside of Chicago. Since the superintendent of Glenwood was also the treasurer for the Louise Juvenile Industrial School, and both were schools for dependent boys sent from the Juvenile Court, the schools became administratively joined, at least for the next three years. According to the Cook County Juvenile Court's annual reports, the number of boys sent to the Louise Manual Training School during this time fluctuated from two in 1918 to ten in 1919. When the school closed in 1920, the children were sent to Glenwood, to relatives, to the juvenile court, or to the Illinois Children's Home and Aid Society. Elizabeth McDonald and her husband moved to California, where she continued her social welfare work.[47]

McDonald's vision for the home and school was steadfast: educating young boys to be good Christians and good workers. As the home's debt grew, however, her mission and strategy shifted more to industrial training. Although O'Donnell has accurately observed how both the Louise Juvenile Home and the Amanda Smith Home drew on the African American tradition of mutual aid, her conclusion that African American professional and club women preferred institutional to boarding home care merits further discussion.[48] The club women were reluctant early on to assist in the sustenance of the Louise Juvenile Home. It was only when the home became state affiliated and thus assured of financial stability, that African American clubs and churches became more fully involved. To ensure the success of their efforts, then, club women carefully chose which facilities to support.

THE AMANDA SMITH HOME AND INDUSTRIAL SCHOOL

The founder of the Amanda Smith Home, Amanda Smith, was considered one of the "Race's foremost evangelist[s] who spent [her] life and fortune in temperance, religion and charitable work." Born in 1837, Smith, along with seven of her siblings, was a slave. In time, her father bought freedom for all of his children, including her. When one of her sisters was later enslaved because she had no proof of her freedom, Smith worked in a kitchen until she could buy her sister's freedom again.[49]

Although Amanda had little schooling, she became an evangelist in the Methodist Episcopal Church. Sponsored by a wealthy Quaker friend, she traveled to England, Scotland, and Ireland, where she participated in religious and temperance conferences, visiting with prominent leaders there. In 1879 she traveled to Bombay and Calcutta, India, to deliver gospel addresses. Many were curious to see and hear an African

American woman who had once been enslaved, but many were likewise swayed by her "sweet power of song" and "keen insight into character." [50] After a successful mission in India, she left for Liberia, where she conducted missionary and temperance work for eight years. She then returned to England and continued to preach, accumulating ten thousand dollars for her addresses. During one temperance speech she heard a voice asking her what she had done for her own people back in America. The vision of an industrial home for children appeared before her, the beginning of the Amanda Smith Home for Colored and Dependent Children. [51]

In 1895 Smith purchased property in Harvey, Illinois, a temperance town outside of Chicago. However, it was not until 1899 that the orphanage home was opened with five children and with funds of $288. One year later, enrollment had increased by sixteen children, fourteen of whom were school-age; by 1903 thirty children resided at the home. The growing number was influenced by the home's connection to the juvenile court. According to McClellan and Bartlett, although no financial support from the county was forthcoming, the children had been referred by the Cook County Juvenile Court. [52] Smith was compelled, as McDonald was, to spend much of her time fund-raising through her evangelistic and temperance engagements. Consequently, the Amanda Smith Home, like the Louise Juvenile Home, was faced with a rising debt. Although inspectors found the home to be "inadequate" according to state standards, because it was deemed the only substantial facility for African American children in the state, it was not closed. [53] This appraisal not only demonstrated the state's willingness to dismiss substandard conditions for dependent children but also indicated the state's unwillingness to assist in the home's improvement.

Such official inspections, however, conflicted with opinion from the African American community. In one anniversary celebration of 1914 sponsored by the Ideal Woman's Club, which more than one hundred persons attended, the home was inspected by the club members. They reported: "The cleanliness and sanitation was without flaw or blemish, the garden work was first class . . . peas, beans, tomatoes, cabbage, potatoes, all the lettuce and radishes were served from the garden." [54] The club women also surveyed the chicken yard and samples of clotheslines, neck halters, and other rope-making products made by the children. After inspection, several club women gave addresses, including Ida

B. Wells, and the children sang. It was not entirely clear whether such pronouncements arose out of race pride or differences between community and state standards, or whether the "cleanliness" of the home masked the financial difficulties that besieged it.

Clearly, though, the Chicago communities were cognizant of the home's need for financial assistance. The home's first public cry for assistance was in September of 1905, when Smith placed a plea in the *Chicago Defender* to help raise at least one thousand dollars for fuel, lumber, hardware, groceries, and plumbing. Smith acutely saw the need to publicize the contributions of the home to the Chicago community, perhaps because the home was located some distance from the city. She announced a "Grand Basket Meeting," in which she hoped that "the pulpit and press, the political, business, legal and social clubs, [would be] fully represented . . . the secret orders, benevolent societies, our boys and girls, juvenile circles, one and all, unite[d] in making this a grand festival day for our work."[55]

The home continued to rely upon the community until January of 1911, when Smith received a windfall of sixty-five hundred dollars from an English friend whom Hallie Q. Brown, the noted African American elocutionist and temperance speaker, had visited in Scotland. It seemed fitting that Brown, in the capacity of a public speaker, had acted as an intermediary between Smith and her English society friends, especially since Smith was experiencing bouts of ill health. Despite her age of seventy-four and her convalescence during the previous summer, Smith supervised the completion of a new dormitory.[56]

Even before this financial grace, unknown to Smith, activities of the West Side Woman's Club were occurring that would change the future of the Amanda Smith Home. At an October 1910 reception of the West Side Woman's Club, over one hundred club women and social reformers convened. Some were deeply involved in facilities for young working girls and dependents, for example, Elizabeth Lindsay Davis of the Phyllis Wheatley Club and Home, Elizabeth McDonald of the Louise Juvenile Home, and Eva Jenifer, future founder and president of the African American YWCA in Chicago. Noted probation officers Joanna Snowden and Ida B. Wells also attended, as did Dr. Anna Cooper of the Dunbar Tuberculosis Sanitarium and Ida D. Lewis, the club's president and state organizer. Although the topics at the reception were not publicized, it is likely, given the women's professional involvement, that child welfare was discussed. In 1912 the club opened a three-story home at 253 Artesian Avenue for girls ages four through fourteen, with Ida Lewis as matron. The home, however, was short-lived. In 1913 it merged with the Amanda Smith Home, and the Amanda Smith Home became the Amanda Smith Industrial School for Girls.[57]

The West Side Woman's Club was only one catalyst, though, in this change. Because of racial segregation, many institutions created for dependent children did not admit African American children. As the African American community interpreted the situation, many young dependent girls were designated "delinquents" and sent to a state school. One newspaper account stated that because of discriminatory practices, "it became necessary at times to send dependent girls to the State School for delinquent girls, when they should have had the care and training of dependent girls."[58] This perception, though, was not entirely accurate. Although there was a county-funded school for African American girls, the Illinois Technical School for Colored Girls, it was established for dependent, not delinquent, girls. Juvenile court records from 1912 through 1918 indicate that African American dependent girls appearing before the court for the first time were sent to the Amanda Smith Industrial School; those dependents who returned to the court one or more times were sent to the Illinois Technical School.[59]

The Illinois Technical School for Colored Girls received further criticism from the African American community because it was maintained under the auspices of the Catholic Church.[60] They argued that not only was the color line drawn but also no respect was given to Protestant girls' religious affiliation. One editorial stated the African American community's feelings succinctly:

> Our people insist that if our girls are to be "Jim Crowed" at all we prefer to have them sent to an institution organized, maintained and controlled by our people, who are directly interested in the welfare of these unfortunates. If we must be segregated, we want to segregate ourselves; we do not want to be "Jim Crowed" by white people and then pay them for doing it.[61]

The situation was resolved in August of 1913 through the joint efforts of African American and white club women, juvenile court representatives, and other race leaders. In the decision to transform the home into an industrial school for dependent African American girls,

African American club women and auxiliaries pledged to "make the school a success" through their support. Consistent with an industrial emphasis, the Amanda Smith Industrial School for Girls opened on Labor Day. Like the Louise Juvenile Industrial School, the Amanda School received county funding; the law stipulated that each dependent girl attending an industrial school receive fifteen dollars. Also like the Louise Juvenile School, the Amanda Industrial School received more than the stipulated amount.[62]

In December of 1913 a committee of eleven members of the West Side Women's Club visited the school. Having inspected the facilities and observed the teachers, they promised to further assist the school. They promptly set up stations in Chicago where toys, candies, and clothing were collected for the girls' Christmas presents. To provide the girls with company and to encourage future donations, the women also encouraged community members to visit the girls. Women's clubs united with the efforts of two previously organized guilds, the Amanda Smith Guilds numbers one and two, to assist the school. For example, the Inter-racial Circle gave a fund-raising "phantom social and conundrum supper," to which guests came dressed in ghost attire and later revealed their identities. A new sewing machine and a bolt of gingham was donated by the Diana Charity Club. The African American and white women's clubs, as well as individuals, pooled their resources to finance a coal fund. The Carter Hair Culturalists in Oak Park donated a ton of coal; the charity committee of the Chicago Federation of Women's Clubs, a white organization, contributed fifty dollars.[63]

Although Amanda Smith had been "relieved" of her administrative responsibilities in 1911, because of ill health, she continued to be active and greatly respected by the African American community. Annual birthday celebrations were given by the women's clubs. When she died in 1915, the African American newspapers recounted her missionary and temperance work, as well as her work at the home and school. She was occasionally criticized by community members for accepting financial support from white philanthropists, but she had not wavered in her determination to keep the home and school open. Even after her death the school remained opened for several years. In 1917 thirty-eight girls, ranging from four to seventeen years of age, attended the school.

Tragically, in 1918 the Amanda Smith Industrial School burned to the ground and two children lost their lives. Some attributed the fire to faulty wiring that the state inspector had "overlooked." As mentioned previously, the home's facilities had been reported as "inadequate" as early as 1905 by Charles Virden, the state inspector. According to Sophonisba Breckinridge, the state was implicated not only in the persistence of segregated facilities but also in the deaths of the two children.[64]

THE PHYLLIS WHEATLEY HOME

Although the Phyllis Wheatley Club was formed in 1896, it was not until 1907 that the home was incorporated and 1908 that it was finally opened. Before that the Phyllis Wheatley Club was concerned with child welfare, having established a day nursery at the Trinity A.M.E. Mission. However, as many young African American women migrated to Chicago, lodging and employment for them became scarce. Many were directed to the Black Belt, where they were beset with the temptations of dance halls, saloons, and movie theaters. Additionally, many who had been promised work as a nurse or a secretary were disappointed to find that no such jobs existed—only domestic or laundry work.

Consequently, the Phyllis Wheatley Home was established to provide a safe and homelike environment for young working girls. In the words of the Phyllis Wheatley Club members, the home sought to "befriend . . . the Colored girls and women who [came] into this great city seeking work, often without relatives, friends or money."[65] Similar to the YWCAs, the home provided a "Christian influence," taught domestic skills, and procured respectable employment for its boarders.[66] Since many young women came with little or no money, the cost for lodging was affordable: $1.25 a week or $.25 a night.

The members of the home's advisory board were prominent African American men, including Julius Taylor, Reverend Carey, and Bernard W. Fitts. The club women, however, were in charge of the committees for fund-raising, tax collection, spring cleaning, and home improvement. The club's motto spoke to its determination: "If you can't push, pull, and if you can't pull, please get out of the way."[67] The Phyllis Wheatley Club began raising funds for the home immediately. As early as 1906 the club sponsored a lawn fete with dancing and other forms of fund-raisers. Hand-made items were raffled, for example, a "beautiful, hand-made lingerie skirt." On another occasion a hand embroidered silk quilt, "made from sixteen gentlemen's handerkerchiefs . . . put together in the most artistic manner" was exhibited and raffled off, netting more than $230.[68]

The Phyllis Wheatley Club also sponsored concerts and dramas. In 1913 a "Celebrity Party" was held, highlighting prominent African American authors and composers. A concert at the Lincoln Center yielded twenty-five dollars for the home. A benefit drama was sponsored by the Elite Social Charity Club, a club that "work[ed] wholly for the Phyllis Wheatley Home." In 1916 the Phyllis Wheatley Club put on a three-act drama, "A Woman's Honor," directed by Madam B. L. Hensley, an organizer with the Elite Social Charity Club and an officer in the Gaudeamus Club. Fenton Johnson, a local writer, donated to the Thanksgiving Day matinee one of his one-act dramas.[69]

Other fund-raising endeavors were smaller and more humble social occasions when club women's camaraderie was expressed simply through "good fun." For example, a "mysterious social" involved the solving of a mystery, with the clue "They are all peaches and herein lies the mystery."[70] The mystery brought in one hundred dollars. Another time, each member earned a dollar and told at an "experience meeting" how it was earned. The money was used for the furnace bill. A Halloween Party was given at the home, where dinner was served and prizes were awarded for the "most artistic and most comical costumes." At another Halloween Party, the person with the most humorous costume was given a prize; admission was five cents.[71]

Like other women's clubs, the Phyllis Wheatley Club held exclusive dances and balls. A pre-Lenten ball in 1915 was considered "the grandest society affair that Chicago has ever had, [and] has taken not only the city but the entire state by storm." Prominent African American citizens participated in the organizing of the event: the niece of Colonel Marshall secured over one hundred patronesses, and Julius Avendorph, "Chicago's arbiter elegantarium," was in charge of the floor committee. The ushers were some of "the most popular and beautiful young ladies and debutantes of the season."[72]

Funds from such events were sorely needed to purchase a larger home, because the present site did not meet the increased demands for lodging. From 1907 to 1914 the home had provided lodging to more than three hundred girls and secured employment for more than five hundred. Through the efforts of the Elite Social Charity Club, which had raised five thousand dollars toward its mortgage, a new home was purchased in 1915 at 3256 Rhodes Avenue. The home eventually accommodated forty-four girls at one time. Many had been referred by the Travelers' Aid, the juvenile court, and the Court of Domestic Relations; some, however, were students at the University of Chicago.[73]

Because there are no records of the young women's lives or of their impressions, it is difficult to ascertain how the "Christian influence" was felt or how the "standards" of domestic service were "elevated." We do not know the degree to which the club women befriended the young women, especially those from the courts, and offered them encouragement and advice. Certainly, club women perceived themselves as exemplary models of womanhood; since the clubs often held their meetings at the home, club women may have been available to offer advice, inspect the girls' work, or discuss related matters. However, the club women did not chaperone or organize parties for the boarders, suggesting that their intent was not social control, as in many of the homes for working immigrant and white girls.[74]

Given the number of lodgers from 1907 through 1914, as well as the home's interactions with the courts, it is feasible that most women's stays were short. This may have been appropriate, because the numbers of children and youths referred to the Louise Juvenile Home and the Amanda Smith Home were also large and their stays short. None of the juvenile court records list the Phyllis Wheatley Home, so it is impossible to know how many young women were referred by the court, or what their dispositions were. As the courts often recommended domestic work for dependent and delinquent girls' rehabilitation, the home may have functioned largely as an employment agency, especially given the large number of women who secured employment through the home. Likewise, it is not clear how many university students boarded at the home, nor what their social relations were with other boarders, especially those from the courts. It is possible that the college women, too, perceived themselves as role models for women referred by the juvenile court.

The dedication of the community of club women to supporting a facility for young working women is undoubted. Many clubs were generous in their collaborative efforts for and donations to the Phyllis Wheatley Home. Often in-kind goods were donated, such as soap, towels, and sheets. A list of requests in 1914 included furniture, bedding, kitchen utensils, and other house materials. In one case Mrs. Eva Jenifer donated a ton of coal. When Dr. Fannie Emanuel visited the club, she "filled five feet of pennies" toward the goal of raising a "mile of pennies." The Gaudeamus Club donated one dozen pillow cases and towels, no doubt made by club members. A davenport, a center table, a rug, small brackets, pillows, bed spreads, couch pillows, and a chenille couch cover were also donated to the home.[75] The annual reports of the clubs, published in the newspapers, listed the varied activities of picnics, dances, matinees, muso-dances, dramatic productions, raffles of embroidered and quilted items, and baseball games. Contributing clubs included the Chicago Woman's Club, the North Side Woman's Club, Hyde Park Woman's Club, Samaritan Club, Lady Elliot Circle C.O.F., and the Necessity Club. Together, the clubs created a network of fund-raisers, as well as social occasions, to ensure the future of the Phyllis Wheatley Home.

THE OLD FOLKS' HOME

The Home for the Aged and Infirm Colored People, known affection-ately as the Old Folks' Home, was one of the first social welfare facilities in Chicago. In 1897 Gabriella Smith had offered to take in four elderly "inmates," with the financial assistance of two prominent African American club women, Mrs. J. C. Stewart and Joanna Snowden. In 1898 a home and its property was donated by an elderly German woman, Bena Morrison, to Gabriella Smith. Because Morrison had stipulated that the African American community manage the home's upkeep, the board of directors and the club women were quite active in its fund-raisers. Through their efforts and a later endowment of property at 620 Fifty-Seventh Street, the Old Folks' Home's finances were secure.[76]

Located at 610 Garfield Boulevard (West Fifty-Fifth Street), the home first accommodated thirteen elders "who had spent their lives in hard toil and deprivation."[77] The inmates' ages ranged from 68 to a self-reported 128 years. Despite their age, the boarders assisted in the general upkeep of the "cosyly furnished" home, along with Smith, who was considered "an all around worker [who] can drive the horse and wagon belonging to the institution as well as a man."[78]

Eligibility for residence in the home in 1901 was contingent upon age (over sixty years) and "good moral character." Upon admission, a payment of one hundred dollars was secured to provide partial living

ILLUSTRATIONS

Anna Elizabeth Hudlin (1840–1914), Chicago, Ill., 1881.
Photographer: Chicago Photographic Studios. By kind permission of the Chicago Historical Society.

Ida McIntosh Dempsey in wedding dress, (n.p.), (n.d.). Photographer unknown.
From Franklyn Atkinson Henderson collection. By kind permission of the Chicago Historical Society.

LOOMIS,

2867 ARCHER AVENUE.
CHICAGO.

Cabinet card photograph, Joanna Cecilia Snowden, by Loomis.
From the Franklyn Atkinson Henderson collection. By kind permission of the Chicago Historical Society.

Ida B. Wells, 1920?. By kind permission of the Department of Special Collections at the University of Chicago Library and the estate of Ida B. Wells.

Indiana Avenue branch YMCA Glee Club girls and their guests at a banquet, Chicago, Ill., 1921. Photographer unknown. By kind permission of the Chicago Historical Society.

HELP OUR OWN

*Residents of the Phyllis Wheatley Home, Chicago, Ill., ca. 1920s. Photographer unknown.
From CHS Library. By kind permission of the Chicago Historical Society.*

Irene McCoy-Gaines and Eleanor Roosevelt, Chicago, Ill., n.d.
Photographer unknown. By kind permission of the Chicago Historical Society.

expenses for the inmate, as well as to guarantee him or her a Christian burial. By 1905 there were more than twenty-five men and women at the home, some of whom were blind or lame and "practically all in [their] second childhood."[79] Three African American physicians—Dr. A. W. Williams, Dr. George Hall, and Dr. A. B. Schultz—volunteered their services, and Provident Hospital supplied pharmaceuticals free of charge. However, because the inmates' medical conditions often strained the staff's ability to care for them, a medical certificate of good health was later required before admission. A policy was also established that if an inmate became so ill that the staff could not care for him or her, financial assistance for another accommodation would be sought. This assistance was often provided through the women's clubs, as was the case with an elderly female inmate diagnosed with an incurable disease. The club women raised one hundred dollars toward her nursing care and formed a committee to visit her twice a month and report on her condition.[80]

The backgrounds of the inmates varied, although most had been slaves. One inmate, Grandma Helen Stewart, claimed to be 128 years old. Having outlived five husbands, she was able to recall with clarity the Revolutionary War, the Mexican War, and the Civil War. Grandma Sophia Job was 120 years old (in another entry, she was estimated to be "somewhat over one hundred"), yet "in full possession of all of her faculties." She remembered George Washington's second inauguration in New York in 1794. Another inmate, Grandma Sarah Ray, 97 years of age, remained active, earning her own pin money by knitting wash cloths. One couple, William and Ann Mues, originally from Virginia, had been married five times to each another. Their first marriage had been the traditional "jumping over the broom" ceremony. When they moved to Canada and later to Chicago, they remarried to legally acquire property.[81]

Although the home sponsored bazaars at which the elderly women sold their handiwork, the club women and the community also organized fund-raising events. Many of these events brought the community together as they celebrated picnics replete with traditional children's games and races. The evenings usually culminated with the Armant Orchestra playing under the stars.[82] Boys from the West Side and the South Side often organized football games; the Grace Presbyterian Church baseball team played the United Presbyterian white team in an effort to expand the home's facilities. It was not unusual for the community to respond to notices requesting donations of ham, bacon, corn meal, hominy, coffee, corn, navy beans, rice, potatoes, cabbage, turnips, coal, cord wood, sheets, foot tubs, cooking pans, rubber shirts, daily paper, desks, and chairs.[83]

When the community response was not as high as expected, the newspaper editors chastised their readers. Julius Taylor criticized African Americans who did not support their own institutions but gave their money to "white store keepers who hate[d] them and always treat[ed] them with the greatest contempt."[84] Like club woman Ida B. Wells, he encouraged African American control of community facilities. In a similar effort, Joanna Snowden appealed to all African Americans in Chicago to support the Old Folks' Home. She calculated that if each citizen contributed a mere twenty-five cents, nearly $12,500 would be raised. More importantly, she stressed the need for community ownership and responsibility. Speaking on behalf of one charity ball, she beseeched: "Let us consider the entertainment ours, this institution and its work ours, its permanency and success ours. Therefore the responsibility our own."[85]

The women's clubs responded to these appeals. In 1910 Anna Hudlin reorganized the Bena Morrison Club to raise funds for applicants for the home. Other women's clubs joined in this effort, particularly the Volunteer Workers' Club, which organized annual festivities, including a Christmas bazaar. Their sixth-month report from April of 1911 indicated the following commitment to the home: "Bought sheets and foot tub, $7.57; rubber shirts, $2.10; sheets and cooking pans, $10.14; Daily paper, $2.20; Christmas Tree, $7.96; Curtains and rods, $28.04; Desk and chair, $30.30; Easter dinner, $6.60; Total Amount spent, $94.91."[86] From 1904 to 1911 this club alone donated more than fifteen hundred dollars to charity, most of it to the Old Folks' Home, the Amanda Smith Home, and the Louise Juvenile Home.

Other women's clubs were also active in the home's support, providing groceries, contributions toward the coal fund, or money to pay the applicants' entry fees. Often the home encouraged such participation by reminding the club women that they, too, would need the support of others in their elderly years. Clearly, unlike the homes for dependent and delinquent children, which received county funds, the institution for the elderly relied upon the goodwill and traditional care-giving of its community members. The Old Folks' Home was also visited by the club women, who brought the "sunshine" of good cheer and entertainment and prepared old-fashioned chicken dinners and ice cream socials. As club women did for the Phyllis Wheatley Home, the women organized committees to clean the home and to decorate during the holidays. Thanksgiving, Christmas, and Easter dinners were prepared, followed by musical entertainment. In common with the other facilities described in this chapter, the clubs formed a collaborative web to ensure that their fund-raising efforts were successful.[87]

The clubs worked individually to meet the home's daily expenses. The Mary Walker Thompson Club donated clothes, food, and money. The Cornell Charity Club sent flour, and the Giles Charity Club, a bushel of potatoes. The Twentieth Century Art Club donated groceries. The Pandora Club members contributed by dressing up in harvest fashions and bringing a fruit or a vegetable to the Old Folks' Home for their November Harvest Home Day. The Clover Leaf Social Club, the Gaudeamus Club, the Fleur de Lis Art Club, the YMLI Charity Club, the Ideal Woman's Club, and the East End Charity Club all contributed to the home.[88]

As usual, not only were funds raised, but also status was bestowed upon the club women. "Grand" charity balls organized by the Silver Leaf Charity Club and by the Triangle and Inner Circle Clubs were attended by "the best class of people." The annual ball started with a "grand march" after the arrival of the mayor and was led by Colonel John C. Buckner of the home's board. The leading club women's attire was described in detail, as for most exclusive events.[89] In other cases prizes were given; for example, at one benefit sponsored by the Chicago Union Charity Club, the highest ticket seller received a handsome table cover and scarf. Theater and musical performances were especially popular and enjoyable fund-raisers. In 1916 the Chicago Women's Amateur Minstrel Club gave an annual performance, described as a "spasm of mirth and merriment for sweet charity's sake." Performances included a screaming farce, music solos, twenty "beauties garbed in pajamas, in original poses and dances," and Mrs. George Cleveland Hall's ventriloquist stunts. The Pekin Theatre, as many times before, provided its facility for the entertainment.[90]

Whereas the homes for children experienced tensions from state and court mediations, the Old Folks' Home's tensions revolved around control of the home. Funding was at the heart of the conflict. The endowment from Bena Morrison, as well as philanthropic efforts of white churches and individuals, reminded the African American community that the home was not fully supported from within. Furthermore, the contingency from Bena Morrison that the home be supported by community efforts may have served not only as an incentive for involvement but as a tacit reminder that African Americans were perceived by white philanthropists as not always capable of holding their own. Despite these tensions, the Old Folks' Home, like the Phyllis Wheatley Home, seemed to prosper because of community-wide efforts, especially those of the women's clubs.

The constraints faced by the founders and supporters of the four homes described above varied. In the homes for dependent children, club women, matrons, and probation officers mediated their influence through the juvenile courts. Despite the efforts of club women to collaboratively raise moneys for the Louise Juvenile Home and the Amanda Smith Home, the debts mounted alongside the homes' physical deterioration. Although they had private and county funding, both homes closed before 1920. Sandra O'Donnell has argued that the self-help traditions of the African American community were greatly weakened by the rise of social service agencies and the attendant professionalism of social work.[91] Although the discussion in this chapter corroborates her argument, there were certainly other factors. An increase of nearly 149 percent in the African American population in Chicago between 1910 and 1920 resulted in further congestion and crowding in the Black Belt.[92] The push–pull factors of migration, racism, and classism were enormous. The women's clubs, along with church societies, settlements, and political branches of the Urban League and the NAACP, could not completely shoulder the mounting demand for housing, employment, and child care facilities. Furthermore, the state was deeply implicated, because it not only condoned the continued segregation of facilities and the exclusion of African American children from mainstream institutions, but also it did little to improve the physical conditions of the existing homes and schools.

The other two homes, the Phyllis Wheatley Home and the Old Folks' Home, were more successful. Part of their success arose from the founders' and the club women's collaborative fund-raising abilities. As mentioned, the multiple club memberships created webs of networking essential for participation in fund-raising events. Another reason for their success was that the Phyllis Wheatley Home and the Old Folks' Home were located in Chicago, rather than outside the city (although the Louise Juvenile Home was originally on the South Side of Chicago). Club women therefore could frequently visit the elderly, rather than taking hour-long train rides to Harvey to visit children at the Amanda Smith Home. Furthermore, these two homes were perceived to be community institutions that were founded, administered, and operated by African Americans. In the case of the Old Folks' Home, the whole community, not simply the women's clubs, was involved in its sustenance, evident in the youth lyceums' and the men's clubs' contributions.

Lastly, the types of fund-raising activities differed for all four homes. For the homes for dependent children, the club women contributed mostly food, small Christmas gifts, clothing, and time. Although the same in-kind donations were provided to the elderly in the Old Folks' Home, there were also fund-raising activities, such as theater productions and charity balls, in which the middle-class status of the club women could be reaffirmed. The Phyllis Wheatley Club, like other sister clubs, sponsored many philanthropic endeavors to which only its members were invited. Three purposes, then, were served through the clubs' fund-raising activities: first, necessary funds were raised for the homes; second, the activities encouraged greater camaraderie among the club women; and third, invitations to the exclusive events (plays, musicals, recitals, and balls) marked the club women's status.

FIVE

AFRICAN AMERICAN

SETTLEMENTS

IN CHICAGO, AS IN OTHER URBAN SETTINGS, SETTLE-
ments were created to accommodate the educational,
economic, and social needs of the rapidly growing number
of immigrants and African Americans. Although many
Chicago settlements opened their doors to immigrants,
most denied access to African Americans. Such exclusion was not
always deliberate; some settlements were circumscribed according to
geographic neighborhoods, specific ethnic groups, or religious denominations. In other cases, however, the color line was distinctly drawn.
Accordingly, African American church leaders, club women, and settlement workers created settlements, missions, and social centers for poorer
African Americans. Although most of these settlements were short-lived,
they pointed to distinct ways in which African American women—as
founders, teachers, supervisors, volunteers, and fund-raisers—shaped
activities and programs to best meet the multiple needs of their communities, particularly those of children and young women.

This chapter focuses on five African American settlements: the Emanuel Settlement, the Negro Fellowship League, the Wendell Phillips Settlement, the Clotee Scott Settlement (formerly the Hyde Park Settlement), and the Frederick Douglass Center. Like most "prototype" settlements in Chicago, particularly Hull House, the Chicago Commons, and the university settlements, the African American settlements were primarily concerned with child welfare, wholesome recreational programs for youths, and domestic and manual training. Lectures, mothers' clubs, and employment bureaus were created, too, as they were in other settlements. However, the African American settlements were unique in the ways in which they interconnected social, economic, and educational aspects of the community.

The analysis begins with the constraints faced by African Americans: exclusion from mainstream settlement activities, mainstream settlement workers' racialized attitudes, and the tensions wrought from scientific models of social reform. Unlike mainstream settlement reformers, African American settlement workers did not distinguish settlement from mission or charity work. All forms of "social uplift" were edifying, evident in the multiple club, church, and political networks of the African American settlement workers. More importantly, the continuum of services and facilities pointed to the tremendous need for such provisions, particularly for poorer African Americans. Although the settlements offered many services, this chapter focuses on three types: child welfare provisions, including kindergartens, nurseries, and clubs; programs for youths, including clubs, classes, and other wholesome forms of entertainment; and domestic training for girls and young women, intended not only for purposes of employment but to inculcate proper attitudes toward homemaking and motherhood.

"LABORATORIES OF SOCIAL SCIENCE": IDEOLOGIES OF MAINSTREAM SOCIAL SETTLEMENTS AND WORKERS

According to Thomas Philpott, more than sixty-eight settlements and neighborhood centers were founded in Chicago between 1895 and 1917. There were undoubtedly more, however, because the National Federation of Settlements, from which Robert Woods and Albert Kennedy drew, acknowledged only secular institutions. Although as Philpott has pointed out, more than two-thirds of the settlements founded before 1917 in Chicago were affiliated with a Protestant denomination, neither

African American, nor Jewish, nor Catholic settlements were usually listed in the *Handbook of Settlements.*[1]

One complication arose from the very definition of *settlement* in contrast to *mission*. Samuel Barnett, for one, distinguished settlements from missions in terms of social proximity between the workers and their ethnic neighbors: "A settlement enables the rich to know the poor in a way not possible for a mission, whose members go about with minds set on their object, and who are often held at a distance because of that object."[2] Jane Addams's own autobiographical accounts of her life at Hull House demonstrated such a position, as she spoke of her learning about "life at its barest and hardest."[3] Despite Addams's insistence upon the settlement's "spiritual force" and familial form of living, her Christian humanism was confounded by images of scientific efficiency and order. This was, of course, not unique to Addams. Carson and other settlement scholars have observed that social gospel melded with "social scientific inquiry and application" as settlement workers mediated their ethical obligations to the poor while also maintaining their class distinctions. In one extreme example, some settlements hired servants who cooked and cleaned the rooms. Despite their efforts to minimize social distance, the settlement workers' backgrounds clearly distinguished them from their clientele.[4]

Despite the settlement workers' conceptions of differences between settlements and missions, there were many similarities in their services. Many missions were accused of proselytizing, but they, like settlements, created kindergartens, nurseries, employment services, and reading rooms. Settlement workers persisted, however, in their view that missions promoted more of a "closed intellectual system," that is, religious dogma, whereas settlements proffered a more "open" system, one based on scientific merits.[5] Not only was such a polarized view unsubstantiated in terms of the actual services provided, but also, in its refusal to acknowledge the multiple roles of churches in various ethnic communities, it was clearly ethnocentric.

So, too, were there tensions between charity and social settlement workers. Like mission workers, charity workers were often portrayed as "outsiders," who simply provided temporary and individual relief. This was in contrast, once again, to the settlement workers, who viewed themselves as engendering the immigrants' self-reliance, independence, and understanding of American life. Rather than "outsiders," who occasionally visited, the settlement workers perceived themselves as building trusting and mutual relationships with their immigrant neighbors. Charity workers thought otherwise. Many were deeply suspicious of settlement workers' radical connections to labor unions.[6]

Social scientific explanations provided the settlement workers with a rationale for excluding African Americans. Many settlement workers thought African Americans could not be "assimilated," in part because of the immense racism they faced from other groups. Settlement workers also argued that slavery had presented African Americans with such an indelible dilemma that the effects could not be easily eradicated nor dismissed. Furthermore, because African Americans had been torn from their original culture, their traditions and taboos had been irretrievably lost. Philpott, in his analysis of settlement workers Addams and Taylor, concluded that they were deeply implicated in keeping the Chicago settlements segregated. On the other side, Allen Davis, Steven Diner, and Rivka Lissak have praised mainstream settlement reformers, such as Addams, as "cultural pluralists."[7]

Although I do not wish to belabor this debate, the controversy over social reform versus control might be further amplified by comparing African American reformers' perspectives with those of mainstream workers. White settlement workers tended to generalize more along racial lines; middle-class African Americans more often cited social class and regional differences. In contrast to white reformers' view that African Americans were unable to be "assimilated," middle-class African Americans framed the dilemma in terms of segregation and adjustment to urban life. Furthermore, when African American workers spoke of the immense burden of slavery, they spoke less in terms of their disconnection from traditions than in terms of a loss of dignity and family life. Despite these differences, white and African American middle-class reformers both spoke of poorer African Americans' lack of "social constraint." As mentioned, the Chicago African American newspapers were replete with "don't do" lists intended to convey socially appropriate forms of behavior to newcomers.[8] Such lists, in the case of the African American middle class, attested to their belief in the educability of all African Americans and their persistence in race advancement.

Exclusion of African Americans from the mainstream settlements was practiced by various and often surreptitious measures. The most obvious form of exclusion was based on religious and ethnic affiliation, as in settlements for Russian Jews or Italian Catholics. Many of these settlements relocated as their ethnic clients moved to other Chicago neighborhoods. Another strategy was to exclude African Americans not demonstratively but by establishing quotas or redrawing geographical boundaries for benefactors. For example, the Chicago Commons drew prescribed boundaries for services to African Americans. When Hull House opened a nursery in 1925, it established a quota for African American children and redrew the neighborhood lines to ensure that the quota would be maintained.[9] In other situations members of ethnic communities, rather than the settlement workers, drew the color line: although some settlements were located near African American neighborhoods, ethnic gangs used physical force and threats to keep African American youths away.[10]

Despite such exclusionary maneuvers, there were multiracial settlements in Chicago, although few in number. Most notable was the Abraham Lincoln Centre, founded in 1905. Mainstream settlements also hired African Americans, further blurring the color line. For example, the University of Chicago Settlement hired an African American manager for its shop; the head of the Boys' Department at Northwestern University Settlement was African American. Such efforts, though, were minimal and did not have far-reaching consequences.[11] Generally, African American facilities were not only segregated but also poorly funded. As of 1930 only one-third of the private agencies in Chicago contributed a meager 1 percent of their budgets to services for African Americans.[12] Although Philpott has argued that scarcity of private societies' funding was intended to keep African Americans in the poorer wards, other smaller ethnic settlements, too, faced the constraints of low allocations and unsalaried staff.

The push and pull factors of discriminatory practices, segregated neighborhoods, and settlement workers' ideologies and backgrounds not only deeply affected poorer African Americans' access to settlements; it also prompted the creation of community institutions by middle-class African Americans. Despite economic hardships, nine settlements were founded by African Americans near or in the Black Belt between 1900 and 1916.[13] Although there were profound differences between the mainstream and African American institutions, as well as in the settlement workers' ideologies and practices, there were also commonalities, particularly with the increased professionalism of African American social workers. Nevertheless, most settlement workers' visions were not secularized but rooted in a Christian communalism and social uplift ideology.

"DOING CHRISTIANITY AND NOT SIMPLY ACTING RELIGION": AFRICAN AMERICAN SETTLEMENT WORKERS' IDEOLOGIES

Compared to the views of mainstream settlement workers, the African American ideologies and practices were not shaped significantly by scientific thought, whether Froebelian pedagogy, Hall's recapitulation theory, or the Progressive Era's preoccupation with vocational aptitudes. Rather, African American settlement reformers and workers, in conjunction with club women, mutually articulated their activities, practices, and perspectives to redefine African American motherhood, womanhood, and home and community life. First, they did not distinguish social or welfare reform from civil reform but webbed child welfare issues to mothers' employment and ultimately to community betterment through women's economic self-determination. For example, the Clotee Scott Settlement offered dressmaking classes so that women's employment opportunities could be expanded beyond domestic and laundry work. Not only did seamstress work encourage women to become entrepreneurs in their own communities, but it also allowed mothers to remain at home with their young children.

Second, African American female reformers' networks drew from the multiple social institutions of churches, clubs, and city chapters of the Urban League, the NAACP, and the Business League. Such networks reinforced African American women's perceptions of their community roles and provided multiple volunteer and fund-raising opportunities. To illustrate, Sophia Boaz, assistant head of the Wendell Phillips Settlement and later a juvenile officer, was an active member of the Alpha Suffrage Club and the University Society Club. Clotee Scott, founder of the Clotee Scott Settlement, was a long-standing member of the West Side Woman's Club. Antoinette C. Cone not only taught music classes at the Clotee Scott Settlement and the Frederick Douglass Center but directed musical and theatrical productions through the Phyllis Wheatley Club.

Third, the club women's and settlement workers' vision of womanhood and motherhood was often imaged in and sustained by a deepseated Christianity. Although there was certainly social class stratification in the African American churches of Chicago—demonstrated by the club women's membership, practices, and rituals—many of the Chicago female reformers explicitly expressed their motives for uplift in terms of their spiritual beliefs. As Lasch-Quinn noted, secular organizations of African American women often demonstrated a "high level of religiosity."[14] Settlement founder Clotee Scott, for one, insisted that her work was "doing Christianity and not simply acting religion."[15] In her appeals to the local churches for donations, she undoubtedly emphasized that basis of her settlement work. When speaking of the Phyllis Wheatley Home for young working girls, Elizabeth Lindsay Davis stressed the importance of a Christian influence.[16] As noted in the last chapter, Elizabeth McDonald and Amanda Smith combined their rescue and mission work with children's welfare, thus conjoining notions of respectability to social, economic, and moral issues. To illustrate further, Clotee Scott promoted dressmaking not only as an economic enterprise but also as a moral one, because in doing so she encouraged young women to aspire to higher goals rather than frequenting the saloons and dance halls.[17]

African American club women's moral and religious tenor often becomes obscured in debates on whether the African American settlements were modeled from church missions or prototype settlements. Rather than classifying African American settlements as secular, we might think of them as nondenominational. In discussing the churches' role in uplifting Southern migrants, Richard R. Wright noted that one of the chief obstacles of the "best social work" was lack of denominational cooperation. Perhaps speaking from his own experiences with the short-lived Trinity Mission in Chicago's Black Belt, Wright explained that the churches should not engage in the businesses of dance halls, gymnasiums, bath houses, or night schools. Rather, church leaders must realign their positions to advocate for the social and economic improvements of African American communities.[18]

When we examine the African American churches' establishment of settlements and missions in Chicago, several patterns emerge that clarify women's later settlement work. During the first decade of the twentieth century, several African American churches formed social centers or missions. The A.M.E. Institutional Church, under the ministry of Reverend Ransom, provided classes and clubs, a day nursery, a kindergarten, and lecture series. Olivet Baptist Church, too, organized classes, clubs, and a literary society.[19] Spear has argued that in providing diverse programs and services, both churches attempted to recruit Southern migrants as new members, as well as to retain their middle-class congregation.[20] Although Spear has underscored the migrants' dissatisfaction with the churches' formal church services, I would note that increased class stratification, as exemplified in church and club memberships, reflected middle-class African Americans' mutual dissatisfaction with associating with the poor. As noted in chapter 2, several of the illustrious African American churches relocated as members of their congregations moved to wealthier neighborhoods.

Class differentiation became further amplified as the churches continued their social uplift and charity activities through their literary societies and clubs. The churches' relocation signified not only a physical but also a social distance, additionally marked by the status and prestige accorded from the literary societies and lyceums. As examined in chapter 6, the youth lyceums, sponsored and organized by leading church women, provided teenagers with diversions from the harmful influences of the dance halls, pool rooms, and saloons. Perhaps more noteworthy, the youth lyceums prepared middle-class adolescents, in true Du Boisian fashion, for future leadership roles. Part of that grooming included the rituals and practices of social uplift.

The female settlement workers adopted a decidedly different strategy from that of the church leaders, both in recreational activities for youth and for all of their programs and clientele. Originally members of the Frederick Douglass Woman's Club, many of the African American female settlement workers increasingly broke allegiances to the center and formed their own establishments. Ida B. Wells resigned from the center and created the Negro Fellowship League; Fannie Emanuel, officer of the club in 1910, founded the Emanuel Neighborhood Settlement while retaining her ties with the center.[21] The location of both facilities—in the heart of Chicago's Black Belt—perhaps reflected both women's disenchantment with the center's focus on middle class clientele. On the other hand, maintaining ties, if not allegiances, to the white and African American middle class was essential for purposes of funding. The Emanuel Settlement's finances were not publicly disclosed, but the Negro Fellowship League was supported by Mrs. Victor Lawson, wife of the publisher of the *Chicago Daily News*.[22] As the examples of Wells and others suggest, African American facilities relied greatly upon white philanthropy. Financial difficulties figured heavily in the league's closing, as they did for the church settlements.

Like the Negro Fellowship League and the Emanuel Settlement, the Wendell Phillips and Clotee Scott Settlements were located in predominantly African American neighborhoods. Unlike the church ministers, who had not deliberated on the problematic "amusement" question, the settlement founders and workers—in the midst of cabarets, saloons, dance halls, and places of ill repute—created dance clubs, singing and drama clubs, and Friday night entertainments to distract youth from these looming temptations. Issues of respectability and morals were inscribed in these events, as well as in the settlements' sewing, embroidery, and cooking classes. Young children's time was consumed in clubs, classes, playground activity, and storytelling sessions.

Although the five settlements examined in this chapter were not affiliated with any church, ministers were certainly invited as guest speakers, as was often the case with the Frederick Douglass Center. Church leaders were prominent members of the settlement boards; their churches were frequently asked to donate, particularly to the Clotee Scott Settlement. Thus, the settlement founders and workers continued to nurture church affiliations, not denominations. Because the need for lodging and employment referrals, child care, and training classes was great, the settlement founders could not afford to choose their sources of financial support.

AFRICAN AMERICAN SETTLEMENTS IN CHICAGO

The five settlements described here were located in or near the African American neighborhoods of Chicago. The Emanuel Settlement and the Negro Fellowship League, in the heart of Chicago's Black Belt, provided basic services such as health care, lodging, and employment referral services. The Wendell Phillips Settlement, on the West Side, and the Clotee Scott Settlement, located in Hyde Park, offered a mix of services reminiscent of earlier African American missions and the prototypical settlements, such as Hull House. The increased professionalism of social and settlement workers through the University of Chicago's School of Civics and Philanthropy undoubtedly influenced their programs. The Frederick Douglass Center was singular in its objective of promoting interracial amity among middle-class Whites and African Americans, although it also offered classes to poorer African Americans. Its location, adjacent to the Black Belt rather than within its boundaries, reflected its preoccupation with social class.

Despite the differences among these settlements, there were striking similarities. First, most relied upon white philanthropy for financial support, although some community support was engendered through the women's clubs. Second, most of the boards of directors were interracial.[23] But because many of the board members were male, a gendered hierarchy of administrative decision making emerged within the settlements, not unlike that in juvenile courts. To illustrate, even though the club women voluntarily served as supervisors, teachers, and fund-raisers for the settlements, prominent African American and white men were charged with administrative and budgetary decisions. The settlement heads, not unlike Elizabeth McDonald and Amanda Smith in their positions, often found their administrative decisions not only questioned but even undermined by the board members. In the case of Birdye Haynes of the Wendell Phillips Settlement, her dual role as head resident and as a student in the University of Chicago's School of Civics and Philanthropy compromised her capacity to create community programming that would ultimately receive board approval. Not only were her decisions questioned and ultimately undermined by William Granes of the Julius Rosenwald Fund, who worked closely with the board of directors; Haynes's programmatic activities were subject to scrutiny by board members Grace Abbott and Sophonisba Breckinridge, professors under whom she studied. Although Haynes was extremely knowledgeable of the African American community's needs, the board repeatedly refused to provide financial backing for her recommended children's and youth services.[24] Despite these conflicts, the Wendell Phillips Settlement, as well as the other settlements, did create a number of services for children, youth, and young women.

Programs for Young Children

Day nurseries, kindergartens, and classes for young children were established by all of the settlements discussed above, with the exception of the Negro Fellowship League. Unlike the kindergartens and their attendant mothers' clubs of the mainstream settlements, however, these services were created primarily to provide safe child care while the mothers worked. As Clotee Scott remarked: "The settlement is considered now as the living home for the children while the parents are at work."[25] It is well documented that many African American women during this time period worked as domestics and laundry women. In 1900 nearly 43 percent of the African American women in Chicago were breadwinners; they evidently had little time for Froebelian pedagogy or the study of child or physical culture.[26] When they did attend mothers' clubs, the more practical matters of hygiene, ventilation, and home life dominated, reflecting the reality of the crowded tenements, unsanitary living conditions, and unsafe neighborhoods of the Black Belt.

In Chicago's Black Belt the Emanuel Settlement sponsored mothers' meetings alongside domestic training and the services of a dental clinic and visiting nurses. This program was consistent with Fannie Barrier Williams's vision that kindergartens build children's character and mothers' clubs teach mothers homemaking skills.[27] In stark contrast, the Frederick Douglass Center sponsored several mothers' clubs for its middle-class members. There, a child culture club, organized by Irene Goins, focused on home life, school and home relations, and child development and psychology. This club was short-lived, perhaps because of the war, but, undaunted, Goins refocused her efforts and established African American Camp Fire Girls and the Girls' Patriotic League units.[28]

Young children participated in a variety of settlement activities. At the Clotee Scott Settlement, classes included manual training for boys and sewing, embroidery, and crocheting for girls. Such classes were common; they were also offered at the Frederick Douglass Center, the Wendell Phillips Settlement, and the Emanuel Settlement. Physical recreation, particularly playground games and gymnastics, were also popular. The Emanuel Settlement offered an athletic club; the Frederick Douglass Center frequently took the children on outings to parks. The Clotee Scott Settlement, though, offered the greatest variety of activities. Physical culture classes were introduced by a University of Chicago student; the white Hyde Park YMCA responded by donating a punching bag, Indian clubs, and dumbbells. The children also congregated each Saturday on the settlement playground, where games were taught. Such recreation was considered very "useful" for children who lived in flats with no open spaces for running and jumping.[29]

The Clotee Scott Settlement was also exemplary in its educative activities. For example, classes were offered in piano, singing, and elocution for "timid, shy children." Most impressive, however, was the reading room, described as "a cosy parlor," which had a collection of more than four hundred books for adults and children. The settlement boasted of the large number of people who used it. One account described the reading room filled with boys and girls who played the piano and played parlor games, rather than congregating on the streets. In one case a twelve-year-old girl wrote a play, performed by the other settlement children.[30]

Another advantage of the Clotee Scott Settlement was a reduction in "prejudice amongst the children."[31] Unlike many of the mainstream settlements, the Clotee Scott Settlement admitted children of all nationalities. In 1913 Clotee Scott spoke of how "both white and colored children have attended the settlement, sitting at the same reading table, singing side by side the same patriotic songs and exercising with the same American flags."[32] Although most of the African American settlements had an open door policy, they did not report the same interracial friendships. Curiously, despite the Frederick Douglass Center's insistence on interracial amity, the color line was distinctly drawn when it came to the children's and adolescents' programs.

The various activities, then, provided safe and wholesome child care. Although no scientific principles were expressed in terms of educating the "whole" child, the classes and recreational activities encouraged the physical, mental, social, and moral development of the children. As Ray Stannard Baker observed, the settlements were "centres of enlightenment and hope," offering a "moral tone" to the community, especially to the children through clubs and classes.[33] However, this "moral tone" was implicit, as settlement workers did not indict parents for their impoverished living conditions but instead provided children with social opportunities not available in their home environment. Rather than rebuking the parents for "disorganized" (and hence "immoral") homes, the settlement workers created mutual social and educative activities.

Programs for Youths

Most of the settlements throughout Chicago were deeply concerned with the youths, particularly their gravitation toward saloons, pool rooms, dance halls, and other places of ill repute. In 1911 the Juvenile Protective Association had documented the existence of more than 328 dance halls in Chicago, which attracted more than eighty-five thousand youths between the ages of fourteen and eighteen.[34] The African American club women and settlement workers were equally concerned with such distractions. Members of the Phyllis Wheatley Club discussed "the temptations that await the girls who go unprotected after dark."[35] Elizabeth Lindsay Davis had recommended a "constant watchfulness," arguing that "all that is noblest and best in them [young girls] must be aroused and developed."[36] The editor of the *Broad Ax* pointed out the dangers especially for young girls in the Black Belt, whom he referred to as "their beautiful daughters, unattended, or in company with sporty young fellows, who are seeking every opportunity, to despoil them, to frequent the lowest and the vilest five cent theaters."[37]

To counteract such dangers, most of the Chicago settlements offered a series of wholesome activities, ranging from dances and sporting events to drama, debate, and singing clubs. Philpott has described the youth dances sponsored by the mainstream settlements in order to prevent bootlegging and to squelch immoral behavior. Detailed guidelines were published on socially appropriate ways of dancing, which meant no cheek-to-cheek caresses or encircling a partner's neck with clasped arms. Lights were usually left undimmed as staff members meandered through the crowd, "prying" young couples apart. Stodgy music was played to prevent girls from "shimmy[ing]" and boys from "rub[bing] it up," "bump[ing]," and "sock[ing] it in."[38] The African American settlements, too, were concerned with such behavior and offered dance classes in waltzing and other traditional dance forms. At one meeting of the Clotee Scott Settlement, the youths wore Japanese costumes "to encourage grace for bodily exercise, and also to provide a clean and safe evening for those young people who work or live in Hyde Park."[39] Great care was taken to sponsor small group activities and to avoid the "idea of a big public dance."[40]

In addition, drama, singing, and sporting clubs were organized to provide other forms of wholesome recreation for African American youths. Once again, the Clotee Scott Settlement led in such activities. In 1914 the settlement organized the Young People's Social Dramatic Club for "any young lady or man of good morals" in order "to encourage the study of dramatic art and the social life of the young people."[41] Three other clubs were also sponsored by the settlement, the Girls' Junior Clover Club, the Boys' Laurel Club, and the Young Men's Glee Club. The Clover Club performed plays and dramatic presentations, as well as drills and gymnastic dances. In the summer, sports activities, including swimming, hiking, tennis, and golf were organized. Although the club was described as "a good club for mothers' daughters who need the right sort of companionship, and who wish to learn the household arts and become useful women," there was little evidence of domestic skills being taught.[42] However, it was likely that many of the young girls also participated in the domestic classes offered through the settlement.

The Young Men's Glee Club participated in singing, dancing, and drama events. Again, such clubs focused not only on developing the artistic skills of youth, but also on providing wholesome recreation: "Look at the well-behaved youth who before had only one or two disreputable saloons, a jim-crow theater and the pool room as the only place as a center." The club clearly achieved its socialization goals: "Parents are proud of the progress these young men are making not only in their singing, but in their general conduct and interest in settlement work."[43]

Reading rooms, too, exerted a positive influence on the youths, especially young boys. The Negro Fellowship League provided wholesome recreation for young boys and men, such as checkers, reading, and writing, so that members would not be "idling away their time in saloons or pool rooms."[44] A 1915 report described the room: "Books, papers and magazines with a comfortable place to sit have made the reading room attractive to hundreds of penniless boys, girls and men who otherwise would have been a public charge."[45] The league's success was evident in its number of visitors, which ranged from seventy-seven during the month of August in 1915 to more than three hundred during one winter week in 1916.[46] The Clotee Scott Settlement also boasted of its reading room's success. It was noted that boys who had dropped out of school were catching up on their reading so they might enroll in the new Hyde Park High School. Hotel waiters, too, began to frequent the reading room instead of the pool rooms.[47]

Despite the settlements' establishment of youth clubs, the inequity in resources and funds, when compared to white youths' clubs, was apparent. Club woman Irene McCoy-Gaines had noted the dearth of adequate resources for youth facilities in the African American neighborhoods in contrast to the white community centers "with cozy clubrooms, well equipped gyms, and swimming pools . . . where a girl could profitably spend her time." She argued that such recreational services were especially needed in the Black Belt for African American girls.[48]

The youth clubs did more than occupy the teenagers' time. The clubs engaged them in the popular culture of dances, songs, and sports. Talented youth were also coached in their budding musical and dramatic skills. Unlike the middle-class youth clubs, which reflected the cultural capital of evening gowns, promenades, and whist and bridge games, the settlement clubs organized social evenings during which one could forget about his or her impoverished home or neighborhood, without the moral overtones often accompanying YMCA or YWCA programs.

Domestic Training for Girls and Young Women

As noted previously, many of the African American settlement workers and club women favored industrial and domestic training for poorer African American women. Fannie Barrier Williams stated in a talk in 1904 that, whereas formerly the apron had been a symbol of "servility" and the kitchen not a place for "ladies," there was now "a new dignity [that] has been added to the occupations that concern our health, our homes and our happiness."[49] Thus, cooking, nursing, and dressmaking were legitimate professions, made "dignified" by industrial education. Such beliefs were not peculiar to Williams but were echoed by other prominent African American women, such as Nannie Burroughs and Elizabeth Ross Haynes.[50] Although ironies and contradictions are apparent to historians today, such an ideology then fit not only within the concepts of social uplift, respectability, the cult of true womanhood, and Christian ideals but also with the harsh realities of discriminatory hiring practices, adjustments to urban conditions, and the lack of educational opportunity for women. Even when young African American women were educated in, say, stenography or bookkeeping, more often than not the color line was drawn, at least in Chicago. Thus, domestic training served multiple purposes: to train for employment as domestic workers, to improve the standards of motherhood and the home, and to occupy young girls' recreational time.

All of the five settlements provided some form of domestic training or employment referral services. With the exception of the Negro Fellowship League, whose clientele were predominantly African American men and boys, all of the settlements offered domestic classes for young girls and women. At the Clotee Scott Settlement sewing classes were taught by teachers from Tuskegee and the Frederick Douglass Center. One teacher, Mrs. C. L. Wilson, was considered an excellent seamstress, especially since she made clothes for the "richest class of white women."[51] Young girls were encouraged to enroll because "we [the settlement] desire our young women to take up this trade." The settlement argued that young women should improve their employment opportunities, rather than relying on laundry or domestic work. Such work was also touted for those "looking for higher things in life and not for those who are looking for big crowds and excitement."[52] Following completion of the class, a diploma was given to girls age fourteen and older. The settlement also provided classes in Irish crochet and cooking to "guarantee work." There is some indication that the settlement functioned as an employment referral agency, especially since it was occasionally unable to procure employment for several dressmakers, because of "many securing white help."[53] However, no public records of employment referrals seem to have been kept.

The Wendell Phillips Settlement, too, taught cooking, sewing, and millinery skills through its night school, although shorthand, Spanish, French, history, and stenography were also taught. The latter classes were most often attended by "prominent women," reflecting social class differences not unlike those at the Frederick Douglass Center. At the center, sewing, cooking, gardening, and dressmaking classes were attended mostly by poorer women, whereas the more academic courses of sociology, English literature, and English grammar were frequented by the middle class. Middle-class women also engaged in sewing and handiwork, but most often through their clubs and for the purpose of charity. For example, a linen chest of bed linen and infant clothing was organized for the poor; so, too, the Woman's Club made garments from cloth provided by the School Children's Aid Society for needy children in various city schools. Thus, the purposes of sewing and handiwork pointed to social class distinctions: those who sewed for charity and those who sewed out of necessity.[54]

Three of the settlements—the Emanuel Settlement, the Negro Fellowship League, and the Frederick Douglass Center—organized employment referral bureaus. None of the settlements reflected the commitment to domestic service training of Flanner House of Indianapolis with its schools for laundry workers and for maids.[55] With the exception of the Frederick Douglass Center, however, most employment services were aimed at African American men. Although there is no direct evidence, it is likely that since much of the settlements' funding was received from white philanthropists and businessmen, many of these jobs were as strikebreakers. I have not been able to document this connection, as Crocker has with the Stewart House in Gary, Indiana, but there is direct evidence that many African American men from the South were hired as "scabs" during the strikes.[56]

Although the Emanuel Settlement and the Frederick Douglass Center organized employment bureaus, I was unable to locate any records pertaining to these services. In the case of the Negro Fellowship League, employment referrals were not enumerated. Rather, services were grouped collectively, as in the 1915 report, which stated that more than "10,000 men, women and children received some type of benefit, be it a job, lodging, or charity."[57] Occasionally, anecdotal reports of the league's intervention were noted, as described in chapter 3.

The domestic classes provided further training toward domestic service for poorer African American women. Yet, there is evidence that a number of middle-class women owned their own millinery, hairdressing, and dressmaking shops or worked from their homes. Thus, it was possible that there was the *perception* that sewing classes might provide upward mobility economically. Indeed, the Clotee Scott Settlement encouraged such thoughts: "The young Negro girl will not always be compelled to hunt for work as laundress if she will only grasp the opportunity to make an honest living by becoming a competent dressmaker."[58] Although the settlements did not organize domestic schools, the handing out of certificates and diplomas pointed to a credentialing process that was reflected in other women's work, such as chiropody, manicuring, and the "mental sciences." It is quite likely that these diplomas were given to young girls who did not complete high school.

By 1919 all of the settlements, with the exception of the Wendell Phillips Settlement, had closed. The Chicago branch of the Urban League, as an umbrella organization, subsumed many of the settlement and club activities. In fact, in 1918 the Frederick Douglass Center became the league's headquarters.[59] Many of the white settlement reformers, such as Sophonisba Breckinridge and Jane Addams, turned their allegiance to the league, as did some of the African American club women. Other club women, however, especially Ida B. Wells, were suspicious of the Urban League's supplanting the smaller community institutions.[60] Wells's suspicions were well founded, because 90 percent of the league's budget was derived from white philanthropy (with Rosenwald providing approximately 33 percent of the budget).[61] Decision-making power was removed from the community, as Weiss has corroborated, in that the league was consumed with immediate problems of housing and employment, rather than political and legal representation.[62]

The league sponsored boys' and girls' clubs, summer camps, kindergartens, nurseries, and lodging and employment referral services, as the settlements had done. Nonetheless, it is questionable whether the league functioned in the same ways as the neighborhood settlements. For one thing, the league was located adjacent to the Black Belt, rather than within it. Furthermore, the league worked in conjunction with a number of institutions, including the juvenile courts, churches, social agencies, and civic organizations. As such, it lost the interdependency of the mutual aid societies and the collaborative networks of the women's clubs, as it functioned with increasingly complex bureaucracies such as the juvenile court.

SIX

LITERARY CLUBS

LITERARY EVENTS, LIKE MANY OTHER AFRICAN AMERI-
can club activities, were not subject to narrow purposes
or expressions. Whether in the form of lyceums, debates,
or essay contests, literary study was often wedded to the
oral traditions of oratory, elocution, recitation, testimony,
and sermons.[1] Likewise, the study of "literature" embraced many
topics, ranging from politics and philosophy to art, religion, travel, and
sociology. The literary artifacts examined in this chapter include essays,
editorials, newspaper columns, addresses, and published speeches, all of
which illustrate club women's versatility. The scope of literary activities
points to the ways in which the club women related the political to the
literary, the secular to the religious, and the written to the spoken word.

The African American literary clubs in Chicago owed their breadth
to a confluence of literary traditions: the African American literary and
church societies, the lyceums, and the Chautauqua movement. Dorothy
Porter's classic study of early African American literary societies has
documented the various genres, topics, and settings in which literary

study occurred.[2] The social and political concerns of abolition, temperance, benevolence, and later, suffrage and political representation were articulated through elocution, addresses, and essays. Even then, such issues were expressed in distinctly gendered ways. Yee has noted that the African American male abolitionist societies emphasized debate, rhetoric, and oratory, whereas women's societies encouraged their members' mental improvement "in order to fulfill their female responsibilities."[3] Such "female responsibilities" were often predicated upon "good moral character," one of the requirements for membership in societies such as the Afric-American Female Intelligence Society of Boston.[4]

Moral fortitude was imperative in that the literary societies were not simply founded for self-improvement but also for future generations. The African Female Benevolent Society of Newport, Rhode Island, raised money for a children's school.[5] The Female Anti-Slavery Society in Salem, Massachusetts, was devoted to self-improvement as well as freedom for all African Americans.[6] Consequently, the societies established reading rooms and libraries to provide educational resources in their communities.[7] The twin efforts of individual and race uplift would be later demonstrated in the women's literary clubs in Chicago.

African American women were also active in the abolitionist societies. Maria W. Stewart and Sarah M. Douglass, among others, delivered antislavery lectures during the 1830s, when public speaking was considered a male activity. Frances Ellen Watkins Harper not only lectured on behalf of abolition but also wrote antislavery poetry. Many women contributed letters, articles, slave narratives, and editorials, albeit often anonymously, to the antislavery newspapers.[8] The lyceums, too, provided opportunity for oratory performance and literary study. In conjunction with the Second Great Awakening, the lyceums' purpose was the "mutual improvement" of both "intellectual and moral faculties."[9] Like the early literary societies, the lyceums bridged from moral character to the intellectual activities of lectures, dramatic performances, and debates. Although the early lyceums were certainly not limited to young women, the moral "improvements" proffered by the lyceums were compatible with those of true womanhood: to "refine their [youths'] feelings, enlighten, elevate and dignify their minds, and soften and purify their hearts."[10]

Nonetheless, the public nature of lyceums prepared women, at least native-born white women, to give addresses on political issues. Anna Dickinson, the "Queen of the Platform," spoke on women's rights and

African American suffrage during the 1860s. Elizabeth Cady Stanton, Susan B. Anthony, and Lucy Stone were likewise ardent in their addresses on temperance, abolition, and women's suffrage.[11] Some African American males, most notably Frederick Douglass, traveled the lyceum circuit and were popular speakers. Douglass frequently entertained his Northern audiences with parodic performances of slaveholding clerics' sermons. As "a masterful Signifier," Douglass caricatured not only the plantation master but also the subservient slave.[12] In a more serious tenor, Douglass lectured on abolition and suffrage for African American men and women. At one lyceum meeting in Cincinnati in 1868, Douglass's delivery was praised as "purer English . . . not a word suggestive of Southern pronunciation, emphasis or manner."[13] So powerful were his words that his speeches and addresses were often recited by others.

Unlike the national lyceum circuit, the first Chicago lyceums were a distinctly male domain. The Chicago Lyceum, the Chicago Mechanics Institute, the Young Men's Lyceum, and the Young Men's Association restricted their membership to men. Women most likely attended the lectures of prominent orators such as Emerson, however.[14] Instead of intellectual study, most Chicago female societies during the 1830s and 1840s performed charity and benevolent work, especially for orphans and the poor. Even when the first white female club, the Chicago Woman's Club, was organized, it still continued to engage in "practical work."[15] The Chicago kindergarten and mothers' clubs, which connected literary and artistic study to child development, continued the two efforts of self-cultivation and maternalistic responsibilities.

Coinciding with the emergence of a growing African American middle class, the first African American lyceums in Chicago were organized in the 1890s. Most of the lyceums, established through the Presbyterian and the American Methodist Episcopal denominations, were located in Englewood, Morgan Park, and Hyde Park. Although the lyceums were originally for adults, youth lyceums soon followed to promote the intellectual and political development of future leaders. The lyceums provided a forum for members to debate and discuss community issues—one that Carter G. Woodson thought particularly appealing for younger persons.[16] Although membership in the lyceums was usually restricted to church members, the lyceums also sponsored Sunday forums, which were attended by many African Americans. Such gatherings served to inform the African American community at large of key political and social issues. Fittingly, speakers were chosen for their national prominence and their oratory skills.

The church lyceums were rooted in African American church traditions. Not only did ministers frequently use the pulpit to deliver political and social commentary; leading community leaders also often stood before the congregation to deliver addresses not unlike the ministers'. Booker T. Washington, for one, spoke the first Sunday of each month before his congregation in Tuskegee, admonishing members to practice the virtues of thrift, industry, and punctuality.[17] Just as political messages were interwoven with religious images, so too were the religious themes of exodus and homeland politically charged. Some scholars have suggested that the distinct genres of dramatic history, poetry, oratory, and philosophical essays developed from these biblical readings and commentary.[18]

Reminiscent of all-day Sunday meetings during slavery, meetings, social gatherings, and fund-raising events occurred in Chicago African American churches throughout the day on Sunday. The lyceums, too, embraced this tradition through their forums on Sunday afternoons. Themes from the morning sermon or the political address of the evening before might be further deliberated, as for the lyceum at St. Mark's Church Literary and Historical Society in Boston, where extemporaneous talking and lively debate from the floor were both frequent and expected.[19] In Chicago the programs often followed a prescribed format, with the keynote speaker preceded and followed by vocal and instrumental performances and poetry recitations. Often the lyceum concluded with a choir or music quartet.

The African American women were particularly active as speakers and organizers in these lyceums. In the case of the Englewood Lyceum, the women's programs were often considered more "original" and successful than those organized with the men. African American women were likely to experience gender tensions like those noted by Higginbotham, and in response they mediated their multiple memberships in their churches, clubs, and political organizations.[20] In some cases these tensions were minimized by organizing forums and occasions, such as a "gala day," when women were the designated speakers and performers. More often than not, though, participation in the lyceums was more egalitarian. For example, most of the debate teams took great care in selecting an equal number of male and female participants. Similarly, prizes were awarded to both the best female and the best male writers in essay contests.

Like the lyceums, Chautauquas reflected a confluence of mainstream and African American traditions. There is evidence that African Americans participated to a limited extent in the national Chautauqua movement, although most were musicians who sang jubilee songs and spirituals. Occasional speakers were selected from the Booker T. Washington camp, for example, Robert B. Moton, principal of the Tuskegee Institute, whose speech "The Black Man and the War" echoed the accommodationist approach. Such speeches were chosen to please a largely white audience.[21] The Chautauqua movement especially held great interest for women who wished to expand their education, albeit informally. Chautauqua organizers, in fact, seized upon this opportunity; an analysis of Chautauqua lectures revealed that over half of the speeches focused on motherhood and the home.[22] White women especially expanded this domestic agenda to include female suffrage, temperance, settlement work, and child labor laws.[23] Although no records of African American female speakers were found, African American women did participate, to some extent, in Chautauqua study courses. In Atlanta's Chautauqua Circle, one of the oldest African American women's clubs in the city, the women moved to the topic of race improvement after studying the Chautauqua courses.[24]

In Chicago the Chautauqua movement was especially popular among mothers and kindergarten educators. The Chautauqua Kindergarten Department in New York, affiliated with the Chicago Kindergarten Institute, offered courses in Froebelian pedagogy and philosophy through the mothers' clubs and kindergarten college. In fact, many nationally renowned Chautauqua speakers hailed from the University of Chicago.[25]

In the African American communities of Chicago, however, Chautauquas held less appeal: the only recorded Chautauqua event occurred in 1906 in the community of Englewood. Under the auspices of St. John's A.M.E. Church, an outside tabernacle was erected to accommodate up to three thousand people. The main attractions were evangelistic sermons, although musical, dramatic and literary works were also performed. During the evenings church choirs entertained the crowds. The Chautauqua events, like some of the lyceums, were charged with a decidedly female influence. Of the ten days, one was designated as "mother's day," on which deaconnesses, nurses, and missionary women throughout the city met to discuss issues of "vital importance to childhood and womanhood." On the following day representatives from nineteen women's clubs sponsored an "elaborate program" as part of Women's Club Day.[26] Such programs were reminiscent of the A.M.E. mission meetings, organized by Rev. Mary E. Lark Hill, at which evangelists and club women took turns speaking on the platform.[27] Although club women did not usually join the storefront churches, such as the Queen Esther Mission, they did become involved in the proselytizing efforts of their denominations.

Several reasons might explain the low popularity of the Chautauquas in the African American communities of Chicago. First, as described in chapter 2, there were demonstrable class distinctions within the African American churches; the Presbyterian and Episcopal churches, often described as more "sedate," may have frowned upon the evangelistic activities and the popular appeal of the Chautauquas. Second, the intellectual and aesthetic needs of many middle-class African Americans were more likely met through their lyceums and clubs. Third, the Chautauqua, at least in the African American communities of Chicago, seemed to concentrate mostly upon religious conversion, paralleling the growing number of storefront churches and gospel tents frequented by Southern African American migrants who settled in the city's Black Belt.

CHICAGO FEMALE LITERARY CLUBS

The women's literary clubs offered an intimate and private audience before which women might offer their own interpretation of works, read their own writings, and translate ideas into uplift practices. Although male writers occasionally read their works before African American women's clubs, I found no accounts of women reading their writings at a men's meeting. Women did, of course, speak publicly on social, political, and educational issues, and such addresses and speeches were original. However, more likely than not, female clubs offered a distinct space where members sharing their interpretations, recitations, and original writings received mutual support and encouragement.

Not only did the literary clubs offer more intimate occasions for sharing perspectives; because of the very nature of their activities, the literary clubs were selective in membership. It was not sufficient for club members to be literate; they must be or at least aspire to be literary.

Such selectivity was evident in the more literary topics at club meetings, in contrast to the practical topics delivered before the general audiences at the Sunday forums. For example, a discussion of Shakespeare or Emerson would not have been held at a forum, not only because it would be considered inappropriate for the occasion, but also because it would have deflated the very selectivity of such study. The study of classical and modern literature served, then, to join club women of like aspiration and social class.

Although many African American women's clubs studied literature, few did so exclusively. Most of the federated clubs included the study of philanthropy, home, education, art, and music. These various strands of study were not treated separately but were interrelated, as club woman Josephine Washington noted: "Here the members study standard authors, read the latest books, discuss current events and compare opinions on questions of interest." [28] As a matter of course, many of the members' original writings focused not on grand literary themes but on the humbler topics of home, domestic art, and child care. [29]

Not only were the literary clubs' topics diverse, but so also was the literature studied. Many of the African American women's clubs read both European and African American literature. Although club meetings might be devoted to Paul Laurence Dunbar's poetry or a novel by Du Bois, it was not unusual for meetings to include a paper on classical art, followed by jubilee singing and a Beethoven piano sonata. [30] Although this assortment of presentations may seem paradoxical, for the club women all of the activities were uplifting and educational. To some extent their reading repertoire—including works by Ruskin, Emerson, Ibsen, Shakespeare, Tennyson, and Eliot—was not unlike that studied by white club women and social and settlement workers. [31] Ruskin and Emerson were especially popular; they were read by the Frederick Douglass Center's sociology class, the Neighborhood and Literary Society, and the University Society Club. [32] The African American club women's cultivation of such literary materials, indeed, reflected their "double consciousness."

The preponderance of European literature, however, did not imply a dearth of African American writing. Prominent male and female African American writers were published in national African American journals and newspapers. Chicago club women Ida B. Wells, Fannie Barrier Williams, Bettiola Forston, and Irene McCoy-Gaines were only a few of the African American literati of the city. Chicago was, in fact, the publishing site for many African American journals, including the *Champion,* the *Half-Century Magazine,* the *Pullman Porter,* the *Fraternal Advocate,* and the *Stroller.*[33] Editorials, essays, and poetry were also often featured in the *Chicago Defender* and the *Broad Ax.*

Unlike the African American women who studied European writers, most white club women in Chicago did not read African American literature—or that of immigrants, for that matter. They limited their study to English and French art, history, and literature.[34] The white women's literary study was considered more formal and systematic, especially through course instruction and lectures. For example, the Chicago Woman's Club's study of literature and art was similar to university extension courses.[35] Occasionally, University of Chicago professors were invited to give lectures. Even when professors were not available, the clubs insisted on "rigor" and "thoroughness." The West End Woman's Club's literary section stipulated that its study be "carried out" through the essay and that the topic be "usually represented by four papers."[36] The Woman's Club of Irving Park, in its presentation of literary papers, attended to style, pronunciation, and substantiation of detail, assigning "one of the best informed members" the role of critic.[37]

Despite their separate paths of study, African American and white club women did create opportunities for joint literary discussion. Reciprocity days were organized for club women to meet and share their ideas. The Ideal Woman's Club sponsored such an event, at which members from twenty African American and white women's clubs convened to discuss Harriet Beecher Stowe. Mrs. T. H. Smith, whose mother had been the model for the character "Emily" read a letter from the author to her mother. (Emily was the mulatto character on the Shelby Plantation in Kentucky.) Her presentation was followed by various talks on the author's life, work, and characters, as well as on the abolitionist movement, by Mary McDowell of Chicago University, Mary Dietz of the Hull House Woman's Club, and Elizabeth Lindsay Davis of the Phyllis Wheatley Club. After the meeting, a motion was passed to honor the birthday of Harriet Beecher Stowe in the Chicago communities.[38]

Although many African American women engaged in some type of literary study, several clubs were considered to be illustrious. One such club, comprised of both men and women, was the University Society.

Members included recent college graduates John Felton, a budding local journalist; Bettiola Forston, a young poet; Sophia Boaz, a social worker at the Wendell Phillips Settlement; and Lenora Curtis, whose essays were occasionally published in the newspapers. Irene McCoy (later McCoy-Gaines), a fiction writer, and Harris Gaines, a lawyer known for his dramatic abilities, also joined.[39] The society was originally formed in honor of its members' "memory of old college days." Although nostalgia was evident in the society decorations of alma mater pennants, the society's primary focus was artistic and intellectual development. One of their first programs showcased the members' musical talents with their solo performances. A series of lectures on "Comparative Religion," included the topics of reincarnation, the Bahai faith, and mental sciences. Although theosophy was of special interest, the members discussed the diverse subjects of self-culture, prejudice, universal languages, and slang.[40]

The Frederick Douglass Center's literary events were also designed for educated, middle-class members. The center organized Sunday forums as the prestigious African American churches did. Unlike the church lyceums, however, the center's forums presented literary and philosophical works. But because the center was not located in the Black Belt and was largely frequented by middle-class clientele, the forums probably did not appeal to poorer African Americans. Celia Parker Woolley, cofounder of the center, often introduced, read, and critiqued European and American writers whose works carried deliberate political and social themes, such as Henrik Ibsen, Jane Addams, H. G. Wells, and Paul Kester. Woolley, herself an author, occasionally read from her own novels.[41] On several occasions an admission fee was charged for her lectures and readings and donated to the center's sewing classes.[42]

As a Unitarian minister, Woolley was greatly interested in philosophical and religious themes. She presented several programs on Emerson, as well as programs on Nietzsche's philosophy and Tennyson's transcendental poetry and a character study of Shakespeare's Shylock.[43] Because the center's aim was to promote better race relations, Woolley invited eminent African American intellectuals to speak at the Sunday forums. The historian Carter G. Woodson outlined his arguments set forth in *The Negro Prior to 1861,* and Major Lynch discussed his most recent publication, *Reminiscences of Reconstruction Days.* Robert Ezra Park, a white sociologist at the University of Chicago, spoke about his book on Booker T. Washington.[44] The orations of Wendell Phillips and Frederick Douglass, as well as the poetry of Paul Laurence Dunbar, were regularly read and performed and occasionally set to music.

The center's Woman's Club, composed of prominent African American and native-born white women, was committed to the study of literature, philosophy, and sociology. Once again, both African American and European literature were studied. Mrs. George Hall presented a character study of Eliot's Adam Bede. Several meetings were devoted to the study of Du Bois's *The Quest of the Silver Fleece*.[45] In 1915 Fannie Barrier Williams organized a Frederick Douglass program, at which she shared her personal memories of Douglass, concluding with a reading of Dunbar's poem for Douglass.[46] Although classes were offered for self-improvement, they also were concerned with social and political uplift. The English class, taught by Ida B. Wells, included the "functions of grammar, the study of the element of good expression, and a further study of the history of English literature."[47] Although diction and fluency were social class markers, their development was also important for public speaking. The sociology classes included on-site studies, exposing the club women to various models of schools and settlements. For example, the women visited several Chicago social settlements and read about the Fireside Schools, with lessons on the merits of thrift and tidiness.[48]

Like the center's Woman's Club, the Phyllis Wheatley Club emphasized literary study and production. As early as 1899 club activities included recitations and addresses, one by a Mr. Moore, who provided an overview of the teachings of Zeno, Socrates, Aurelius, Seneca, and other "profound" thinkers and writers. Mr. Moore stressed that such historical study was crucial for any race to "reach the highest goal." In elaborating on this theme, he argued that those with "brains" ruled the "brainless." Thus, mothers should keep "good" books in the home for the children. However, he continued, books alone were not sufficient; children needed worthy role models. He instructed the women to "cease from 'apeing' women whose highest ambition was wearing fine clothes but whose minds were aimless."[49] Unfortunately, no records were kept of the discussion that followed. Mr. Moore was not the only male speaker to lecture the club women on their behavior. At another meeting in 1899 Dr. Jeffrey, after speaking on the "formation of the brain" and philanthropy, advised the women to behave according to such love and to "cease from being puffed up and self-conceited creatures."[50]

Overall, however, the club women themselves directed their course of study and discussion. Elizabeth Lindsay Davis presented a synopsis of "The Black Fairy," a story written by the young Chicago author Fenton Johnson. In 1913 the club organized a program devoted exclusively to African American writers and composers, featuring Paul Laurence Dunbar, Fenton Johnson, Frances Harper, Samuel Coleridge-Taylor, and Alfred Anderson. A visiting club woman presented her original paper on "The Women Writers of the Colored Race," considered "very interesting from start to finish." The poetry of club women—Mrs. Birdie White Cook, Mrs. E. Wright, and Mrs. Moore, considered a poetess of "no little ability"—were read, although not available in publication.[51] Such examples supported the club's dictum that the "intellectual side [was] not neglected."[52]

Literary study was performed as well as being discussed. Theater productions were most often popular comedies and dramas and religious dramas, such as those by George Middleton.[53] The women also designed the stage settings and costumes, often quite intricate. In one of the Chicago Union Charity Club's plays, "The Bulgarian Princess," the lead character, "attired in a Bulgarian robe of oriental pattern," began the production with a grand march of characters while the audience sung "Onward Christian Soldiers." This performance collected nearly twenty-three dollars for the Phyllis Wheatley Home.[54]

Although there were ample records of literary study and events, the content and context of the meetings were unfortunately not documented. What did African American club women think of Ibsen's portrayal of women? How was Emerson's transcendental thought interpreted in the context of the African American experience? What female African American authors did the club women read and discuss? The lack of public records on the study of women writers was not unique to African American female clubs; native-born white women's clubs, too, failed to list female authors for study, with the exceptions of George Eliot and Jane Addams. Even though Victoria Earle Matthews insisted that women's role in race literature was "the most important part and has been so in all ages," club records seem to indicate differently.[55] Clearly, the persona of a "black Shakespeare or Dante" was not perceived as a female.[56]

CHURCH LYCEUMS AND LITERARY SOCIETIES

As noted, the Chicago communities of Englewood, Morgan Park, and Hyde Park were reputed for their church lyceums and literary societies. The membership pattern—mostly young adults and youths—was the same as that of the lyceums in the early 1800s. As in the earlier lyceums, intellectual development was linked to deportment, although the later emphasis was social, not moral. The Englewood Lyceum's purpose was not only to "rais[e] the standard of its literary work, making it more attractive, more beautiful and more artistic" but also to build the young women's confidence before an audience.[57] Great progress was evidently achieved because the coverage of a 1913 program noted the self-assured stage presence of young ladies who only several months before had been "too bashful and unaccustomed to the stage."[58]

Even though the Englewood Lyceum and other church lyceums were composed of young men and women, the female influence was pervasive and even expected. As noted, Sunday lyceums in Englewood were occasionally reserved as "Ladies' Day" or "gala day," occasions when women's issues were addressed by female speakers. At one such lyceum program in 1913, Mrs. Jeffries provided the welcome address, followed by talks on "My Ideal Woman" and "Two Pioneer Women," tributes to Harriet Tubman and Sojourner Truth. Notwithstanding the well-informed nature of the women's speeches, the African American newspapers depicted not their content but their delivery. One presenter was extolled for her "queenly manner . . . so natural to her sex"; the other female presenters were "arrayed in all their glory. The question of woman's rights was not discussed because there was no need of it."[59]

Despite such coverage, women continued to present issues of concern at the lyceums. Before the St. Mark's Lyceum, Fannie Barrier Williams spoke on "woman's work," presenting two alternatives for most young women: "domestic service and idleness."[60] The St. Mark's Literary Society featured papers on prison reform, the experiences of probation officers, and the moral development of children. Even though women were active in the lyceums, there were times when their views were noticeably missing. At one debate, deliberated by the St. Mark's Literary Society, only male participants discussed the subject, "Resolved, That Women Should Be As Highly Educated As Men."[61]

Women speakers, however, frequented the podium of the Bethel A.M.E. Literary Club, founded in 1909. At the club's first meeting more than three hundred persons convened to hear Ida B. Wells's report of her investigations of the recent lynchings in Cairo, Illinois.[62] The club was known both for its political speakers and for its social protests. In 1912 the club gathered to protest the Hyde Park Protective League's support of segregated schools.[63] At another meeting Miss Smith, Dean of Girls at Wendell Phillips High School, was invited to speak on her decision to segregate the social evenings of African American and white students.[64]

The club women established youth lyceums not only as "an outlet for their artistic propensities" but also to socialize adolescents into community forms of knowledge and activism.[65] The most prominent youth lyceum was that of the Grace Presbyterian Church, established by club woman Mrs. Carey Lewis. This lyceum rapidly became so popular that the "social side was eliminated because of increased attendance."[66] The lyceum sponsored a series of speakers, many of whom were known nationally, including Emmett Scott; Dr. Tobias, the international secretary of the YMCA; and Booker T. Washington.

Speeches often focused on discrimination and segregation; one was the talk by Dr. Carey, titled "Have We Followed the Flag?" Dr. Carey, minister of the Institutional Church in Chicago and a "natural orator," contended that African American servicemen had fought for a country that still denied them their rights. The audience's response was favorable to his comments: "Dr. Carey brought down the house when he asked for protection from the flag that Black men had supported, but attacked the idea that there should be a 'Jim Crow' section for training men who are to shoulder guns."[67] Charles Satchel Morris, known as the "boy orator," also addressed this issue, arguing that African American men must enter businesses after the war. But to do so, he continued, they need to first be given their full rights and to have the "southern racist laws wiped out."[68] As evident in his example, youths were not only keenly aware of political issues but also were skilled orators.

Other churches, too, organized youth lyceums and clubs for intellectual development and social entertainment. The Young People's Lyceum offered wholesome recreation for teenagers on Friday evenings. There, high schoolers wrote and presented their plays and other writings. Most impressively, its founder, Bertha Moseley, organized a two-day Douglass anniversary with addresses, songs, and recitations, culminating in an address by Ida B. Wells.[69] The Bethel Sunday School, too, formed a

Young Women's Patriotic Club, which participated in essay contests and musicales. Quinn Chapel and the Berean Baptist Church also created youth clubs "to better the church and self."[70]

The youths' political consciousness was frequently conjoined to community activism. For example, the Grace Presbyterian Church Lyceum often took up collections for the Provident Hospital, the African American hospital. At one meeting more than thirty dollars was raised. On another occasion, the lyceum delivered a ton of coal to the Amanda Smith Home. Mrs. Adah Waters, organizer of the Girls' Patriotic Service League, spoke before the lyceum, encouraging the girls "to render greater service." The girls responded by sewing and knitting clothing for the African American servicemen of the 365th Infantry at Camp Grant.[71]

One of the most notable annual literary events for youths was an essay competition organized by Irene McCoy-Gaines. The contest was established not only to "inspire the youth of Chicago to a higher and better life" but also to "cause a widespread [sic] of reading and literary research."[72] The 1913 topic, "What Has the Negro Contributed to the World for the Advancement of Civilization?" drew much excitement as representatives from eight clubs presented their writings. The *Chicago Defender* printed the winning essay, by Lenora Curtis, whose research had ranged from ancient African civilizations to the contemporary accomplishments of African American inventors, scientists, literary figures, and musicians.[73]

Although Du Bois had expressed concern that the African American churches did not challenge the "intellectual needs" of their youths, this was certainly not true in Chicago.[74] Through the church lyceums, youths listened to prominent national and community leaders speak about political issues; they debated and wrote on these issues as well. The lyceums not only intellectually engaged the youth but also appealed to their "social inclinations."[75]

African American literary clubs in Chicago persisted in the dual purpose of self-improvement and community uplift. Like the members of the early literary societies, the Chicago club women were educated and privileged. Yet they did not consider their literary study idle or self-serving; rather, they sought to broaden their knowledge of literature, philosophy, and politics in order to act socially and politically. As noted, the dramatic productions organized by the clubs were instrumental in raising funds for community institutions. The lyceums, too, had two functions. Although the members were middle-class and educated, the audiences of the Sunday forums drew from the community at large. Members developed and showcased their talents in music, oration, and recitation, but they also, in "talented tenth" fashion, provided learning opportunities for the community.

For the women the literary clubs seemed to provide a distinctly feminized sphere, in which they encouraged one another to articulate new ideas, support their interpretations, write their own words, and critique one another. Very little elaboration was given on their "lively discussions." Nor are we able to read the works of the poetess of "no little ability." It is as if the intimacy and privacy of such occasions allowed access only for those who were present. What is revealing, however, is that women did not publicly read their poetry and that they designated distinct days on which only their addresses would be heard. Such activities indicate that women consciously created and defined a literary space for themselves.

SEVEN

SOCIAL CLUBS

ALTHOUGH MOST CLUBS ENGAGED IN SOME FORM OF social uplift, there were other clubs whose primary purpose was social. This was especially true of dancing clubs, whist clubs, and matrimony clubs, which were often criticized for their superficiality and lack of community commitment. Nannie Burroughs expressed dismay at what she called the "mania for club life" among African American women; she thought whist clubs were especially nonsensical.[1] Katherine Tillman, too, criticized African American women who aspired to be or were "society women," characterizing them as "fashionable Afro-Americans, like her Caucasian sisters [who] spends [sic] her time in novel reading, card playing and in whirling through the intricate mazes of the dance."[2] Other club leaders, such as Addie Hunton, dismissed the frivolity, pointing out that most African American female clubs did not indulge in such activities: "Such may be the clubs of the idle rich, of the self-indulgent votaries of fashion; and doubtless there are, in some of the large cities, Afro-American women who ape the follies of this class, but the average club woman, certainly the club woman of this section [the NACW], is a creature of another type."[3]

Despite Hunton's observations, many such clubs did exist, not only in Chicago but in other American cities. The exclusivity, as well as the social cast, of these clubs was demonstrated by their nomenclatures of "Elite," "Elete," "Unique," or "Uneek." As Gatewood has astutely commented, such names brought into question the clubs' very selectivity, for if they were truly elite, why did they ostentatiously name themselves so?[4] In Chicago the whist clubs that proliferated before and during the war years reflected an exclusivity reminiscent of the elite clubs during the 1880s and early 1890s. However, the women who joined the whist clubs were not from Chicago's first families but were middle-class women who resided within a two-mile radius of the Black Belt. Members of these whist clubs did not belong to federated clubs that engaged in political reform and social uplift. Conversely, members of the Phyllis Wheatley Club, the Alpha Suffrage Club, the Cornell Charity Club, and other "wide awake" clubs did not join the whist clubs. Although the whist clubs constituted a separate and distinct group, given their prevalence in Chicago, an analysis of African American women's clubs would not be complete without their inclusion.

In examining clubs that engaged primarily in social pastimes, the economic and social relations that undergirded the cultural capital of their events—the charity balls, the box parties, the weddings, the whist contests, and the dancing parties—must also be considered. More specifically, these social events supported the predominantly female businesses of dressmakers, milliners, chiropodists, hairdressers, and manicurists. Such businesses provided alternative forms of employment to African American women who faced discrimination in the workforce. There were, then, various economic spheres embedded in the clubs' social pastimes: the "Elite 400," who sponsored charity balls; the poor who benefited from the proceeds; and businesswomen whose livelihood relied in part upon such social occasions.

"GENTEEL PERFORMANCE": CHARITY BALLS, DANCES, AND PARTIES

As discussed in chapter 2, although class distinctions remained drawn between the elite and middle class in the 1890s, all were selected to join Chicago's "Elite 400." Invitation and guest lists definitively cast one's social fate, as noted at one 1905 charity ball, sponsored by the Frederick Douglass Center: "All society is waiting to see who is who, and who will be debarred on account of their social standing or lack of social standing."[5] That invitations mattered was evident in a 1908 controversy in which a Mrs. Manning's invitation to the Grand Free Ball was questioned. Apparently, some of the wives of the Fellowship Club members (who were sponsoring the ball) did not want her present. Regardless, she was offered a verbal invitation and even went to great lengths to sign an affidavit that declared that she had been invited, although not formally. When Mr. and Mrs. Manning promenaded into the hall, the women threatened to leave if she did not admit to concocting a bogus invitation. The event culminated not only in the Mannings' departure, but also in the arrival of a policeman, who warned "the highly cultured ladies and gentlemen that they must behave themselves and that he was good and ready to take care of all those who wanted to do any fighting."[6] Although most balls did not end in such disagreements, this incident demonstrates the exclusivity and selectivity of many such events.

Newspapers published the attendance list of charity balls and also reported in great detail the guests' attire. At the 1905 Frederick Douglass Center event mentioned above, Mrs. Emanuel Williams's dress was described as adorned with "costly Bettenberg lace [and] lavender trimming" and purported to have cost at least five hundred dollars. Mrs. Moseley's dress was trimmed with a "lavender mull velvet," while Hattie Claybrook's gown was of a "pale blue silk and lace."[7] The guests' stately deportment and bearing were depicted as follows: "It can be truthfully said, that each lady and gentlemen were gowned so faultlessly that without the slightest embarrassment, they could have been ushered into the presence of the President of the United States or participated in the most exclusive receptions and functions that could be gotten up as far as dress and deportment are concerned."[8] Such reportage was not uncharacteristic of portrayals of race progress. Nonetheless, despite the attention given to dress and deportment, invitees were certainly selected for their financial contributions. In the case of the 1905 charity ball, enough money was secured to purchase a new residence for the Frederick Douglass Center on 3032 Wabash Avenue.[9]

During the same year the Frederick Douglass Center sponsored another grand ball at the new Pekin Theatre. Recently opened by Mr.

Mott, the Pekin Theatre claimed to be the only theater owned, operated, and managed by an African American. More than one hundred patrons were invited. Jane Addams, who assumed the cost of the drama troupe, was joined in her box seat by African American club women Ida B. Wells, Mrs. Moseley, Mrs. George Hall, and Fannie Emanuel. Despite the financial success of the production, the event took a decidedly polemical turn when, after the performance, Ida B. Wells was escorted to the front stage. She thanked the patrons for their support and then proceeded to lambast several of the African American ministers who had criticized the event "upon purely selfish or personal grounds." Many in the audience not only nodded but even cheered.[10] Although the ministers' objections were not stated, many had openly opposed theaters, alongside dance halls and saloons, arguing that such amusements led to vice. Unvoiced was their concern that their congregation's loyalty, and thus their financial commitment to the church, would be diminished.

The ministers, however, were not alone in receiving indictments. Following the 1905 charity benefits, the *Broad Ax* published a series of scathing articles against the Frederick Douglass Center, particularly targeting Celia Parker Woolley and her "silk stocking followers." The editor, Julius Taylor, criticized the center not only for its lack of assistance to the poor in the Black Belt but also for its largely white administration. This accusation was true, because Woolley had designated herself as president, even though the *Broad Ax* had submitted Ida B. Wells's name for the office.[11] African American representation would become a contentious issue at a later date, one that would prompt Wells to leave the center.

Although the Frederick Douglass Center's balls received negative publicity, other charity balls were praised, especially those that contributed to the African American community. In 1908 a "grand" charity ball was organized for the only African American hospital in Chicago, Provident Hospital. Again, the headlines spoke in grand language; the event was described as "the most brilliant affairs every [sic] held by the Afro-American race in Chicago." Unlike the center's event, invitations were granted to "the great mass of our citizenship," including persons from neighboring states.[12] Because the need for health care was particularly urgent and the hospital had expanded its services to include free surgical treatment for the poor, the invitation list was less selective.[13] In order to continue these services, then, the organizers beckoned to the civic and charitable spirit of the larger African American community.

In addition to the grand-scale balls, there were smaller dances sponsored by the women's clubs. Again, much attention was given to attire and deportment. The women attending the Jolly Twenty Club's annual dancing party in 1913 were portrayed as "superbly gowned" and their escorts "gallant."[14] Members at a West Side Woman's Club meeting were "gowned beautifully."[15] The Volunteer Workers' Club sponsored a social affair in 1910, replete with an "elaborate spread." Most interesting, though, was the description accorded the hostess: "the charmingly dressed hostess was as the evening glory, for when she greeted you, you felt lifted up with that real balm of life that only she has."[16] Although such descriptions were overwrought, the club women's behavior was not a matter of external trappings only. Rather, this "genteel performance" was developed through a conscious cultivation of aesthetics, fine manners, and character.[17]

Charity balls and dances were not the only exclusive events to which the elite and the middle class were invited. Weddings, anniversaries, and birthday parties were also extravagant in their decor, apparel, and gifts. One of the most publicized weddings was that of Jesse Binga and Eudora Johnson. Because of Binga's prominence as a banker, his wedding was considered one of the "most elaborate and the most fashionable in the history of the Afro-American race in the Middle West." The bridal gown created from "Modiste's art," the classical music of Ferullo's Band and Tomaso's Orchestra, and the decor of "evergreen, palms, and pink carnations" trailing from the billiard parlor to the balcony were described in flourishing detail, as were the "rare and expensive" wedding presents. In the newspaper coverage of a wedding anniversary, the gift list occupied nearly two full-length columns of the front page.[18]

As noted, various economic spheres were embedded in these social events. In the case of charity balls, the philanthropic results were obvious: the cultural capital of the middle class and the elite became the social machinery through which moneys were raised for those less fortunate. Furthermore, as mentioned, the economic benefits were not only earmarked for charity but also dispersed to entrepreneurs in the community, most notably dressmakers, milliners, manicurists, and hairdressers. Young women were encouraged to take up dressmaking and hairdressing as profitable forms of employment, particularly because African American women preferred to patronize other African Americans, especially if their work was considered "first class."[19]

"First class" work entailed both creativity and technical knowledge. A good milliner, according to Tillman, studied the facial features and complexion of her customers, in addition to matching the hat's style to the gown. Hairdressers not only considered the clients' features and attire but also were versed in a knowledge of herbal and chemical treatments for the scalp and hair.[20] A beauty culturist's skill and experience were measured by the results obtained through facials, toilet waters, beauty creams, mole banishers, and the ubiquitous facial bleaches. A chiropodist's reputation was built from his or her original creations of balms, powders, and soaking solutions. Katherine Dunham's account of her uncle's admixtures, derived from African American and Choctaw herbal remedies, pointed to the skill and art of chiropody, as well as the high demand for such services by leading society women.[21]

Many of the Chicago women, even some of the club women, were successfully employed in chiropody, hairdressing, and manicuring businesses. The Burnham Beauty College graduated its first African American student, Grace Garnett-Abney, in 1896. Although most known for her "hair tongs," which stimulated the hair growth of African American women, Garnett-Abney also opened two beauty shops for white women.[22] Carrier Warner, a vice president of the Phyllis Wheatley Club, learned manicuring and facial treatments through the Moler College of Chicago. She opened her own chiropodist and manicure parlors, which were acclaimed as frequented by "the best and wealthiest white ladies of this city."[23] Others were reputed for their special treatments and cures, such as Minnie Sinclair, who treated facial blemishes, or Alice Bemby, whose tonsorial parlor, the Palace of Art, specialized in manicures.[24] Women, though, were not the only clients of beauty services. Irene Goins's husband, known as the "Father of Manicurists" on Chicago's South Side, owned many shops where men could get haircuts, singes, shampoos, shaves, massages, witch hazel steams, and manicures. Female manicurists were employed in his shops, in part to curb the male clienteles' "profane language, loud talking, lounging and sleeping."[25]

African American women were also successful as milliners. Hattie Arrant, formerly a teacher in Kansas City, took up millinery work when she moved to Chicago in 1901. By 1910 she had become so well known that she created hats for the leading women "of both races."[26] Maude Seay, another milliner in demand, was known for her French-style hats, which many women wore to the charity and New Year balls.[27] Her protégée, Mayme Clinkscale, opened her own shop of "imported French patterns" on fashionable State Street.[28]

Most of these entrepreneurs were educated at proprietary colleges and institutes that cropped up in Chicago at the turn of the century. Some institutes wedded technical skills to traditional female traits and roles. Poro College, for example, included the study of chemistry but also emphasized the female attributes of "dignity, grace, and beauty."[29] The Clio School for Mental Science and Character Analysis taught not only character analysis and vocational guidance but also "poise, individuality, and wide-awakeness."[30] Other institutes stressed the scientific basis of their studies. Estelle Kenton, principal of the Enterprise Institute's Beauty Culture Department, insisted that beauty culture was not mere "vanity" but promoted "health and comfort." Accordingly, the institute offered courses in chiropody, electrolysis, facial massage, and scalp treatments as well as in hairdressing and manicuring.[31] The Provident School of Beauty Culture also emphasized the healthful effects of its treatments, which were prepared in its own laboratory. Under the directorship of Mme. E. M. Scott, a certified chiropodist, the school's courses were purported to be "as thorough and complete as the schools of the opposite race."[32] The recruitment strategies of the Universal College of Beauty Culture were more pecuniary. Students who enrolled in their home study courses of "hair culture, scalp treatment, facial massage, and maniculture" were supplied with the college's products: "1 hair straightening comb, 6 boxes Universal Hair Grower, 1 Manicuring Set and a Diploma."[33]

In catering to the clubs' social events, the businesswomen were doubly advantaged. Not only were the club women regular customers, but the events also served as venues for advertising the businesswomen's services. Each individual seamstress's gowns no doubt were marked by her particular designs and skills, especially because a great deal of handwork was involved in lace trimming, embroidery, and crocheted collars.[34] Undoubtedly, women exchanged information about the services of various beauty culturists, manicurists, and chiropodists. For the club women who were also dressmakers, manicurists, and chiropodists, their club memberships carried both social and economic advantages.

Whist clubs were extremely popular in Chicago from 1914 through 1918. During this period at least eighteen new clubs were formed, as indicated by their names. There were many other social clubs that also frequently played whist, progressive whist, and bridge. The Necessity Club, the Oriole Whist Club, the East End Whist Club, the Friday Afternoon Whist Club, the Superior Whist Club, the Piquet Whist Club, the Rainbow Whist Club, and the Wednesday Afternoon Whist Club were only a few of the whist clubs. Even the Clotee Scott Settlement organized its own whist club, the Glee Club. Most curiously, these clubs proliferated during the war years, suggesting that preoccupation with social engagements may have been one way to allay war-time tensions and anxieties.

An analysis of whist clubs reveals that most members did not participate in social uplift activities or war-time efforts, such as knitting sammies for the soldiers. On the other hand, the most prominent club women—such as Ida B. Wells, Irene Goins, Irene McCoy-Gaines, Elizabeth Lindsay Davis, Fannie Emanuel, Mary Waring, and Fannie Barrier Williams—did not belong to whist clubs, although they were occasionally invited as guests. The whist clubs seemed to function as neighborhood clubs did: most women joined several whist clubs, and they generally resided within several miles of the Black Belt.[35]

These clubs' whist tournaments were marked especially by expensive prizes. For example, the prizes offered by the Saturday Afternoon Whist Club included "a cut glass compote, a cut glass vinegar bottle, a hand-painted tea strainer, a cut-glass sherbet glasses, a cut-glass vase, and two steins."[36] A 1914 Billiken Hoop and Needle Club's whist party listed the prizes of "a glass olive dish, two sterling silver hat pins, and gold cuff buttons."[37] The Fortnightly Whist and Literary Club awarded the prizes of a cut-glass salad bowl, a cut-glass compote dish, and a hand-painted bonbon dish to its winners.[38] Most likely these prizes were purchased from the club dues; in essence, then, the money simply circulated within the club.

The menus of six-course luncheons, partners to the whist contests, were often highlighted in the newspaper. One Volunteer Workers' Club's menu, considered "par excellence," included chicken croquettes, French peas, creamed potatoes, biscuits, pineapple sherbet, and caramel cake.[39] The Social Eight Whist Club offered a banquet where guests were welcomed with "a bower of roses," then had a dinner of cream of tomatoes, broiled whitefish, sherry wine, fillet of beef and mushrooms, champagne, salads, ice cream, and cakes.[40] The Progressive Whist Club served a "bountiful repast in modern style," after which the latest dances were introduced.[41] A five-course luncheon was served and valentine favors given at one Social Eight Whist Club meeting. The valentine scheme was repeated at a S. Q. J. Whist Club luncheon, described as "charmingly pretty" and held at a "palatial residence."[42]

The club women went to great efforts to achieve the desired ambience through lavish decor. The University Society Club often held its meetings in beautifully decorated rooms of pink and green, where lunch was served, followed by games of amusement, including progressive whist.[43] At the Twilight Social Club events, the tables were decorated with green and pink, again, the club colors. One of the club's social occasions was held at a house decorated with "palms, ferns, and water lilies with pictures of noted men and statues of noted women."[44] Most extravagant, though, was a whist lawn party, where the hostess "opened the gates of their beautiful lawn, bedecked with over 300 yards of pink ribbons and about 1,000 yards of peach blossoms. Fifty pink Japanese lanterns canopied the beautiful grass covered back yard."[45]

Men also participated in whist clubs, although their tournaments were less lavish. The Englewood Country Club, designated for men only, sponsored shirtwaist dances and minstrel shows and held boxing, checkers, and whist matches regularly.[46] The Nonpareil Club, a men's club that opened its membership to women, also engaged in luncheons, card games, whist, and "joyful singing."[47] Such comemberships undoubtedly provided the opportunity for eligible men and women to meet. When the Orchid Whist Club organized a pre-Lenten dance at the Kenwood parlors, it was intimated that some of the "leading young men" would be present.[48] Such events were similar to those organized by the matrimony clubs, which ensured that men and women of like social standing would socialize together.

Despite the preponderance of cultural capital, not all whist clubs dedicated their energies solely to entertainment. As in many other clubs, charitable deeds were embedded within the club activities. Although the juxtaposition of cultural capital and charity might seem incongruous, the numerous examples in the newspapers indicated its social acceptance. For instance, coverage of the Clover Leaf Social Club noted that Mary

Johnson was voted the "most charming hostess," then mentioned the club's discussion on how to help the poor.[49] The Thursday Evening Whist Club's decision to limit its membership so that more could be spent on their gowns and the "sumptuous dinner" was tempered by regular purchases of groceries for the Old Folks' Home.[50] In one breath, the Volunteer Workers' Club made arrangements for a future whist party and gave "immediate attention" to four charity cases. Receipts from 1914 indicated that whist parties were one source of funds that the Volunteer Workers' Club used for charitable purposes. That year the club had raised forty-six dollars through its whist contests.[51]

MATRIMONY CLUBS

Another popular type of social club was the matrimony club, expressly formed to find suitable and like marriage partners for young African American men and women. Curiously, most were started by men. For example, the aim of the Matrimonial Club, founded by Dr. Harry Garner, was to help find men who were "prosperous enough to marry a desirable young woman, provide for her and make her home a little haven."[52] Most members of this club were prominent young men in Chicago, including Booker T. Washington, Jr., who then attended Northwestern University. Perhaps because of the men's procrastination, new rules were established by the Matrimonial Club in 1915 that if any member became engaged, he must marry.[53] With much tongue-in-cheek humor, the club provided news on dating partners and which bachelors would be "getting off." The club's decided goal in 1916 was to "get Walter Anderson off." In 1917 Mr. Milton, a post office worker, was "unanimously voted" as the next person to be married. Dr. Cornelius Lowe was next on the list. Even the club president, Dr. Garner, reported that he would "get off" in the spring and hinted that she would be a "dashing widow." Walter Anderson had apparently not fulfilled the club's 1916 goal, as a 1917 club vote dictated that he must "make it" this season. Toward this end Mr. Anderson spoke to a group of eligible young women, asking for their assistance in "ridding" themselves of "several worthy candidates for matrimony."[54]

The Young Men's Matrimony Club also passed a resolution that "a drive" be launched to marry off some of the "older girls."[55] For this purpose Benjamin Martin was voted eligible and ready to "step off" by Christmas. To encourage such partnerships, club members attended recitals at Lincoln Center and participated in debates with the young women's clubs. The Pre-Nuptial Club, a young women's club, challenged the Matrimony Club in 1917 to a debate on the subject "Should the Woman Predominate in Household Affairs?" Two of the "smartest" girls were selected. Unfortunately, the arguments and the results of the debate were not published.[56]

Like the men's matrimony clubs, the women's Pre-Nuptial Club was organized with the specific goal of "matronizing young women." However, the language was decidedly gendered, as betrothed young women were handed a "certificate of honor" as they were "passed on." Although occasional references were made to girls "getting off" or to the "new stunts" conjured by the young women, more often the language was more serious, referring, for example, to Miss Ida Taylor's "marching to the altar."[57]

Even in the nonmatrimony clubs, persons were occasionally described as potential marriage partners. For example, the Clover Leaf Social Club was entertained by a Mr. Arthur Norse, heralded as a "coming young man." In reciprocal manner, the young ladies of the club were referred to as "society buds of Lake Forest wearing unusual smiles for the handsome Norse." Not only were their smiles charming, but also their "costumes were exquisite creations beyond description. One could shut his eyes and pick blindly, awakening to find he had a veritable fairy by his side."[58] A similar description was given for a "little dancing party" sponsored by the Entre Nous Club: "The affair was glorious in every respect, informal, and the ladies present so bewitchingly attired in a riot of beautifully colored gowns that they might have been taken for fabled goddesses who had condescended to descend from their lofty heights to mingle their destinies with those of men."[59]

This chapter has examined clubs that were primarily engaged in the social pastimes of card playing, dancing, and luncheons. Although other clubs occasionally chastised these clubs for their frivolity and self-indulgence, they did often dispense charity and donate fees to community facilities. For the most part, however, these clubs constituted a distinct membership and social intent.

Such clubs' popularity did not diminish. Drake and Cayton, in their later sociological study of Bronzeville, documented how fashionable card-playing and dancing clubs had become. The names of some of the 1930s social clubs—Amicable Twelve, Peppy Ten, Thirteen Congenial Girls, Merry Ten, Smart Debs, and Personality Eight, to name only a few—attested to their frivolity and social emphasis.[60] Reminiscent of the whist clubs in the first decade of the century, these clubs were limited to members of exclusive social networks. The middle-class norms of respectability and control of behavior were not only stressed but also, in some cases, even written into the clubs' constitutions and bylaws.[61]

Similar to those of 1910, the dancing events of the 1930s clubs prescribed formal behavior and protocol. Invitations were exclusive, with the exception of large public dances that were organized to raise funds. Unlike the earlier charity balls and dances, however, the dancing parties organized in the 1930s dispensed little of their money to charity. More often than not, the moneys were invested in clubhouses or savings clubs.[62] Thus, the clubs functioned less to assist those in need than to reaffirm the middle-class status of their members.

CONCLUSION

THE ONCE MIDDLE-CLASS AFRICAN AMERICAN COM-
munities of Woodlawn, Englewood, and Morgan Park in
Chicago are now known more for their rival gangs and
their segregated islands of poverty. In 1992 the district of
Wentworth, in the heart of what was once called the Black
Belt, had the highest violent crime rate in Chicago; Englewood rated
fourth.[1] Although the *Chicago Tribune* recently reported that African
Americans lived in nearly every neighborhood in Chicago, percentages
overwhelmingly demonstrate that most African American communities
are still highly segregated. The Near South Side's and the Far South
Side's African American populations are respectively 98 percent and 91
percent.[2] Although the African American population in the Hyde Park–
Kenwood area is only 53 percent, one has only to walk or drive
through Hyde Park to notice the "dividing lines" between the illustrious
University of Chicago, with its turn-of-the-century refurbished homes,
and the adjoining poorer African American neighborhoods, with their

abandoned stores and vacant lots. Once the home of philanthropist Julius Rosenwald, Kenwood, too, is distinguished by its contrasting restored mansions and its poverty line.

Much has changed in the seventy-five years since the African American club women were first granted the right to vote in the national elections of 1920. Waves of Southern migration surged to 179,000 African Americans during the 1940s and to 157,000 in the 1950s.[3] Once again, many newcomers joined relatives, friends or former neighbors in the southside neighborhoods. Others applied for residence in the newly developed public housing high-rises, the first of which, ironically, was named after Ida B. Wells. So segregated and isolated were some individuals' lives that even though they had been born in Chicago, they had never been as far north as downtown.

Yet, despite the profound changes, much has not changed. In spite of the amount of attention devoted to the underclass, gang violence, and cases of child abuse, there is still a tremendous amount of social uplift and community activism in the African American southside neighborhoods. In an effort to "take back their streets" from gang members and drug dealers, citizens from Rogers Park to Humboldt Park held twenty-four-hour vigils, at which they sang gospel songs, prayed, and encouraged one another. Many of the churches continue in the tradition of former missions and settlements in their outreach programs of day care, children's baseball teams, and scouting units. In the Washington Park neighborhood, St. Edmund's Episcopal Church not only offers job training, affordable housing, support block clubs, and community policing but has also opened its own academy. In Woodlawn, renovation projects sponsored by the churches and local businesses provide jobs and are helping to revitalize the community.[4] As in the early 1900s, Washington Park is still a community site for summer outings, baseball games, picnics, and community festivals and gatherings.

Clearly, there are other community projects too numerous to detail. What such projects illustrate are not only the troubling conditions of violence and crime but also a community responsiveness and leadership not unlike those of the early twentieth century. It would be too simplistic, however, to equate contemporary forms of uplift with those engendered by middle-class leaders "upon" the poor and the underclass. As Mitchell Duneier has observed in his study of working-class African American men in Hyde Park, contemporary ethnographies and studies of African American communities have polarized African American communities into the middle class and the poor and have neglected the influence of their "respectable" working-class citizens.[5] In creating such divisions, he argues, there has been the implicit assumption that the poor, who have no values, need middle-class role models. Englewood, most publicized for its homicide rate and its gang-bangers, surely has a strong working-class presence. Not only do three-fourths of its residents have jobs, but one-third also own their own homes.[6] As one community member phrased it, "You can live *in* the ghetto but you don't have to be *of* the ghetto."[7]

Duneier's criticism of the underrepresented working class might be extended to poorer African Americans. Even in Chicago's public housing units, known for their poverty and violence, there is a strong, albeit invisible, leadership. That leadership is female. As presidents of the local advisory councils in their housing units, many of the females wield more influence in their neighborhoods than local alderpersons do. Like the club women, women such as Cabrini-Green's Hattie Calvin and Washington Park's Artensa Randolph are not paid employees but volunteers.[8] In a spirit similar to that of the club women, both women speak and act on behalf of the children's and mothers' welfare. Unlike the club women, however, they live in the very projects and neighborhoods they represent.

In pointing to contemporary examples, I do not intend to undermine the remarkable activism of Fannie Barrier Williams, Irene McCoy-Gaines, Joanna Snowden-Porter, Ida B. Wells, and the other club women of the early twentieth century. Nor do I mean to imply that the legacy of the club women is being "carried on." Certainly the social, political, and economic conditions and constraints of today differ from those of the Progressive Era. So, too, do the roles of women, inscribed within these contexts, vary. This points to other untold histories of African American women's uplift activities in Chicago. Beginning in the 1920s, another intricate layer of activism on Chicago's South Side emerged through the interstitial and short-lived sites of storefront churches, missions, and evangelistic homes. These sites were also "feminized," as many female preachers and evangelists, perhaps returning to the earlier rescue activities of Elizabeth McDonald, sought to uplift the lives of poorer migrants. Hence, African American women not only worked within their own established clubs and community institutions, through the incipient bureaucracies of the juvenile court and the Urban League, but also through these nonformal sites of agency. Although no study has examined these multiple layers where social uplift was enacted, negotiated, and no doubt compromised, contemporary versions of women's community roles might be rooted in these various contested sites.

The early African American women's clubs of Chicago, by design and perhaps by necessity, were marked by distinctions in social class. The Du Boisian prescriptions of leadership had, in fact, called for such separation. But the intrinsic and extrinsic rewards of class—status, prestige, cultural capital, camaraderie, and respectability—carried with them the responsibilities of social obligation, race progress, and responsive leadership. Although social uplift was carried out within this context, it also occurred against the backdrop of increased racism, discrimination, and segregation in Chicago. For African American females, then, the distinct qualities not only of class and gender but also of the persistence of discrimination determined their gendered community practices. As moral guardians and caretakers of children, youths, and the elderly, they reenacted roles that were socially appropriate for women during the Progressive Era. The specific contexts, rituals, and practices of such roles were nurtured both by historical and cultural continuities and by classed positions, which were, in part, shaped by the women's club movement at large. In essence, what emerged was a series of dialectics—manifested in the gendered tensions between African American men and women; in the class distinctions between the African American elite, middle class and poor; and in the ideological, organizational, and cultural differences between African American and white club women. In navigating these immense and often turbulent waters, the African American club women created their own privileged space and identities and at the same time linked various constituencies and audiences.

AFRICAN AMERICAN

WOMEN'S CLUBS,

CHICAGO, 1890-1920

Clubs are coded according to types of activities published in the *Chicago Defender* and the *Broad Ax*. This does not necessarily mean that the clubs did not participate in other pursuits than the ones listed below; they may have publicized particular activities and events in other ways. In cases where no code is given, no specific activities were mentioned in the newspaper or other accounts.

Abbreviated codes are as follows: A = Art (classical); CH = Charity (for individual families or children); D = Dancing (social); DA = Domestic Arts (embroidery, sewing, knitting, and crocheting); E = Economic; L = Literary; M = Musical; P = Political; S = Suffrage; SO = Social; SU = Social Uplift (contributing mainly to community institutions); W = Whist; Y = Youth.

A

Acme Club (D, L, W)
Adelphic Club
Afro-American Mothers' Council
  (P, SU)
Alba Rose Social Club (CH, L, S)
Alloha Suffragist Club (S)
Alpha Suffrage Club (S, P, SU)

American Beauty Culture Club (SO)
American Rosebud Club
American Rose Fine Art Club
  (CH, DA, L, S)
Arbor Vitae Club (SO)
Arts and Letters Club (A, L)
Astra Club (SO)
Autumn Leaf Social Club (W)

B

Bedfordine Hair Culture Club (SO)
Belgian Whist Club (W)
Beryle Pleasure Club
Bethel Literary Club
Biligan Whist Club (W)
Billiken Hoop and Needle Club
   (DA, S)
Billiken Whist Club (W)
Blue Bird Art Club
Book Lovers' Club (L, M)
Boulevard Whist Club (W)
Brown's Progressive Crochet Club
   (DA, W)
Busy Bee Club (SO, SU)

C

Calendar Club
Carnation Art Club (D)
Carnation Whist Club
Carpathia Literary Club (L)
Carter Charity and Benevolent
   Association (CH)
Carter Hair Culturalist Club (CH)
Chevalier Club (L, W, SO)
Chicago Armstrong League
Chicago Hampton Club
Chicago Tuskegee Club (L, SO)
Chicago Union Charity Club
   (CH, L SU)
Chicago West Lawn Club (Y)
Chicago Women's Christian
   Association
Children's Aid Auxiliary (Red Cross)
   (SU)
Choral Study Group (M)
Chrysanthemum Whist Club (W)
Clara Jessamine Club (SU)
Clover Leaf Social Club (CH, SO)
Coleridge-Taylor Choral Society (M)
Colored Women's Business Club (E)
Cornation Whist Club (W)
Cornell Charity Club (CH, L, SU)

Coterie Club (L)
Criterion Club (later called Le
   Volvaire) (M, SO, SU, W)
Culture Assembly Club

D

Daughters of American Flag
Elizabeth Lindsay Davis Club
   (CH, SU)
Dearborn Whist Club (W)
Des Jeunes Aspirant Club (L, SO)
Diana Charity Club (SU)
Dressmaker and Milliners' Club (E)
Drexel Whist Club (W)
Dunbar Club

E

East End Charity Club (CH)
East End Whist Club (W)
Easter Lily Club (E)
East Side Woman's Club
Edgewater Embroidery Club (DA)
Elite Social Charity Club
   (CH, DA, L, SU)
Emergency Charity Club (CH, W)
Englewood Culture Club
Entre Nous Club (SO)
Equal Rights League
Etavirp Club (CH)
Etude Club (M)
Eureka Fine Art Club (L)
Euterpean Club (SO)
Eutopa Whist Club
Excelsior Whist and Industrial Club
Exquisite Club (SO)

F

Fisk Club
Five Hundred Club
Fleur de Lis Art Club (DA, SU)
Fortnightly Whist and Literary Club
   (DA, L, W)
Frederick Douglass Child Culture
   Club (L, SU, CH)

Frederick Douglass Woman's Club
(CH, DA, L, P, S, SO)
Friday Afternoon Embroidery Club
(DA)
Friday Afternoon Whist Club (W)

G

Gaudeamus Club (CH, L, S, SU, W)
Giles Charity Club (CH)
Girls' Cleanup Club (SU, Y)
Girls' Lyric Literary Club (L, Y)
Girls' Patriotic Service League
(SU, Y)
Golden Link Club (CH, W)

H

Half-Century Club (SO)
Harmony Club No. 1 (CH)
Harmony Whist Club (W)
Hazel Hurst Club
Heart and Hand Club
Heliotrope Club
Henrietta P. Lee Comfort Club
Hesperian Whist Club (W)
Home Economic Club
Hoop Club
Household of Ruth
Hyacinth Charity and Art Club
Hyde Park Literary Club (L)
Hyde Park Woman's Club (Nos. 1
and 2)

I

I.B.C.T. Club
Ida B. Wells Club (CH, M, L, P)
Ideal Embroidery Club (DA)
Ideal Woman's Club (CH, L, S, SU)
Idle Hour Art Club (SO, W)
Imperial Art Club (L)
Independent Art Club (A)
Ingram's (Mrs. Grace) Knitting Club
(DA)
Inter-Racial Circle (SU)

Intra-Mural Art Club (A)
Iroquois Community League (SU)

J

Jewell Club (for girls)
Joan of Arc Club
Jolly Eight Whist Club (W)
Jolly Twelve Whist Club (W)
Jolly Twenty Club (SO)
Julia Gaston Club (L)

K

Kings Daughters' Council
Knit and Comfort Club (DA)

L

Labor of Love Club
Ladies' Art and Culture Club
Ladies' Auxiliary of the Eighth
Regiment Illinois National Guard
(SU)
Ladies Home Club
Ladies of Love Club
Les Fillias Gais Club
Lincoln Savings League (E)
Lona Camp Fire Girls (SU, Y)
Lyric Literature Club (L)

M

Madame C. J. Walker Club
Malay Social and Charity Club
Mary Walker Thompson Club (CH)
Mayflower Club (E)
Mental Pearl Charity Club
Modern Priscilla Club (DA)
Mothers' Aid Club (DA)
Mothers' Council (CH)
Motley (Pearl T.) Social Uplift Club
Mozart Club (M)
Mystic Social Club (L, M, SO)

N

Necessity Club (CH, M, W)
Negro Women's Civic League

None Such Club
Nonpareil Club (SO, W)
North Side Woman's Club (SO)

O

O.E.S. Club
Orchid Whist Club (W)
Oriole Whist Club (W)

P

Pandora Club (CH, SU)
Patria Club No. 1
Peerless Club (L, SO, W)
Philomathian Dramatic Club (L, Y)
Phyllis Wheatley Club
(CH, L, M, P, S, SU)
Phyllis Wheatley Juniors (S, Y)
Pink Rose Club
Pioneer Girls (Y)
Pioneer Lodge
(of the Theosophical Society)
Piquet Whist Club (W)
Poinsettia Embroidery and Art Club
(DA)
Poro Club
Pre-Nuptial Club (SO)
Priscilla Art and Social Club (DA)
Progressive Art Club
Progressive Charity and Art Club
Progressive Embroidery Club (DA)
Progressive Literary Club (L)
Progressive Whist Club (W)

R

Rainbow Whist Club (W)
Raymond Dancing Club (D)
Red Cross Auxiliary No. 411 (SU)
Rosary Social Club
Royal Art and Social Club (DA)

S

Samaritan Club (A, DA)
Saturday Afternoon Whist Club (W)
Sawolka Club
Semper Fidelis Club

Sigma Beta Club
Silver Leaf Charity Club (CH)
Silver Spray Club
Sionilli Girls' Social Club
(DA, SO, Y)
Smart Set Whist Club (W)
Snow Club
Social Eight Whist Club (W)
South End Children's Aid Society
(CH)
S.Q.J. Whist Club (W)
S. S. and E. Club
Sunday Afternoon Club
Superior Social Club
Superior Whist Club (W)
Swastika Whist Club (W)

T

Thallis Girls' Club (Y)
Theosophical Society (L)
Three Arts Club
Thursday Evening Whist Club (W)
K. D. Tillman Club (L, SU)
Toussaint Literary Club (L)
Town of Lake Charity and Art Club
Town of Lake Woman's Club (S)
Turquoise Cluster Club
Twelve Matrons' Club
Twentieth Century Art Club (DA, A)
Twentieth Century Penny Club (E)
Twilight Social Club (SO)
Tyree Circle

U

Umbria Glee Club (Y)
Uneek Club (Evanston)
University Society Club (L, SO)
Utopia Club (SO, W)

V

Verdi Art Club (L, M)
Violet Whist Club
Volunteer Workers' Club
(CH, DA, L, SO, SU)

W

Wednesday Afternoon Whist Club
(W)
West Side Woman's Club
(CH, P, S, SU)
White Rose Club
Wide Awake Club
Widows' Club
Wild Rose Whist Club (W)
Fannie E. Wilson Matron's
Improvement Club
Woman's Aid Club
Woman's Utile Dulce Club (DA)
Women's Civic League (SU)
Women's Service League
Women's Study Club (L, M)
Women's University Ward Club

Y

YMLI Charity Club (CH, DA, SU)
Young Girls' Literary Club (L, Y)
Young Matrons' Culture Club
Young Peoples' Improvement Club
(Y)
Young Women's Christian Associa-
tion (YWCA) (D, SO, SU, Y)
Young Women's Patriotic Club (Y)

**AFRICAN AMERICAN SETTLEMENTS
AND MISSIONS (WITH WHICH CLUB
WOMEN WERE AFFILIATED)**

Butler Mission
Clotee Scott Settlement (formerly
Hyde Park Settlement)
Emanuel Neighborhood Settlement

Frederick Douglass Center
Lexington Social Center
Negro Fellowship League
Trinity A.M.E. Mission
Turner Mission
Wendell Phillips Settlement
West Side Settlement

AFRICAN AMERICAN HOMES

Amanda Smith Home for Colored
and Dependent Children (later
Amanda Smith Industrial School
for Girls)
Hannah Griffin Home
Home for the Aged and Infirm
Colored People (Old Folks'
Home)
Louise Juvenile Home (later Louise
Juvenile Industrial School for
Boys)
Phyllis Wheatley Home
West Side Home (later merged with
Amanda Smith Industrial School
for Girls)

**AFRICAN AMERICAN CHURCH
LYCEUMS AND CLUBS**

Bethel A.M.E. Literary Club
Englewood Lyceum
Grace Presbyterian Church Lyceum
Silver Spray Club (St. Mark's)
St. Mark's Lyceum (Literary Society)
Young Peoples' Improvement Club
(Quinn Chapel)
Young Peoples' Lyceum

BIOGRAPHICAL SKETCHES

OF PROMINENT AFRICAN

AMERICAN CLUB WOMEN,

CHICAGO, 1890–1920

Note: Information is derived from newspaper club records and annual reports and from primary material on the clubs and their members, including *Lifting As They Climb,* by Elizabeth Lindsay Davis; *Intercollegiate Wonder Book,* volumes 1 and 2; and *The Story of Seventy-Five Years of the Chicago and Northern District of Club Women, Inc., 1906–1981,* by the Chicago Northern District Association. Club membership and official roles are noted, as well as significant club and community service. No dates are given for membership or offices held in the clubs, nor does the list purport to be complete. The multiple club memberships of women point to how collaborative activities and club networks expanded.

Adams, Sadie. Born in Staunton, Virginia. President of the Chicago Federation of Colored Women's Clubs; president, recording secretary, and charter member of the Gaudeamus Club; charter member of the Clara Jesamine Club; member of St. Thomas Church; member of the Inter-Racial Circle (formed to assist the Amanda Smith Home); associate member of the African American YWCA and the Chicago Urban League; treasurer of the building fund for the Amanda Smith Home; member of the Illinois Home and Aid Society Board; delegate for the Alpha Suffrage Club for the suffrage march in Washington, D.C., and one of the club's presidents and corresponding secretaries; vice president and secretary of the Easter Lily Club.

Anderson, Mrs. J. C. President of the Women's Civic League.

Anderson, Martha B. Secretary of the Illinois Federation of Colored Women's Clubs; noted vocalist who performed for many of the clubs' charitable events.

Anderson, Violet. Born in London. Former court stenographer and business-woman; first African American lawyer in Illinois to be appointed assistant city prosecutor; secretary of the Alba Rose Club; president of the Elite Social Charity Club.

Arnold, Mrs. M. President of the Mary Walker Thompson Club.

August, Mrs. E. I. President of the Gaudeamus Club.

Avendorph, Mrs. Julius. Member of the African American "Elite 400" and prominent in organizing many of the charity balls. During the war years, wrote a newspaper column, "Fancy Work," which provided instructions for knitting clothing for the soldiers.

Beasley, Laura. Treasurer of the Alpha Suffrage Club; teacher of domestic science at the Frederick Douglass Center.

Bell, Amanda. President of the Hyde Park Woman's Club.

Berry, Ella. Born in Stanford, Kentucky, and educated in Lexington. President of the Cornell Charity Club; investigator for the Chicago Commission on Race Relations.

Blackburn, Mrs. M. President of the Clover Leaf Social Club.

Boaz, Sophia. Graduate of the School of Civics and Philanthropy, University of Chicago, through a scholarship from the Rosenwald Fund. Social worker with the Wendell Phillips Settlement; member of and critic for the University Society Club; juvenile officer, 1913 to 1925.

Boody, Mrs. Organizer and chaperone for the Philomathian Dramatic club (for youth).

Brown, Adelaide. Treasurer and charter member of the Gaudeamus Club; secretary of the Alpha Suffrage Club.

Buckner, Mrs. John. Organizer of the Knit and Comfort Club, which provided knit goods for the soldiers of the Eighth Regiment (an African American unit) during the war. Married to Maj. John C. Buckner of the Eighth Regiment, member of the Illinois legislature.

Caldwell, Alice. President and chair of the Charity Committee of the Volunteer Workers' Club; chair of the Charity Section of the Chicago Federation of Colored Women's Clubs; member of the board of directors for the Children's Aid Society (affiliated with the Illinois Children's Aid and Home Finding Society); secretary and journalist of the Phyllis Wheatley Club.

Caldwell, Emma. Matron of the Fidelia Industrial Orphans' Home.

Calloway, Fannie. Charter member and president of the Gaudeamus Club.

Carter, Ezella. Founder of the Carter Charity and Benevolent Association in 1917 (an organization of hairdressers); president of the Giles Charity Club; member of the Chicago Urban League; probation officer.

Chandler, Emma. President of the Volunteer Workers' Club and of the Chicago Union Charity Club.

Chapman, Lillian. Member of the board of directors of the Children's Aid Society (affiliated with the Illinois Children's Home and Aid Society); sewing teacher for the Clotee Scott Settlement, the Emanuel Settlement, and the Frederick Douglass Center.

Claybrook, Hattie. President of the Hyde Park Literary Club; member of the Frederick Douglass Woman's Club.

Coleman, Genevieve. President of the Samaritan Club and the Cornell Charity Club; member of the Clover Leaf Social Club.

Collins, Minnie. Chair of the board of managers of the Phyllis Wheatley Home; chair of the executive board of the Phyllis Wheatley Home; one of the founders of the Clara Jessamine Club (formed to aid the Phyllis Wheatley Home).

Cone, Antoinette C. Teacher of music classes at the Clotee Scott Settlement and the Frederick Douglass Center; member of the Phyllis Wheatley Club.

Cooper, Dr. Anna B. Came to Chicago in 1898 after courses at Wilberforce University and the University of Medicine and Surgery in Cleveland. President of the board of the Paul Dunbar Tuberculosis Sanitarium in Chicago; member of the Phyllis Wheatley Club; regular speaker to women's clubs on medical and social reform issues.

Covington, Laura. President of the Alpha Suffrage Club.

Crawley, Elizabeth. Born in Kentucky. President of the East Side Woman's Club; vice president of the Chicago Federation of Colored Women's Clubs; president of the Ideal Woman's Club; member of the board of directors of the Phyllis Wheatley Home.

Curtis, Lenora. Corresponding secretary of the University Society Club; known essayist and writer.

Davis, Elizabeth Lindsay. President of the Illinois Federation of Colored Women's Clubs of Illinois; president of the Phyllis Wheatley Club and founder of the Phyllis Wheatley Home; member of the Chicago Woman's Club; member and secretary of the Ida B. Wells Club; president of the Daughters of American Flag, Company B/Eighth Illinois Regiment; member of the Western Advisory Board of the Chicago School of Mental Sciences; officer with the Children's Aid Society (affiliated with the Illinois Children's Aid and Home Finding Society); member of the Hyde Park Woman's Club; member of the Volunteer Workers' Club; reporter for the Swastika Whist Club; author of several books on the African American club movement.

Davis, Fidelia. Organizer and founder of the Fidelia Industrial Orphans' Home at her residence, 3152 Dearborn Street.

Dempsey, Ida McIntosh. President of the Old Settlers' Club (until her death); secretary of the Republican Suffragist Convention; board member and corresponding secretary of the Frederick Douglass Center.

Dunmore, Mrs. Head of the Industrial Section and charter member of the Phyllis Wheatley Club.

Emanuel, Fannie. Born in Cincinnati, came to Chicago in 1881; educated at the Jenner Medical College and the Chicago Hospital of Medicine, where she received her M.D. in 1912. Conducted a charity home for young children on Armour Avenue (Emanuel Settlement Home), from 1909 to 1910. Organized neighborhood settlement community clubs from 1908 to 1912; founder of the Emanuel Neighborhood Settlement; president of the Alpha Suffrage Club; organizer of two New Year charity balls for the benefit of Provident Hospital, the Old Folks' Home, and the Emanuel Settlement; charter member, president, and secretary of the African American YWCA; president of the Education Section of the Frederick Douglass Center and president of the Frederick Douglass Woman's Club. A member of the "Elite 400," she was described as the "new queen of four hundred among the Afro-Americans in Chicago." Her husband, Professor William Emanuel, started his business of chiropody and manicuring parlors in Chicago in 1887.

Everage, Mrs. B. President of the Ideal Woman's Club.

Farmer, Lula. Spearheaded the idea of the Phyllis Wheatley Home.

Fischer, Mary. One of the presidents of the Phyllis Wheatley Club.

Fisher, Mrs. J. E. President of the Lincoln Savings League.

Fitts, Annie B. President of the Progressive Circle of the King's Daughters Council. Worked at the Home Visiting Department of the Illinois Public Welfare Service. Her husband, Bernard Fitts, was owner and printer of *The Searchlight,* a weekly newspaper.

Forston, Bettiola. Born in Kentucky in 1890; at the age of twelve came to Chicago to live with her aunt, Toreada Mallory, a well-known soprano in Illinois. Attended Keith School and was appointed poet laureate of her class; in 1910 learned the "feather trade" and opened a millinery business. Wrote more than one hundred original poems; called "the new poetess of the Afro-American race in the middle west." President and journalist of the University Society Club; second vice president of the Alpha Suffrage Club; city organizer of the Chicago Federation of Colored Women's Clubs.

Garnett, Isabella. Educated at Provident Hospital's Nursing School; a school nurse in Evanston. Received her M.D. from the Physicians and Surgeon's College and the University of Illinois College of Medicine. Married Dr. Arthur Butler, with whom she founded the Evanston Sanitarium.

Garnett-Abney, Grace. Sister of Dr. Butler of Evanston; the first African American graduate of the Burnham Beauty College; in 1896 opened a beauty parlor for both African American and white women. Claimed to have introduced the two-room kitchenette apartment in Chicago.

Goins, Irene. Born in Quincy, Illinois. Owned a millinery business in Chicago. Board member of the Illinois League of Women chapter; president and chair of Civics of the Chicago Federation of Colored Women's Clubs; chair of the Suffrage Committee of the Phyllis Wheatley Club; supervisor for the Lona Camp Fire Girls; president of the Chicago and Northern District; president of Illinois State Federation of Colored Women's Clubs; member of women's trades union and of the Urban League; started a child culture club and girls' club at the Frederick Douglass Center. Her husband owned a number of manicuring parlors throughout the city.

Golden, Carrie. Medical doctor; member of the Phyllis Wheatley Club who oversaw the committee that inspected African American tenements.

Gordon, Mrs. One of the presidents of the Ida B. Wells Club.

Green, Mrs. Philip. Attended Moler College to study chiropody and manicuring; owned a beauty and manicuring parlor in downtown Chicago.

Hall, Mrs. George Cleveland. Considered one of the "queens" of the Chicago's "Elite 400"; described as "represent[ing] the highest type of Afro-American womanhood"; organizer and patroness of charity balls for the Frederick Douglass Center; president of the African American YWCA; member of the Chicago Women's Amateur Minstrel Club. Noted elocutionist who performed for many charity events. Her husband, George Cleveland Hall, was a physician.

Hampton, Alice. Sewing teacher at the Frederick Douglass Center.

Harris, Eliza. Vice president of the Afro-American Mothers' Council.

Hawkins, Cora. Founder of the Volunteer Workers' Club; member of the Alba Rose Social Club.

Hawkins, Louise. Secretary of the Easter Lily Club.

Haynes, Birdye. Graduate of the School of Civics and Philanthropy, University of Chicago, through a scholarship from the Rosenwald Fund. Supervisor at the Wendell Phillips Settlement.

Hensley, B. L. President of the Elite Social Charity Club (for the Phyllis Wheatley Home); secretary and member of the Phyllis Wheatley Club; theater director for benefit productions for the Phyllis Wheatley Home; chair of the board of directors for the Phyllis Wheatley Home; president of the Gaudeamus Club.

Hill, Rev. Mary E. Lark. An evangelist and composer of camp meeting songs; founder of the Queen Esther Mission (5040 State Street) in 1905; owner of a cafe.

Hill, Viola. Second vice president of the Alpha Suffrage Club.

Holloway, Mary. Instructor for sewing classes for the Phyllis Wheatley Home.

Holt, Nora. Writer for the *Chicago Defender,* especially on lyceum and musical activities.

Hooper, Eva. President of the Carter Hair Culturalist Club; executive board member and head of the Committee for Churches, Chicago Uurban League.

Hudlin, Anna Elizabeth. Member of the Old Settlers' Club, a club for the first African American residents of Chicago; organized the Bena Morrison Club, which assisted the elderly in the Home for the Aged and Infirm. Married to Joseph Hudlin, another member of the Old Settlers' Club.

Hunter, Anna. First matron of the Phyllis Wheatley Home.

Jackson, Charlotte. Head of the Court Records Department of the juvenile court.

Jackson, Fannie. Noted elocutionist.

Jackson, Mary. First vice president of the Phyllis Wheatley Club; member of the West Side Woman's Club; president of the Illinois Federation of Colored Women's Clubs.

Jackson, Mrs. M. B. Treasurer of the Afro-American Mothers' Council.

Jemison, Hattie. Teacher of dressmaking classes, Frederick Douglass Center.

Jenifer, Eva. Born in Kaskaskia, Illinois. President of the Frederick Douglass Woman's Club; founder and president of the African American YWCA, Chicago; chair of the trustee board for the Phyllis Wheatley Home; member of the Phyllis Wheatley Club, until members asked her to resign over YWCA controversy.

Johnson, Clara. Born in Columbia, Missouri. President of the Chicago Federation of Colored Women's Clubs and the Phyllis Wheatley Home; charter member and president of the Volunteer Workers' Club; charter member and editor of the Gaudeamus Club.

Johnson, Eliza. One of the presidents of the Phyllis Wheatley Home.

Johnson, Florence E. One of the superintendents of the Phyllis Wheatley Home.

Johnson, Jessie. One of the founders of the Clara Jessamine Club; president of the Chicago Federation of Colored Women's Clubs; head of the Home Service Branch of the Red Cross during the war; first secretary of the Phyllis Wheatley Woman's League; secretary of the Phyllis Wheatley Club.

Jones, Anna. Member of the Urban League.

Jones, Ida Taylor. One of the first African American female high school teachers in the Chicago public schools; taught at Wendell Phillips High School. Vice president of the Phyllis Wheatley Club; also taught dressmaking at the Clotee Scott Settlement.

Jones, Jessie. Teacher of stenography at the Frederick Douglass Center.

Jones, Nettie. President of the Cornell Charity Club.

Joyner, Marjorie Stewart. Born in Monterey, Virginia; one of the first African American graduates of Moler Beauty School. Opened a beauty shop in 1916; in 1919 became the vice president and national supervisor for Madam Walker's chain of beauty schools, which recruited "Walker agents." In 1928 received a patent for a permanent hair wave machine.

Kennedy, Emma. President of the Cornell Charity Club.

Kinney, Ellen. President of the American Rose Fine Art Club.

Lawson, Lulu. Born in North Carolina; a graduate of Howard University. Worked with the Rosenwald Fund as a social worker; chair of the YWCA, 1921–23; field worker for the Chicago Red Cross during the war; member of the Chicago Women's Amateur Minstrel Club.

Lewis, Carey. Member of the executive board of the Urban League; member of the Phyllis Wheatley Club; founder of the Grace Presbyterian Church's youth lyceum.

Lewis, Ida D. Born in Crawfordsville, Indiana. Founder of the West Side Woman's Club, which founded the West Side Home (for young working girls, later merged with the Amanda Smith Industrial School for Girls); president of the Illinois Federation of Colored Women's Clubs.

Lewis, Irene. Writer of social columns for the African American newspapers.

Liggins, Emma. President of the Gaudeamus Club.

Livingston, Lucy. President of the Chicago Union Charity Club.

Loomis, Eva. Recording secretary of the Phyllis Wheatley Home Association.

Lyles, Alice. Member of the Ideal Woman's Club.

Macon, Theresa. Born in Louisville, Kentucky. President of the State and City Federation of Colored Women's Clubs; charter member of the Ida B. Wells Club and of the Cornell Charity Club; recording secretary of the NACW;

member of the board of directors of the Phyllis Wheatley Home Association; vice president of the Amanda Smith Home; member of the executive board of the Chicago Urban League.

Marshall, Mrs. John R. Wife of the commander of the Eighth Regiment Illinois National Guard.

McCoy-Gaines, Irene. Born in Ocala, Florida; educated at Fisk University and at the School of Civics and Philanthropy, University of Chicago; president of Colored Women's Republican Clubs of Illinois; industrial secretary of the YWCA; secretary of the juvenile court; president of the Theosophical Society; reporter for the University Society Club; chair of the committee for the Bethel Literary Essay Contests. She herself won several literary prizes. Married to attorney Harris Gaines.

McCracken, Ethel. President of the Illinois Federation of Colored Women's Clubs; treasurer of the Phyllis Wheatley Club.

McDonald, Elizabeth. Born in Kentucky. In 1901 became a volunteer probation officer for the juvenile court; known rescue worker and missionary; founder of the Louise Juvenile Home (and later Industrial School for Boys); member of the Volunteer Workers' Club; president of philanthropy for the Frederick Douglass Woman's Club.

McKinley, Ada. Board member of the Illinois League of Women chapter; president of the Citizens Community Center.

Mcpherson, Mrs. J. H. Quarantine officer in the Chicago Health Department in 1918; first woman to have such a position in Chicago.

Merriweather, Mrs. Albert. President of the Twentieth Century Art Club.

Minott, Adena. Graduate of the American Institution of Phrenology and Psychology in Washington, D.C., and of the Fowler and Wells American Institute of Anthropology in New York City; mental scientist, phrenologist, and child culture specialist; founder of the Clio School of Mental Sciences and Character Analysis in Chicago.

Moore, Gertrude. One of the presidents of the Phyllis Wheatley Home.

Moore-Smith, Alberta. President of the Colored Women's Business Club, Chicago; county probation officer in 1912; member of the African American YWCA; president of the South End Children's Aid Society.

Moseley, Bertha Lewis. Daughter of B. F. Moseley, Chicago attorney and colonel; graduated with honors from Englewood High School in 1910; graduated from Chicago University with a master's degree at age twenty-two, having received four diplomas in seven years; president of the Grace Presbyterian Church Lyceum and founder of the Young People's Lyceum; in charge of the Farren Community Center, Recreation Division; teacher at Whitney School.

Overton, Eva. Secretary of Upsilon Kappa Sigma.

Patterson, Mrs. Minnie. Sewing teacher for the Idle Hour Art Club and the American Rose Fine Art Club.

Pemberton, Mrs. President of the Ideal Embroidery Club.

Perry, Helen. One of the first African American female high school teachers in the Chicago public schools; taught at Wendell Phillips High School.

Perry, Lena LeGrand Belle. A truant officer, appointed in 1918. Secretary of the Necessity Club, which sponsored a day nursery.

Ralston, Fanny. President of the Penny Club.

Richards, Fannie. President of the Phyllis Wheatley Home Association.

Ridley, Rebecca. Matron of the Home for the Aged and Infirm Colored People.

Rouse, Eva. President of the Iroquois Community League in Evanston.

Sampson, Edith. Lawyer; in 1924 appointed probation officer.

Sayre, Helen. Born in Canada. President of Wendell Phillips High School Parent-Teacher Association; social worker.

Schultz-Knighten, Anna B. A doctor "well known for her charity, and [who] is now educating an orphan girl, who promises to be as capable as the doctor"; later studied law. Married to D. J. Knighten, the only African American livestock broker in Chicago.

Scott, Clotee. Founder of the Clotee Scott Settlement in Hyde Park; probation officer in 1926; founder of the Harmonia Ethical Club (for children).

Scott, Madam E. M. Held an Illinois state certificate for teaching chiropody; founder and manager of the Provident School of Beauty Culture in 1910, the only school in the United States operated by an African American woman "where the course of study is thorough and complete." (The school taught chiropody, manicuring, marcel waving, hair dressing and pressing, shampooing, hair dyeing and bleaching, hot oil treatment, singeing and clipping, facial massaging, mud and French pack, and high frequency and body massaging.)

Scott, Lucia H. Superintendent of the Boys' Clean Life Club.

Scott, Luna. Piano teacher at the Clotee Scott Settlement; Milwaukee correspondent for the *Chicago Defender.*

Seay, Madam Maude. A milliner, owner of a millinery shop. "Some of the most elaborately plumed hats worn at the Thanksgiving K. P. Ball were fashioned by her." Specialized in French-style hats.

Simpson, Dorothy. President of the Phyllis Wheatley Juniors.

Sinclair, Minnie. Owner of popular beauty shop.

Smith, Amanda. Born in Long Green, Maryland; an evangelist, missionary, temperance activist, and founder of the Amanda Smith Home (and later Industrial School for Girls) in Harvey, Illinois.

Smith, Emma. President and founder of the Easter Lily Club and the Mayflower Club, two savings clubs for women.

Smith, Gabriella. One of the founders of the Home for the Aged and Infirm Colored People; matron of the home.

Smith, Geneva. Leader in the community of the Town of Lake; active worker with the Berean Baptist Church.

Smith, Gertrude. Probation officer with the juvenile court from 1912 to 1914.

Smith, Maude. President of the Illinois State Federation of Colored Women's Clubs.

Snowden-Porter, Joanna. Born in Chicago. Juvenile probation officer; member of the board of directors and one of the founders of the Old Folks' Home; officer of the Juvenile Protective Association; treasurer and member of board of directors for the Phyllis Wheatley Home; president of the Northwestern Federation of Colored Women's Clubs; bookkeeper for the Chicago Recorder's Office, Chicago.

Stewart, Mrs. H. E. President of the North Side Woman's Club.

Stewart, Mrs. J. C. President of the Town of Lake Woman's Club; missionary worker with the Olivet Baptist Church.

Taylor, Mrs. Julius. President of the Afro-American Mothers' Council; charter member of the Phyllis Wheatley Club; wife of the editor of the *Broad Ax*, Julius Taylor.

Taylor, Mollie. One of the presidents of the Ida B. Wells Club.

Teney, Mrs. A. President of the Swastika Whist Club.

Thomas, Jessie. A probation officer for the juvenile court, beginning in 1910.

Thomas, Lillian. A sewing teacher at the Clotee Scott Settlement.

Thornton, Bishop Mattie. Founder of the Holy Nazarene Tabernacle Apostolic Church in 1913; she conducted camp meetings at Morgan Park, Evanston, and Milwaukee in 1912; one of the founders of the Home for the Aged and Infirm Colored People.

Tivis, Nina. Director of several young girls' literary clubs; active member of the Frederick Douglass Center.

Turner, Fannie. Charter member and president of the Ideal Woman's Club; vice president of the Chicago Federation of Colored Women's Clubs; president of the K. D. Tillman Club; treasurer of the board for the Paul Laurence Dunbar Sanitarium.

Vance, Alice. President of the Lincoln Savings League.

Walton, Martha. Chair of the Mortgage Fund for the Phyllis Wheatley Club and Home; secretary and president of the Volunteer Workers' Club.

Waring, Mary Fitzbutler. Graduate of Louisville National Medical College and Chicago Medical School. Teacher at Wendell Phillips High School. In charge of the Dunbar Sanitarium; captain of canteen of uniformed workers (who met trains of soldiers) with the Red Cross Auxiliary; national organizer of war camp commmunity work; secretary, statistician, and chair of education and of health for the Illinois State Federation of Colored Women's Clubs; president of the Necessity Club; director of the Children's Aid Auxiliary; head of the Woman's Second Ward Suffrage League; officer of Children's Aid Society (affiliated with the Illinois Children's Aid and Home Finding

Society); chair of health and hygiene, NACW. Married to Frank Waring, LL.B.

Warner, Mrs. Carrie. Vice president of the Phyllis Wheatley Club. A graduate of Moler College, she owned chiropody and manicure parlors in downtown Chicago. One newspaper highlighted her work: "[Her] parlors are frequented by hundreds of the best and the wealthiest white ladies of this city which is sufficient to prove that Mrs. Warner is a successful business woman."

Waters, Adah. Studied at Fisk University, where she taught printing, and at Northwestern University; editor of the Woman's Department, *Afro-American Budget,* Evanston; editor of the A.M.E. Sunday School Union's children's periodical; organizer of the Girls' Patriotic Service Leagues in Chicago during the war years; supervisor of the Amanda Smith Home (and later Industrial School) in Harvey, Illinois; superintendent of the Friendship House, Chicago.

Watkins, Mrs. S. A. T. Head of prominent whist clubs; prominent member of St. Thomas Church. Her husband was a lawyer.

Watson, Cora. One of the founders of the Iroquois Community League in Evanston (which established a home for working girls in Evanston in 1917).

Webb, Rhoygnette. Graduate of Provident's Nursing School and of the Purdue University School of Pharmacy; Head nurse at Dr. Butler and Dr. Garner's Sanitarium in Evanston.

Webster, Lucy. Chair of the Charity Committee, Volunteer Workers' Club.

Webster, Mary. Chair of the Press Committee and sewing teacher for the Volunteer Workers' Club.

Wells, Ida B. Born in Holly Springs, Mississippi. Founder of the Negro Fellowship League; cofounder of the Frederick Douglass Center; founder and president of the Ida B. Wells Club, the Ideal Woman's Club, and the Alpha Suffrage Club. Speaker for the Anti-Lynching Bureau of the National African American Council; vice president of the Frederick Douglass Woman's Club; first African American woman appointed as an officer in the Adult Probation Department. Her husband, Ferdinand Barnett, was a lawyer and an assistant state attorney.

Wells, Ophie. Supervisor of the sewing activities of the Phyllis Wheatley Club; known musician who performed at many of the church lyceums and clubs; taught music classes at the Frederick Douglass Center.

West, Cordelia. Chair of the House Committee, African American YWCA; president of the Volunteer Workers' Club; president of the Northern District of Colored Women's Clubs.

Williams, Bertha. First African American woman to graduate as a stenographer before the twentieth century; the only African American female notary public as of 1896.

Williams, Mrs. Daniel. Charter member of the Phyllis Wheatley Club. Her husband was the founder of and a doctor at Provident Hospital.

Williams, Fannie Barrier. Born in New York; attended New England Conservatory of Boston and the School of Fine Arts in Washington, D.C. Former teacher in Washington, D.C., and painter. Charter member of the Phyllis Wheatley Club and of the Prudence Crandall Study Club; one of the founders of Provident Hospital; member of the Chicago Library Board and of the Chicago Woman's Club. Prominent speaker in the female club movement and member of Chicago's "Elite 400." Writer of numerous essays, articles, and speeches on the African American women's club movement and on the role of women in uplift work. Her husband, S. Laing Williams, was a judge.

Williams, M. C. President of the Clover Leaf Club.

Wilson, Mrs. C. L. Sewing teacher at the Clotee Scott Settlement.

Wilson, Grace. Attended the School of Civics and Philanthropy, University of Chicago. Member of the Chicago Union Charity Club; worked for the investigation department of the Negro Fellowship League; "mother" at a home for incorrigible girls in Glencoe, Illinois (1918); matron for State Training for Girls at Geneva (the first African American woman to hold a civil position in such an institution); the first African American female police officer.

Wright, Mrs. E. H. Member of the Phyllis Wheatley Club and the Urban League; chair of the Home Section of the Frederick Douglass Woman's Club. Also considered a fine poetess, her works were read at several women's clubs. Her husband was a judge.

Young, Lou Ella. President and recording secretary of the Eureka Fine Art Club; officer of the True Reformers; chair of the Urban League's Committee for Fraternal Organizations; corresponding secretary of the Chicago Federation of Colored Women's Clubs.

NOTES

NOTES TO INTRODUCTION

1. Weber, *Sociological Writings;* Gerth and Mills, *From Max Weber;* R. Collins, *Three Sociological Traditions.* See also W. J. Wilson, *The Declining Significance of Race,* for the prominence of social class in sociological analyses.

2. *Broad Ax,* October 10, 1914.

NOTES TO CHAPTER 1

1. The term *progressive maternalism* is taken from Ladd-Taylor's *Mother-Work,* wherein she distinguishes between feminists and progressive maternalists during the Progressive Era. Perhaps the most cited works on the cult of true womanhood ideology are by Welter. See *Dimity Convictions;* "The Cult of True Womanhood," 151–174. For other works on the cult of domesticity and on the nurturance of the domestic sphere, see Rosenberg, "The Female World of Love and Ritual," 1–29; Cott, *Bonds of Womanhood;* Ryan, *Womanhood in America.* The resurgence of the Republican motherhood in the Chicago women's movement was particularly pronounced in the kindergarten movement; see, for example, E. Harrison, *A Study of Child-Nature.* Seminal scholarship on the earlier versions of Republican motherhood includes Kerber, *Women of the Republic;* S. M. Evans, *Born for Liberty.*

2. The merging of Washingtonian and Du Boisian ideologies is also noted

by Higginbotham, *Righteous Discontent,* and Gatewood, *Aristocrats of Color.* My analysis indicates a split in the club women's ideology along class lines. That is, Washington's industrial education model was most often recommended for poorer African Americans, while Du Bois's model of leadership and aristocracy was practiced by the club women. See Gaines, *Uplifting the Race,* for further discussion of the uplift ideologies and male and female models of leadership; and Smith, "The Black Women's Club Movement."

3. For this term I draw from P. H. Collins, *Black Feminist Thought.* I extend her concept of "other mothers" to "other homes," most prominently in the club women's establishing of day care facilities, such as nurseries and kindergartens for younger children and homes for young working girls, the elderly, and orphaned and dependent children. That the club women perceived these facilities as "other homes" is evident in the nomenclature, that is, the Phyllis Wheatley Home, the Amanda Smith Home, the Old Folks' Home, as well as in goals set forth under the NACW category "Child": to create home-finding organizations and to assist dependent and delinquent children. E. L. Davis, *Lifting As They Climb,* 101.

4. There are many fine pieces on the history of ideas concerning the concepts of race and its attendant racist practices. Among these, see Jordan, *White over Black;* Newby, *Jim Crow's Defense;* Meier and Rudwick, *From Plantation to Ghetto.*

5. For examples of literature documenting race progress and exemplary leaders, see Alexander, *History of the Colored Race in America;* Brawley, *Negro Builders and Heroes;* Brawley, *Women of Achievement;* H. Q. Brown, *Homespun Heroines;* Culp, *Twentieth Century Negro Literature;* Daniel, *Women Builders;* Hopkins, "Famous Women of the Negro Race," 273–277; Kletzing and Crogman, *Progress of a Race;* Mossell, *The Work of the Afro-American Woman;* Richings, *Evidence of Progress among Colored People.* Most works featured the lives and accomplishments of men; as a case in point, those works featuring women were mostly written by female writers. Scholars, too, have documented the Victorian ideals to which many African American club women subscribed. See Carlson, "Black Ideals of Womanhood in the Late Victorian Era," 61–73; J. M. Wilson, "Domestic Feminism, Conservatism, Sex Roles, and Black Women's Clubs," 166–177; Dickson, "Toward a Broader Angle of Vision," 114–115.

6. There are numerous scholarly references to this incident. The most complete documentation of the NACW's history is Wesley, *History of the National Association of Colored Women's Clubs.* See also Kendrick, "They Also Serve," 817–825; B. W. Jones, "Mary Church Terrell and the National Association of Colored Women, 20–33." For primary documentation of the NACW, nationally and regionally, see Chicago Northern District Association, *The Story of Seventy-Five Years;* E. L. Davis, *Lifting As They Climb;* Yates, "The National Association of Colored Women," 283–287.

7. Giddings, *Where and When I Enter,* 99.

8. Higginbotham, too, in *Righteous Discontent*, 207, has noted the two tiers within the NACW's motto.

9. For scholars who argue that African American gendered roles were more egalitarian and culturally informed, see Yee, *Black Women Abolitionists;* Perkins, "The Impact of the 'Cult of True Womanhood,' " 17–28; White, *A'rn't I a Woman;* White, "The Cost of Club Work," 247–269. Hewitt, in "Beyond the Search for Sisterhood," 299–321, argues that despite a similarity in the rhetoric of the cult of true womanhood among ethnic women, the material conditions of women's lives differed greatly; thus, their expressions of true womanhood were not monolithic. For a Marxist analysis, especially the patriarchal positions of men, see hooks, *Black Looks;* A. Y. Davis, *Women, Race, and Class.*

10. Yee, *Black Women Abolitionists,* 40. Harley has argued that historically African American women's sphere was separate, confirmed by White's elaboration of intergenerational female trash gangs during slavery. Harley aptly distinguishes between this separate sphere and that of domesticity. See Harley, "For the Good of Family and Race," 159–172.

11. Cited in B. W. Jones, *Quest for Equality,* 24.

12. Yates cited in Culp, *Twentieth Century Negro Literature,* 21–28.

13. F. B. Williams, "The Accusations Are False," 165.

14. Cooper, "The Colored Woman Should Not Be Ignored," 573.

15. Alexander, *History of the Colored Race in America,* 592. Guy-Sheftall has noted how ministers employed the cult of true womanhood ideology to protect their own positions. See *Daughters of Sorrow,* 72.

16. Higginbotham has astutely argued that African American men reinstated their manhood and their own dignity through promoting a female domestic sphere; "Beyond the Sound of Silence," 58. See also Friedman, in *White Savage, Racial Fantasies.*

17. F. B. Williams, "The Woman's Part in a Man's Business," 544–545. Williams was not alone in beseeching men for their protection. See also Cooper, *A Voice from the South,* 18, 25. See the July 1904 issue of the *Voice of the Negro,* which is devoted to African American women's perspectives on womanhood, character, and status.

18. Baker cited in Gatewood, *Aristocrats of Color,* 97.

19. J. Thorne, "A Plea for Social Justice," 2–6.

20. Alexander, *History of the Colored Race in America,* 592.

21. See Anderson, *The Education of Blacks in the South;* Thrasher, *Tuskegee.*

22. The home economics movement permeated vocational, as well as higher, education for women. See Solomon, *In the Company of Educated Women;* Powers, *The 'Girl Question' in Education.* See also Fuell, "The Value of Domestic Science," 429–430.

23. Freeman, "The Home-Making Arts," 427–428. One of the more fascinating, and least examined, aspects of the domestic arts were their effects on standards of character and beauty. According to Kenton, principal of the Beauty

Culture Department of the Enterprise Institute in Chicago, "beauty, health and comfort" made up a "magic trio," cultivated alongside the domestic arts; Dr. Jefferson argued that housekeeping was not only an artistic endeavor but also resulted in "beauty and neatness, harmony and sweetness." Alongside reports of the latest housekeeping technologies in the women's columns were beauty and health "hints." Some advertisements even stated that wife abandonment resulted from imperfect housekeeping. *Broad Ax* (hereafter referred to as *BA*), May 14, 1911, June 14, 1913, July 2, 1910. Not all African American women subscribed to these notions. Mossell, for one, chided those offering such advice, pointing out that a clean house would not "keep a man home"; furthermore, she argued, character, not cheerfulness, was most important. See Mossell, *The Work of the Afro-American Woman*, 115–125.

24. *Chicago Defender* (hereafter referred to as *CD*), July 2, 1910.

25. Nichols and Crogman, *Progress of a Race*, 199–200.

26. Cited in Sterling, *We Are Your Sisters*, 435.

27. Brawley, *Negro Builders and Heroes*, 260. Terborg-Penn discusses Brawley's traditional views of womanhood in "The Historical Treatment of Afro-Americans in the Woman's Movement," 245–259.

28. Kletzing and Crogman, *Progress of a Race*, 222.

29. Alexander, *History of the Colored Race in America*, 599.

30. Ibid.

31. *CD,* June 14, 1913.

32. *BA,* November 10, 1904.

33. Gibbs, "Woman's Part in the Uplift of the Negro Race," 264–265.

34. Kletzing and Crogman, *Progress of a Race*, 216.

35. F. B. Williams, "The Colored Girl," 400.

36. hooks, *Black Looks*, 94.

37. White, *Ar'n't I a Woman?* 56.

38. Terrell cited in E. L. Davis, *Lifting As They Climb*, 86. The NACW divided the category of "Mother" into three areas: parent education, "wholesome attitude," and health. In a questionnaire designed to elicit general information, mothers were asked questions about their parenting practices, questions that evoked responses about middle-class practices, for example, Are you your child's "companion"? Do you conduct a story hour with your children? Do you visit their schools? Do you subscribe to any parents' magazines? See E. L. Davis, *Lifting As They Climb*, 98–101.

39. Yates, "Kindergartens and Mothers' Clubs," 306–307. See also Graves, "Motherhood." As Ladd-Taylor has noted, the Republican motherhood, which echoed the cult of domesticity, was reinstated by many club women during the early twentieth century; *Mother-Work*, 4–6.

40. Nichols and Crogman, *Progress of a Race*, 226.

41. Kletzing and Crogman, *Progress of a Race*, 197–198.

42. Culp, *Twentieth Century Negro Literature*, 184.

43. E. L. Davis, *Lifting As They Climb*, 18. See also Crummell, "The Black Woman of the South."

44. Scholars have elaborated on the professionalization of domestic work, as well as on Nannie Burrough's leading role in the education of domestic workers. See particularly Barnett, "Nannie Burroughs and the Education of Black Women," 97–108. Higginbotham's suggestion that African American domestic workers were respected because of their church-going practices and hard work is evident in quotes such as the following by Katherine Davis Tillman: "Let no one scorn the vast army of domestics who dwell in the land, for in God's sight there is as much honor in doing one's best in that sphere as in any other." Tillman, "Afro-American Women and Their Work," 89; Higginbotham, "Beyond the Sound of Silence," 58. For a comprehensive history of African American female employment, including domestic service, see J. Jones, *Labor of Love*.

45. F. B. Williams, "The New Black Woman," 575.

46. Du Bois, *The Black North in 1901*. Social distinctions assumed various prescriptions and requirements, including such nuances as the "proper selection of dinner guests," the "art of tea making," and "how to eat roasting ears [of corn]." *BA*, December 2, 1905, September 9, 1911.

47. B. W. Jones, *Quest for Equality*, 22, 26.

48. Harley, "Beyond the Classroom," 480. My analysis of respectability is built not only from the club women's perspective but also from Higginbotham's *Righteous Discontent* and from Scott's *Natural Allies*. Scott has noted that African American club women's motivations were ones of respectability and race uplift. I particularly stress the dialectical relationship between the two.

49. Cited in Wesley, *History of the National Association of Colored Women's Clubs*, 48. Such descriptions were corroborated by white club women, such as Blauvelt's observations of the Michigan State Federation of Colored Women's Clubs: "These were ladies in every sense of the word. They had the faces of ladies—strong, sweet, thoroughly refined faces" (662). Blauvelt, "The Race Problem As Discussed by Negro Women," 662–672.

50. Hine, "Rape and the Inner Lives," 912–920.

51. Higginbotham, "Beyond the Sound of Silence," 56. Higginbotham's "bicultural voice" is not unlike Du Bois's "double consciousness"; see Du Bois, *Souls of Black Folk*.

52. To protest African Americans' exclusion from the Chicago World's Fair in 1893, Ida B. Wells wrote and distributed a pamphlet, *The Reason Why the Colored American Is Not in the Columbian Exposition*. See Massa, "Black Women in the 'White City,'" 319–337. In 1894 Fannie Barrier Williams was recommended for membership in the Chicago Woman's Club. Celia Parker Woolley had presented a resolution that year that club membership be based on "character and intelligence, not color or race." In 1895 a resolution was passed that no one be denied membership because of race or color, and Williams was admitted;

Chicago Woman's Club Records, 1895–96. However, there were no African Americans represented in the City Club or the Woman's City Club. When questioned why these clubs did not address the "Negro question," the president of one of the branches of the Illinois Federation of Women's Clubs responded: "Most of the presidents expressed themselves as against the discussion of the Negro question because as women's names come out as being against negroes these women and others of the club would have to live in fear of the negro men. A woman must be careful not to put herself in a position of causing them to regret to have a grudge against her, as you know a white woman has to fear a colored man." Chicago Commission on Race Relations (referred to hereafter as Chicago Commission), *The Negro in Chicago*, 440. See also Terborg-Penn, "Discrimination against Afro-American Women in the Woman's Movement."

53. F. B. Williams, *The Colored Woman and Her Part in Race Regeneration*, 426.

54. Ruffin cited in E. L. Davis, *Lifting As They Climb*, 17. The club women, in a vein similar to that of the literature that documented race progress, confirmed their role in advancing the race. See, for example, A. H. Jones, "A Century's Progress," 631–633; A. H. Jones, "The American Colored Woman," 692–694; Terrell, "The Progress of Colored Women," 291–294; F. B. Williams, "An Extension of Conference Spirit," 300–303; "The Club Movement among the Colored Women," 99–102; "The New Black Woman," 575–576.

55. F. B. Williams, *The Colored Woman and Her Part in Race Regeneration*, 384. For excellent histories of African American female organizations, see, among others, Lerner's *Black Women in White America*, which I have cited extensively; Lowenberg and Bogin, *Black Women in the Nineteenth Century American Life;* Noble, *Beautiful, Also, Are the Souls of My Black Sisters;* Porter, "The Organized Educational Activities of Negro Literary Societies," 555–576; Sterling, *We Are Your Sisters;* and the multiple volumes in *Black Women in United States History,* edited by Hine et al.

56. F. B. Williams, *The Colored Woman and Her Part in Race Regeneration,* 382–383.

57. Gordon, "Black and White Visions of Welfare," 559–590.

58. Thornbrough, "The History of Black Women in Indiana," 650; Harley, "Beyond the Classroom," 254–265.

59. F. B. Williams, *The Colored Woman and Her Part in Race Regeneration,* 424.

60. Gordon, "Black and White Visions of Welfare," 578.

61. One of the more notable examples was Kathryn Johnson, who volunteered endlessly for the NAACP, yet she was not rewarded with a formal leadership position. Salem, *To Better Our World,* 159–161.

62. B. W. Jones, *Quest for Equality,* 21.

63. The names of the probation officers and the police officer are listed in appendix 2. Arguments for African American female police officers were predicated not only on equal representation in the workforce but also upon municipal housekeeping and moral guardianship, especially for young girls. The

subtitle of one newspaper article noted, "Women Are in the Lead in Everything of Uplift—They Bear Our Children, Then Protect Them from the Lynch Hounds, Some Even Find the Board and Bed for the Family—Now They Are the First to Lead in Defense of Our Girls in the 'Red-Light Flate' [sic] Where Many Are Turned Out as Damaged Goods." *CD*, January 15, 1916. I would add that police positions were salaried positions, unlike probation work, which either was funded through private charities or was considered volunteer work. Although three African American women passed the police examination, only one, Grace Wilson, was given a position. For further articles on African American women in the Chicago police force, see *CD*, March 13, December 11, 1915, April 1, 1916, March 31, 1917. See Dulaney, *Black Police in America,* and Shaw, *What a Woman Ought to Be and to Do,* for further examination of issues of employment.

64. "Carrie Pearl Pleads Cause of Neglected Working Girls," *BA,* April 4, 1914; "Play Grounds in Great Demand," *CD,* February 12, 1916; Irene McCoy-Gaines, "A Plea for Our Girls," *CD,* February 28, 1920.

65. The settlement workers' and social workers' ideologies are treated more extensively in chapter 5. My argument is similar to Ralph Luker's, that many of the African American settlements were modeled from missions and functioned in a similar way. Luker, "Missions, Institutional Churches, and Settlement Houses," 101–113.

66. Chicago Commission, "The Migration of Negroes from the South, 1916–1918," 44–45.

67. *CD*, October 20, 1917. Such advice on public behavior, especially speech, dress, and forms of amusement, was not new. See Kletzing and Crogman, *Progress of a Race,* 208–209. The NACW, too, was concerned with the influence of unwholesome amusement on young people. That concern was expressed in its efforts to "eliminate forms of entertainment that diminish . . . the vitality of the moral life of our young people." Aptheker, "The National Association of Colored Women, 1904," 890.

68. *CD*, July 22, 1911. See also the articles "Young People Have Bad Deportment," *CD,* June 2, 1917; "Children of the Street," *CD,* June 8, 1918; Mrs. B. S. Gaten, "Standards of Looseness in Public Places," *CD,* July 13, 1918.

69. See, in particular, Grossman, *Land of Hope.*

70. See, among many scholarly works, E. B. Brown, "Womanist Consciousness," 208–223; P. H. Collins, *Black Feminist Thought;* Dill, "The Dialectics of Black Womanhood," 543–555; Gilkes, "Holding Back the Ocean with a Broom," 217–231; Gordon, "Black and White Visions of Welfare," 559–590; Knupfer, "'Toward a Tenderer Humanity and a Nobler Womanhood,' " 58–76; Perkins, "The Impact of the 'Cult of True Womanhood,' " 17–28; White, *Ar'n't I a Woman;* White, "The Cost of Club Work," 247–269; Yee, *Black Women Abolitionists.*

1. Spear, *Black Chicago,* 11; Chicago Commission, "The Migration of Negroes from the South, 1916–1918," 44. Perhaps the most complete source on the Great Migration is Grossman, *Land of Hope.* Class differentiation among African Americans increased in most Northern cities during the late nineteenth century. See Kronus, *The Black Middle Class;* Kusmer, *A Ghetto Takes Shape;* Lammermeier, "Cincinnati's Black Community," 24–28; Osofsky, *Harlem;* Scheiner, *Negro Mecca.*

2. Spear, *Black Chicago,* 8.

3. Drake, *Churches and Voluntary Associations,* 33, 37, 46, 59.

4. Massey and Denton, *American Apartheid,* 10.

5. Drake, *Churches and Voluntary Associations,* 70–75.

6. Ibid., 104–110. See also Fisher, "Negro Church in Illinois," 552–569. For further information on churches, see the 1927 *Intercollegiate Wonder Book,* 1:171, 191. Spear has argued that the secular programs of these churches resembled those of middle-class white urban churches. However, it should be noted that literary societies, forums, recitations, and addresses were long-standing traditions in the African American churches.

7. Drake, *Churches and Voluntary Associations,* 86.

8. Branham, "Black Chicago," 215.

9. Dempsey, *An Autobiography of Black Chicago,* 1.

10. Spear, *Black Chicago,* 15.

11. A value of less than 50 percent signified that African Americans were more likely to have Whites as neighbors than African Americans. See Massey and Denton, *American Apartheid,* 24–27, where they cite Lieberson's isolation indices. Branham, too, has argued that by 1900 African American "enclaves" had been established, in that sixteen Chicago wards were 99.5 percent to 100 percent white and more than 50 percent of the African Americans lived in three adjacent southside wards. His analysis, however, does not differentiate between native-born and foreign-born white populations. See Branham, "Black Chicago," 212–262.

12. Spear, *Black Chicago,* 4.

13. Zorbaugh, *The Gold Coast and the Slum,* 11, 38, 45. Recent studies by Philpott, *The Slum and the Ghetto,* and Massey and Denton, *American Apartheid,* have reconfirmed Zorbaugh's study.

14. Zorbaugh, *The Gold Coast and the Slum,* 148.

15. Massey and Denton, *American Apartheid,* 24–27.

16. Drake, *Churches and Voluntary Associations,* 11; Diner, "Chicago Social Workers and Blacks in the Progressive Era," 393.

17. Gatewood, *Aristocrats of Color,* 194–195; Dempsey, *An Autobiography of Black Chicago,* 16. For information on Englewood and Morgan Park, see the 1927 *Intercollegiate Wonder Book,* 1:229; on Evanston, see Leonard, "Paternalism and the Rise of a Black Community." Chicago was not the only city with an African American "Elite 400." See also Cromwell, *The Other Brahmins.*

18. Frazier, "Chicago Black Belt," 74.

19. *BA,* August 28, 1909. In the suburb of Wilmette, where African Americans did not live but worked, an Anti-Negro Committee was organized, which advised that all African American gardeners and domestic workers be fired because their presence would lower land values. See Bowen, *Colored People of Chicago,* n.p.

20. Drake and Cayton, *Black Metropolis,* 62–64, 178–179; Spear, *Black Chicago,* 177–178; Philpott, *The Slum and the Ghetto,* chap. 6; Bowen, *Colored People of Chicago,* n.p. See also Tuttle, Jr., "Contested Neighborhoods and Racial Violence," 266–288; Tuttle, *Race Riot.* For newspaper coverage on the residential tensions in Hyde Park and Woodlawn, see *BA,* August 18, September 18, 1909.

21. Drake and Cayton, *Black Metropolis,* 74.

22. F. B. Williams, "Social Bonds in the 'Black Belt' of Chicago," 40.

23. Cited in Gatewood, *Aristocrats of Color,* 121.

24. Ibid.

25. Williams cited in Gatewood, *Aristocrats of Color,* 232.

26. Avendorph, "Chicago's Social Condition Today and Twenty Years Ago," *CD,* October 6, 1917. See also by Avendorph, "Should Show Proper Interest in Dress at Formal Affairs," *CD,* December 2, 1916.

27. Spear, *Black Chicago,* 72.

28. "Most Magnificent Function Ever Held among Afro-Americans in Chicago. Dr. D. H. Williams and Mrs. Andrew L. Smith Led the Grand March Who Were Followed by the Cream of the Four Hundred," *BA,* January 25, 1908. See also Phelps, "Negro Life in Chicago," 12–14.

29. Marks, "The Social and Economic Life of Southern Blacks," 47–48.

30. Gatewood, *Aristocrats of Color,* 221, 228.

31. This was true in other cities as well. See Gatewood, *Aristocrats of Color,* 211–212.

32. *BA,* November 4, 1899.

33. Drake, *Churches and Voluntary Associations,* 141–142.

34. Branham, "Black Chicago," 229. For a fuller examination of Provident Hospital and the creation of other health-related facilities for African Americans nationwide, see Smith, "Sick and Tired of Being Sick and Tired."

35. Duster, *Crusade for Justice,* 249.

36. *BA,* May 3, 1919.

37. See the section in chapter 4 on the Old Folks' Home.

38. See Phyllis Wheatley Association Papers.

39. Drake, *Churches and Voluntary Associations,* 102, 146; *CD,* March 4, 1916; Chicago Commission, *The Negro in Chicago,* 149–150; Drake and Cayton, *Black Metropolis,* 55.

40. Fenton Johnson, a popular journalist and poet, occasionally wrote a "who's who" column for Benton Harbor, discussing who was vacationing there, as well as the friends and relatives accompanying Chicagoans. See "The

West Michigan Resort," *CD*, July 22, 1911. See also Gatewood, *Aristocrats of Color*, 201–202.

41. F. B. Williams, "Social Bonds in the 'Black Belt' of Chicago," 40.

42. L. W. Washington, *The Chicago Negro Business Men and Women*. For further biographical information on prominent African Americans in Chicago, see "Some Chicagoans of Note," 234–242.

43. See Frazier, "Chicago Black Belt," 70–80; Spear, *Black Chicago;* Drake and Cayton, *Black Metropolis;* Landry, *The New Black Middle Class;* Spear, "The Rise of the Chicago Black Belt," 57–69.

44. Frazier, "Chicago Black Belt," 76.

45. Spear, *Black Chicago*, 174–179. This was not peculiar to Chicago alone. See Landry's account of Detroit churches, where they rented pews to keep poorer African Americans out of their more "sedate" churches. Landry, *The New Black Middle Class*, 34. See also Philpott, *The Slum and the Ghetto*, 165–167.

46. Hine, *Hine Sight*, 98.

47. Gatewood, *Aristocrats of Color*.

48. Ibid., 303–304; *CD*, November 22, 1913.

49. Spear, *Black Chicago*, 68.

50. Drake, *Churches and Voluntary Associations*, 125.

51. See Drake and Cayton, *Black Metropolis;* Spear, *Black Chicago;* Philpott, *The Slum and the Ghetto*.

52. Drake and Cayton, *Black Metropolis*, 47.

53. Ibid., 48.

54. Branham, "Black Chicago," 216.

55. Chicago Commission, *The Negro in Chicago*. On housing conditions in Chicago, see Abbott and Breckinridge, *The Tenements of Chicago;* Comstock, "Chicago Housing Conditions, 6," 241–257; Breckinridge, "The Color Line in the Housing Problem," 575–576; Duke, *The Housing Situation;* Philpott, *The Slum and the Ghetto*, 159–160.

56. Abbott and Breckinridge, *The Tenements of Chicago*, 123.

57. Chicago Commission, "The Migration of Negroes from the South, 1916–1918," 44–45; Marks, "The Social and Economic Life of Southern Blacks," 46.

58. Zorbaugh, *The Gold Coast and the Slum*, 148.

59. Ibid.

60. Chicago Commission, "The Migration of Negroes from the South, 1916–1918," 54.

61. Zorbaugh, *The Gold Coast and the Slum*, 147.

62. Stehno, "Public Responsibility for Dependent Black Children," 488.

63. F. B. Williams, "Social Bonds in the 'Black Belt' of Chicago," 40.

64. *Chicago Tribune*, August 11, 1889, 12.

65. Bowen, *Colored People of Chicago*, n.p.

66. Meyerowitz, *Women Adrift*, 24–25.

67. Bowen, *Colored People of Chicago,* n.p.

68. Ibid.

69. Spear, *Black Chicago,* 29; Jackson, "Black Charity in Progressive Era Chicago," 402; W. L. Evans, "The Negro in Chicago Industries," 15–16.

70. Hall, "The Health or the Sanitary Conditions of the Negro in Chicago," *BA,* December 31, 1904.

71. Tuttle, "Contested Neighborhoods and Racial Violence," 271.

72. Hall, "Sound Hints to the Afro-Americans of Hyde Park," *BA,* July 28, 1906.

73. *CD,* July 1, 1911.

74. *CD,* October 20, 1917.

75. Drake, *Churches and Voluntary Associations,* 33.

76. Chicago Commission, *The Negro in Chicago,* 149.

77. See Vandewalker, *The Kindergarten in American Education,* 73–74.

78. Dempsey, *An Autobiography of Black Chicago,* 2; Spear, *Black Chicago,* 95–96, 106; Bowen, *Colored People of Chicago,* n.p.; Chicago Commission, *The Negro in Chicago,* 147; F. B. Williams, "Social Bonds in the 'Black Belt' of Chicago"; Luker, "Missions, Institutional Churches, and Settlement Houses," 101–113; Kletzing and Crogman, *Progress of a Race,* 144.

79. Spear, *Black Chicago,* 105. For information on the Hyde Park Neighborhood Settlement, see *CD,* September 27, 1913; *BA,* August 16, 1913; for the Clotee Scott Settlement, see *CD,* March 27, 1915; for the Emanuel Settlement, see *CD,* June 25, 1910; *BA,* September 7, 1910.

80. For information on the types of activities carried out by the Negro Fellowship League, see the 1915 annual report published in *CD,* January 15, 1916. The Frederick Douglass Center's activities were numerous and published weekly, beginning with the *BA,* January 6, 1906. The political activities of these settlements are featured in chapter 3; the literary activities of the Frederick Douglass Center are examined in chapter 7.

81. Spear, *Black Chicago,* 327.

82. F. B. Williams, "Social Bonds in the 'Black Belt' of Chicago," 41.

83. Strickland, *History of the Chicago Urban League,* 45.

84. Duster, *Crusade for Justice,* 372–373.

NOTES TO CHAPTER 3

1. E. B. Brown, "Womanist Consciousness," 218.

2. In using the term *voluntary space* I refer to questions raised by S. M. Evans in her essay, "Women's History and Political Theory," 119–140.

3. Chestnutt, "Women's Rights," 182–183.

4. Du Bois, "Votes for Women," 234.

5. Clifford, "Votes for Children," 185.

6. A. H. Jones, "Woman Suffrage and Social Reform," 190.

7. Logan, "Colored Women as Voters," 242.

8. Grimke, "The Logic of Woman Suffrage," 178. hooks has argued that

many African American men did not believe in equal rights, especially suffrage, for African American women. See *Black Looks; Ain't I a Woman*.

9. Withers, "Jim Crowism vs. Woman Suffrage; Slavery before and after the War," *BA*, March 24, 1914.

10. Waring, "Training and the Ballot," 185–186.

11. Logan, "Woman Suffrage," 488.

12. Bruce, "Colored Women's Clubs," 190.

13. Burroughs, "Black Women and Reform," 187.

14. *BA*, April 4, 1900.

15. *BA*, November 26, 1910. Such traditionalism was reflected in stories published in African American women's magazines. For example, in "The Suffragette" by Bettie Mason, a young lady challenged her boyfriend to a debate about female suffrage. Whereas he waxed eloquent on the subject, she was characterized by her beauty and dress, not her convincing arguments. At the story's end, the boyfriend admitted that his girlfriend "has enough sense to vote" but told her, "You're so pretty you don't have to use it." She coyly hinted that if she had a home where she could exercise her cares, she might learn how to use that "good sense." The story concluded with the young lady's statement: "Careers may be for some women, Bob, but this [a home] is my proper place." See Mason, "The Suffragette," 6.

16. *BA*, June 6, 1903.

17. *BA*, October 15, 1904.

18. Ibid.

19. *BA*, February 24, 1906.

20. *BA*, November 7, 1914.

21. *BA*, October 10, 1914.

22. *CD*, March 7, 1906.

23. *BA*, March 24, May 5, 1906.

24. *BA*, July 16, 1912.

25. *BA*, March 14, June 27, April 4, 1914.

26. *BA*, June 27, 1914. The African American and white women's suffrage movements were largely segregated, as were their club movements because of discrimination by white women, predominantly those from the South. For further insights into the tensions and conflicts between white and African American suffragists see Flexnor, *Century of Struggle;* Kraditor, *The Ideas of the Woman Suffrage Movement*. Other notable works on white women's attitudes toward African American women include Guy-Sheftall, *Daughters of Sorrow;* Terborg-Penn, "Discrimination against Afro-American Women in the Woman's Movement," 301–316; Terborg-Penn, "The Historical Treatment of Afro-Americans, 245–259." Giddings has astutely noted how white women, in fact, undermined their own agenda because of their racism; see *Where and When I Enter,* 6. For information on conflicts within the Illinois suffrage movement, see Wheeler, "Conflict in the Illinois Woman Suffrage Movement of 1913," 95–114.

27. *BA,* April 9, 1912.

28. *CD,* February 11, 1911.

29. *CD,* December 2, 1911.

30. K. E. Williams, "Alpha Suffrage Club," 12.

31. *CD,* March 27, 1915.

32. *CD,* March 8, 1913; *BA,* March 18, 1913; *CD,* March 29, 1913. See Ida B. Wells Papers, Alpha Suffrage Record, box 5, folder 1.

33. *BA,* November 15, 1913.

34. *CD,* August 23, 1913; K. E. Williams, "Alpha Suffrage Club."

35. *BA,* April 11, 1914. See also de Priest, "Chicago and Woman's Suffrage," 179; Hendricks, "Vote for the Advantage of Ourselves and Our Race," 171–184; Hendricks, "The Politics of Race."

36. *BA,* October 13, 17, 10, June 27, July 25, 1914; *BA,* February 12, 1915.

37. *BA,* February 12, 1915.

38. *CD,* March 23, 1918.

39. *CD,* May 16, 1916; *BA,* November 22, 1913; *CD,* August 1, 1914. The suffrage movement in Chicago was largely successful because of the formation of coalitions between African American and white reformers and club women, evident in the number of white women who were invited to speak at the African American women's club meetings. Because I have not examined the white women's club records, it is not clear whether reciprocal invitations were extended to African American women to speak at white women's club meetings. For an examination of the history and the larger statewide structure of the suffrage movement, see Buechler, *The Transformation of the Woman Suffrage Movement.*

40. *CD,* October 11, 1913.

41. *BA,* October 13, 1913, January 10, October 4, February 14, October 7, 1914; *CD,* May 29, June 26, July 13, 1915.

42. *BA,* March 7, 1914.

43. Stovall, "The *Chicago Defender* in the Progressive Era," 159–172.

44. *BA,* March 13, 1915; *CD,* June 3, 1916.

45. *CD,* May 20, 1916.

46. *CD,* September 2, 1916.

47. Salem, *To Better Our World,* 39.

48. *BA,* December 31, 1910.

49. Ibid.

50. *CD,* June 6, 1918. Primary sources on the antilynching campaigns include Wells-Barnett, *On Lynchings, Southern Horrors;* Duster, *Crusade for Justice.* For a fine collection of Ida B. Wells's writings, as well as an analysis of her life, see Thompson, *Ida B. Wells-Barnett;* Townes, "The Social and Moral Perspective of Ida B. Wells-Barnett." For a critical work on Wells's speaking career, see Campbell, *Women Public Speakers in the United States, 1800–1925,* 462–475. Other historical essays on Wells's antilynching campaign include Tucker, "Miss Ida B. Wells and Memphis Lynching," 112–122; B. Aptheker, *Woman's Legacy,*

chap. 3; Bederman, "'Civilization,' the Decline of Middle-Class Manliness," 5–30; Terborg-Penn, "African American Women's Networks in the Anti-Lynching Crusade," 148–161. See Stephens, "Anti-Lynching Plays by African American Women," 329–339, for a discussion of antilynching plays written by African American women.

51. *CD*, August 14, June 26, 1915, May 20, 1916, March 16, May 4, April 27, June 8, May 25, 1918. Ferdinand Barnett, Ida B. Wells's husband, was one of Joseph Campbell's lawyers; see *CD*, June 10, 1916.

52. *CD*, May 18, February 17, February 21, 1918.

53. *CD*, February 20, January 16, 1915.

54. *BA*, November 15, 1916; *CD*, August 14, 1915.

55. Ibid.

56. Moore-Smith cited in Wesley, *History of the National Association of Women's Clubs*, 58; Benson, *Counter Cultures*, 206–209.

57. *CD*, July 15, 1916.

58. *CD*, June 17, 1917.

59. *CD*, June 22, 1918; *BA*, November 7, 1917. Marshall Field and Company and Libby Company were not alone in discrimination against African American women. See "Race Women Refuse Automatic Telephone Because Company Would Not Employ Colored Agents nor Advertise in Their Race Newspapers," *BA*, July 22, 1911; "Chicago Tribune Calls College Graduate Negress and Black Mammy," *CD*, October 28, 1911. So, too did club women protest when they were not waited on in department stores; see *BA*, June 11, 1916. In one case young women walked out of their jobs when the Chicago Mercantile Company refused to hire other African Americans; see "Girls Quit Downtown Firm When Color Line Is Drawn," *CD*, July 13, 1918.

60. *CD*, June 25, 1910.

61. Ibid.

62. *CD*, January 23, 16, 1915, October 5, August 24, 1918. Other articles on Wendell Phillips School's racial tensions included "No More 'Jim Crow' Social Affairs at Wendell Phillips," *CD*, April 17, 1915; "Color Line Again at Wendell Phillips," *CD*, October 6, 1917; "Color Line Bobs Up in High School Again," Wendell Phillips, *CD*, March 17, 1917.

63. *CD*, August 24, 1918.

64. *CD*, September 23, 1911.

65. *CD*, August 9, 1913. See also "Amanda Smith School for Girls Formed in Court Room," *CD*, August 16, 1913.

66. *BA*, August 19, November 4, 1911, May 25, 22, 1915. See also Cripps, "The Reaction of the Negro to the Motion Picture *Birth of a Nation*," 344–362.

67. *CD*, June 12, 1915.

68. *CD*, May 20, 1911.

69. Ibid.

70. *CD*, February 12, 1916. In 1892 Wells had argued before a group of Memphis African Americans that they should save their nickels so that they

would become financially independent of Whites. She would continue the theme of economic self-determination in Chicago, urging African Americans to support community businesses and institutions. See Wells-Barnett, "Let the Afro-American Depend but on Himself," 539–540.

71. E. B. Brown, "Womanist Consciousness."

72. *BA,* December 31, 1904.

73. *BA,* December 31, 1904.

74. Ibid.

75. Ibid.

76. *CD,* July 10, 1920. For a complete list of members in the Easter Lily Club, see *BA,* December 21, 1918.

77. *CD,* July 20, 1918.

78. *BA,* November 1, 1916.

79. *CD,* July 10, 1920.

80. *BA,* November 1, 1916; *CD, BA,* July 15, 1916; *CD,* July 20, 1918, July 10, 1920.

81. *BA,* November 19, 1916.

82. *CD,* August 18, 1917.

83. *CD,* August 18, 1917.

84. Ibid; *CD,* September 28, 1918.

NOTES TO CHAPTER 4

1. There were no comprehensive lists of African American probation officers. This list is derived from club records and newspaper articles; as such, it is most likely incomplete. Jeter mentions five African American officers, four of whom worked only with African American families. See Jeter, *The Chicago Juvenile Court,* 32. My tally of names includes Elizabeth McDonald, Ida B. Wells, Joanna Snowden-Porter, Clotee Scott, Alberta Moore Smith, Gertrude Smith, and Jessie Thomas as probation officers; Lena Perry and Sophia Boaz as truant officers; Irene McCoy-Gaines, a stenographer with the court who later became a probation officer; and Grace Wilson, who moved from the position of matron at the Home for Incorrigible Girls in Glencoe to police work. See *CD,* April 6, 1918. Police work for African American women was especially promoted after immigrant women were hired. Most arguments were predicated upon municipal housekeeping and moral guardianship. See *CD,* March 13, 1915; *BA,* May 9, 1914; and *CD,* December 11, 1915. Female police officers were thought to be particularly effective with delinquent girls. See Lou, *Juvenile Courts in the United States,* 79.

2. See, for example, Schlossman, *Love and the American Delinquent;* Platt, *The Child Savers;* Youcha, *Minding the Children;* Ladd-Taylor, *Mother-Work;* Abramovitz, *Regulating the Lives of Women;* Skocpol, *Protecting Soldiers and Mothers;* Boris, "Reconstructing the 'Family,' " 73–86.

3. Bowen, "The Early Days of the Juvenile Court," 299.

4. Boris, "Reconstructing the 'Family,' " 73–75. See also Gordon, *Pitied but Not Entitled,* 55–56.

5. See *Proceedings of the Conference on the Care of Dependent Children.*

6. See Abbott and Breckinridge, *The Administration of the Aid-to-Mothers Law in Illinois;* Bogue, "Mothers' Allowances in Cook County, Ill.," 67–90; Goodwin, "An Experiment in Paid Motherhood," 323–343; Leff, "Consensus for Reform," 397–417; Gordon, *Pitied but Not Entitled,* 45–46.

7. Crawley, "Dependent Negro Children in Chicago in 1926," 58. This small number of mothers' pensions was not unique to 1920. An examination of Cook County Juvenile Court 1918 and 1919 Annual Reports revealed only nineteen pensions given to African American families; Cook County Juvenile Court will hereafter be referred to as CCJC.

8. Wald, "Chicago House Conditions," 458.

9. There is little information on the instruction of probation officers, perhaps because it was sporadic. Probation officer meetings were held monthly to "unify" the work. In cooperation with the Chicago Institute of Social Science, the chief probation officer set up lectures on the historical, legal, and practical aspects of probation work. See 1906 CCJC Annual Report, 4–7.

10. The multiple roles of probation officers have been variously described by social and child welfare reformers, as well as historians. See, for one, Schlossman, *Love and the American Delinquent,* 61–62. Probation officers worked with parents, children, teachers, employees, ministers, settlements, and club organizers. See Abbott and Breckinridge, *Truancy and Non-Attendance in the Chicago Schools.* Perhaps the most stringent articulation of the probation officers' qualities was expressed by Louise de Koven Bowen: "They must be men and women of many sides, endowed with the strength of a Samson and the delicacy of an Ariel. They must be tactful, skillful, firm and patient. They must know how to proceed with wisdom and intelligence and must be endowed with that rare quality—common-sense." See Bowen, "The Early Days of the Juvenile Court," 300.

11. Zaretsky, "The Place of the Family in the Origins of the Welfare State," 218.

12. Lou recommended that probation officers be paired with children according to language, "racial psychology," and religion; see Lou, *Juvenile Courts in the United States,* 89.

13. See Crawley, "Dependent Negro Children in Chicago in 1926," 86. There were various statistics and figures regarding dependency and delinquency of African American children in Chicago during this period. Breckinridge and Abbott cited the percentages of African American dependents and delinquents collectively as 3.8 percent boys and 6.2 percent girls, although the designation "Negro" also included other groups, such as Chinese. Crawley noted that 6.7 percent of dependent children were African American; by 1920 there were, however, more delinquent than dependent African American children. According to Gittens, one-third of the girls and women in the Cook County jail were African American. My examination of CCJC Annual Reports from 1917 to 1919 indicated that of thirty-one ethnic classifications for delinquency,

African Americans ranked second in 1917; in 1918, of thirty-nine groups, African Americans ranked sixth; and in 1919 African Americans ranked eighth out of thirty-four ethnic groups. See Breckinridge and Abbott, *The Delinquent Child and the Home*, 62; Crawley, "Dependent Negro Children in Chicago in 1926," 53; Gittens, *Poor Relations*, 43; CCJC Annual Reports, 1917–19. What has not been adequately addressed in the literature is the treatment of the youths by police officers or juvenile court officials. See *CD*, June 22, 1918, for one example of the Chicago Urban League's advocacy of an African American youth beaten by police officers.

14. Jackson, "Black Charity in Progressive Era Chicago," 405; *CD*, February 12, 1916. Examples of women's clubs devoted specifically to child welfare included the Children's Aid Society, the South End Children's Aid Society, and the Giles Charity Club. However, most federated clubs included children's welfare work under the philanthropy or home department.

15. *BA*, February 3, 1900.

16. Hine, "Rape and the Inner Lives," 914.

17. Grossman, *Land of Hope*, 134–135.

18. Quote by Elizabeth Lindsay Davis cited in Meyerowitz, *Women Adrift*, 54.

19. *BA*, September 18, 1909.

20. Gaten, "Standards of Looseness in Public Places," *CD*, July 13, 1918.

21. Meyerowitz, *Women Adrift*, 68. Louise de Koven Bowen, under the auspices of the Juvenile Protective Association, published two monographs that documented the unwholesome and dangerous influences of dance halls upon youths. See *Our Most Popular Recreation Controlled by the Liquor Interests;* and *The Public Dance Halls of Chicago.*

22. *BA*, November 14, 1903.

23. Hurley cited in Lubove, *The Professional Altruist*, 140.

24. 1906 CCJC Annual Report, 4.

25. Ibid.

26. *BA*, November 14, 1903.

27. Ibid.

28. Cited from "An act to regulate the treatment and control of dependent, neglected and delinquent children," *Revised Statutes of the State of Illinois*, chap. 23, cited in Bremner, *Children and Youth in America*, 506–511.

29. Ibid.; *BA*, November 14, 1903.

30. *BA*, November 14, 1903. In the 1905 examination, twenty-three officers were certified as probation officers. CCJC Annual Report, 1913, 9.

31. Du Bois, *Efforts for Social Betterment among Negro Americans;* Jackson, "Black Charity in Progressive Era Chicago," 408; 80–81; Crawley, "Dependent Negro Children in Chicago in 1926," 83–84. The number of children attending the school that year was recorded elsewhere as twenty-three. See "Louise Juvenile Home Opening," 339.

32. *BA*, October 5, 1907.

33. Du Bois, *Efforts for Social Betterment among Negro Americans,* 81.

34. Ibid., 61.

35. *BA,* December 25, 1909.

36. Ibid.

37. *CD,* January 7, 1911; *BA,* December 30, 1911, December 16, 1913.

38. *BA,* December 30, 1911, January 4, 1913.

39. *BA,* July 26, 1913.

40. *BA,* October 4, 1914.

41. *CD,* September 20, 1913; *BA,* October 4, 1914.

42. CCJC Annual Report, 1919, 130–132; CCJC Annual Report, 1912, 90–91.

43. Bowen, *Safeguards for City Youth at Work and at Play,* 174–176.

44. See CCJC Annual Reports, 1918, 37; 1919, 35; 1917, 22.

45. See CCJC Annual Reports, 1918, 39; 1919, 43.

46. *BA,* December 16, 1913; *CD,* September 20, 1913; *BA,* June 6, 1914.

47. Crawley, "Dependent Negro Children in Chicago in 1926," 85.

48. O'Donnell, "The Care of Dependent African American Children in Chicago," 763–776.

49. Cited in a tribute to Smith in *CD,* March 6, 1915. For biographical information and tributes to Amanda Berry Smith, see H. Q. Brown, *Homespun Heroines,* 128–132; Majors, *Noted Negro Women,* 278–282. See also Smith, *An Autobiography.*

50. H. Q. Brown, *Homespun Heroines,* 130.

51. Ibid.

52. McClellan and Bartlett, *The Final Ministry of Amanda Berry Smith.*

53. Spear, *Black Chicago,* 102–103.

54. *BA,* June 20, 1914.

55. *BA,* September 30, 1905.

56. *CD,* January 28, 1911.

57. *CD,* October 8, 1910, May 25, 1912; *BA,* August 17, 1913.

58. *BA,* August 17, 1913.

59. See CCJC Annual Reports, 1906, 27; 1912, 18, 52–53, 55; 1915, 34; 1917, 25, 48.

60. See Bowen, *Colored People of Chicago,* n.p.

61. *BA,* August 17, 1913.

62. See also *CD,* August 9, 17, 1913 for information on the court proceedings of the Amanda Smith Home. See CCJC Annual Reports, 1918, 39; 1919, 43.

63. *CD,* December 20, 1913, April 22, November 18, 1916; *BA,* February 15, 1913, January 26, 1917.

64. Breckinridge, cited in Gittens, *Poor Relations,* 44. See the "Report on Amanda Smith Industrial School for Girls," by Charles Virden, State Agent, June 18, 1915, copy in Rosenwald Papers. Cited in Spear, *Black Chicago,* 102;

McClellan and Bartlett, *The Final Ministry of Amanda Berry Smith*, 12. See *CD*, November 30, 1918, for coverage of the home's fire.

65. *BA*, March 27, 1909. See the pamphlet, "The Phyllis Wheatley Home for Girls," in the Phyllis Wheatley Association Papers. See also Lerner, "Early Community Work of Black Club Women," 158–167; F. B. Williams, "Colored Women of Chicago," 564–566.

66. *BA*, April 14, 1914.

67. *BA*, July 28, 1906.

68. *BA*, July 28, 1906, March 23, 1912; *CD*, December 30, 1913; *BA*, March 14, 1914. See Knupfer, "If You Can't Push, Pull."

69. *CD*, October 11, 1911; *BA*, November 15, 1913; *CD*, June 28, 1913; *BA*, June 5, 1916.

70. *BA*, July 13, 1912.

71. *BA*, October 29, 1916, October 21, 1911, November 26, 1910.

72. *BA*, February 11, 1917.

73. *CD*, February 7, 1920.

74. Here I refer particularly to Kunzel, *Fallen Women, Problem Girls*. Although her work focuses on "problems girls," she details the various forms of social control used to reform the young women.

75. *BA*, May 2, 1914; *CD*, February 17, April 6, May 4, 1912; *BA*, March 17, 1914.

76. *BA*, December 27, 1902; Lewis, "The Old Folks' Home of Chicago," 329–335; Du Bois, *Efforts for Social Betterment among Negro Americans*, 75.

77. "Home for Aged Colored People," 5.

78. *BA*, December 27, 1902.

79. *BA*, November, 18, 1905; Lewis, "The Old Folks' Home of Chicago," 330.

80. Lewis, "The Old Folks' Home of Chicago," 331; *BA*, April 25, 1914.

81. *BA*, December 27, 1902; Lewis, "The Old Folks' Home of Chicago," 333–334.

82. See, for example, Du Bois, *Efforts for Social Betterment among Negro Americans*, 61; *BA*, August 8, 1900, August 12, 1913. The two newspapers advertised many such events, including the Old Folks Home Day Basket Picnic, the home's Annual Bazaar, and the Harvest Home Day.

83. *BA*, August 8, 1900.

84. *CD*, February 12, 1910.

85. *BA*, November 25, 1905. Snowden's arguments were used to further encourage attendance at a charity ball sponsored by the Triangle and Inner Circle Clubs.

86. *BA*, April 22, 1911.

87. At the bazaars the home's inmates, as well as the club women, sold handmade articles, such as hand-painted china, embroidery, and artwork. For an example of in-kind food donations, see *BA*, March 21, 1903. In autumn

two days were set aside: one for raising moneys for the coal fund and one as "canning day." See Du Bois, *Efforts for Social Betterment among Negro Americans,* 61; *CD,* June 18, 1918. The women's club weekly records in the newspapers were replete with activities directed toward the Old Folks' Home, including visits, entertainment, preparing dinners, and other forms of "good cheer."

88. *BA,* January 11, 1916; *CD,* November 26, 1910; *BA,* February 14, 1914, January 1, 1913.

89. *BA,* February 24, 1900, November 18, 25, 1905; Lewis, "The Old Folks' Home of Chicago," 334–335.

90. *CD,* September, 24, 1910, June 3, 1916.

91. O'Donnell, "The Care of Dependent African American Children in Chicago," 763–776.

92. Chicago Commission, "The Migration of Negroes from the South, 1916–1918," 44–45.

NOTES TO CHAPTER 5

1. Philpott, *The Slum and the Ghetto,* 79, 81; Woods and Kennedy, *Handbook of Settlements.* See also Head, *Chicago Social Settlements.* Only recently have scholars focused on African American settlements. See Lasch-Quinn, *Black Neighbors;* Luker, "Missions, Institutional Churches, and Settlement Houses," 101–113; Crocker, *Social Work and Social Order.* Although not included in this chapter, the YMCAs' and YWCAs' programs and services closely resembled those offered at the African American settlements. See Mjagkij, *Light in the Darkness.*

2. Cited in Carson, *Settlement Folk,* 58.

3. Cited in Weiss, *The National Urban League, 1910–1940,* 55. See also Addams, *Twenty Years at Hull-House.*

4. Carson, *Settlement Folk,* 15. Davis and Trolander portray the prototypical settlement workers as middle-class, college-graduate females, who often remained unmarried, yet looked upon the settlement as a form of family life. See A. H. Davis, *Spearheads for Reform,* 87; Trolander, *Professionalism and Social Change,* 12–13.

5. Carson, *Settlement Folk,* 66–67.

6. A. H. Davis, *Spearheads for Reform,* 20.

7. Diner, "Chicago Social Workers and Blacks in the Progressive Era," 393–410; Philpott, *The Slum and the Ghetto;* Lissak, *Pluralism and Progressives.* See also Addams, *The Spirit of Youth and the City Streets;* A. H. Davis and McCree, *Eighty Years at Hull House;* Sklar, "Hull House in the 1890s," 658–677.

8. Grossman, *Land of Hope,* 170–174; Philpott, *The Slum and the Ghetto,* chap. 13.

9. Philpott, *The Slum and the Ghetto,* 316, 334.

10. Ibid., 322.

11. Ibid., 317.

12. Ibid., 304.

13. Ibid., 317.

14. Lasch-Quinn, *Black Neighbors,* 118.

15. *CD,* March 27, 1915.

16. *BA,* March 27, 1909.

17. *CD,* November 1, 1913.

18. Wright, "Social Work of the Negro Church," 81–93.

19. Spear, *Black Chicago,* 92, 95–96; Lasch-Quinn, *Black Neighbors,* 68.

20. Spear, *Black Chicago,* 96.

21. *CD,* January 1, 1910.

22. Upon Mrs. Lawson's death, Ida B. Wells applied to the Rosenwald Fund. However, a racist joke from one of Rosenwald's employees prompted her to rebuke his distasteful humor. Needless to say, she did not receive Rosenwald's endorsement. See Jackson, "Black Charity in Progressive Era Chicago," 400–417; Spear, *Black Chicago,* 106; Philpott, *The Slum and the Ghetto,* 322.

23. Many of the African American settlements were short-lived largely because of lack of funding. Most depended upon white philanthropy, especially the Julius Rosenwald Fund. Rosenwald provided 25 percent of the revenue for the Frederick Douglass Center and the Wendell Phillips Settlement. See Julius Rosenwald Papers, box 14, file 3; Fitzpatrick, *Endless Crusade,* 182. Interracial boards allowed for further control by white philanthropists.

24. Carlton-LaNey, "The Career of Birdye Henrietta Haynes," 259–263.

25. *CD,* October 18, 1913. See also Hunton, "Women's Clubs," 78–79.

26. Bowen, *Colored People of Chicago,* n.p.; Spear, *Black Chicago,* 29; Jackson, "Black Charity in Progressive Era Chicago," 402.

27. There is little information on the Emanuel Settlement or on Fannie Emanuel, its founder. Dr. Emanuel was a president of the Frederick Douglass Center prior to her founding the settlement, which was, in actuality, a large house on Armour Avenue in the Black Belt. See *BA,* January 10, 1910; *CD,* May 29, 1915; Philpott, *The Slum and the Ghetto,* 321. Williams was not alone in her endorsement of kindergartens. However, there was little written information on the activities of African American kindergartens. Although Yates spoke highly of Froebelian pedagogy, the mainstay activities in African American settlements were manual training, domestic training, physical exercise, and club work. Dunbar noted that mothers were often suspicious of kindergarten teachers. See Yates, "Kindergartens and Mothers' Clubs," 304–311; Emerson, "Children of the Circle," 81–83; Dunbar, "A Kindergarten Club," 386–390; Rouse, "Atlanta's African American Women's Attack on Segregation," 511–518; Barrett, "Social Settlement for Colored People," 511–518.

28. *CD,* April 24, 1918, April 19, 1919. For a contrast, see Neil, *Our Little Men and Women.* As father of the mothers' pension system, Neil stressed not only physical activity for girls but also instruction in domestic arts and hygiene.

29. *CD,* March 20, February 20, 1915. Physical culture was more prevalent in the mainstream settlements, although the African American newspapers did

advise mothers to engage their children in such exercises. See *BA,* January 21, 1905, September 8, 1910.

30. *CD,* October 18, November 1, December 22, 1913.

31. *CD,* August 9, 1913.

32. Ibid.

33. Baker, *Following the Color Line,* 138.

34. Philpott, *The Slum and the Ghetto,* 281.

35. From brochures cataloged under The Phyllis Wheatley Association Records.

36. *BA,* February 3, 1900.

37. *BA,* March 5, 1910.

38. Philpott, *The Slum and the Ghetto,* 281–282. See also Dubin, "The Moral Continuum of Deviancy Research," 75–94.

39. *CD,* May 15, 1913.

40. Ibid. Folded into the settlements' concern with adolescence was the teaching of "social hygiene," a combination of moral talks, physical hygiene, and sex education. Many of the ethnic settlements in Chicago dispensed such information through physicians, visiting nurses, settlement workers, and club women. Often such lessons were taught in domestic classes and the youth clubs. See Clarke, "Social Hygiene in Settlement Work," 383–434. Although I found no such activities in Chicago, the Tuskegee Women's Club did establish "social purity clubs" for young girls, as did some of the African American YWCAs. See Richings, *Evidence of Progress among Colored People,* 198; Batterham, "Negro Girls and the Y.M.C.A.," 439. Mothers' lectures were also given on "social and sex hygiene" at the Mary Walton Free Kindergarten for Colored Children (formerly the Free Kindergarten Association for Colored Children) in New York. See Scheiner, *Negro Mecca,* 147–148.

41. *BA,* April 11, 1914.

42. *BA,* February 14, February 28, 1914.

43. *CD,* March 27, January 23, 1915. Although Hine has astutely suggested that boys' clubs were formed to protect young girls, there is greater evidence that the boys' clubs were formed to offset the growing number of delinquent boys brought before the juvenile court. My preliminary research into the juvenile court's deliberations on African American boys and girls indicates that many dependent children were classified as delinquent in part because facilities were unavailable to them unless they were classified as such. Additionally, there were more settlement clubs and classes for girls than for boys in Chicago. From an early age girls were socialized into future roles as mothers and keepers of the home. Hine cited in Gordon, "Black and White Visions of Welfare," 579.

44. *BA,* July 20, 1913. Wells, in her earlier days at Memphis, had also established a club for young men there. See Decosta-Willis, *The Memphis Diary of Ida B. Wells.*

45. *CD,* January 13, 1916.

46. *CD,* August 14, 1915, February 19, 1916.

47. *CD,* September 6, 1913.

48. *CD*, February 28, 1920.

49. F. B. Williams, "Industrial Education," 492.

50. Burroughs, *Ten Reasons Why We Should Have a Trade School;* Burroughs, "Industrial Education," 188–190; Haynes, "Negroes in Domestic Service," 384–442. For further information on Burroughs, see Higginbotham, *Righteous Discontent,* 211–221; Barnett, "Nannie Burroughs and the Education of Black Women," 97–108. For recent scholarship on the increased professionalization of domestic work, see Neverdon-Morton, *Afro-American Women of the South;* Powers, *The 'Girl Question' in Education.* For excellent histories of African American women's employment as domestic workers, see Burgess and Horton, "African American Women and Work," 53–63; Harley, "When Your Work Is Not Who You Are," 42–55.

51. *CD*, October 18, 1913.

52. *CD*, May 31, August 9, November 1, 1913.

53. *CD*, May 31, December 22, 1913.

54. On classes and programs at the Wendell Phillips Settlement, see Grossman, *Land of Hope,* 140, 143; Spear, *Black Chicago,* 105, 171, 174; *CD,* May, 20, 1911; *BA,* September 29, 1916. Information on the Frederick Douglass Center's classes was published in the weekly columns of the *CD* and the *BA.* Further information on the center is available in Bowen, *Colored People of Chicago;* F. B. Williams, "The Frederick Douglass Centre," 602–603; F. B. Williams, "Social Bonds in the 'Black Belt' of Chicago," 40–44.

55. Crocker, *Social Work and Social Order,* 88–93.

56. Ibid., 186–197. For the situation in Chicago, see Wright, Jr., "The Negro in Times of Industrial Unrest," 69–73; Grossman, *Land of Hope,* chap. 7.

57. *CD*, January 13, 1916.

58. *CD*, September 20, 1913.

59. Spear, *Black Chicago,* 170.

60. Duster, *Crusade for Justice,* 372.

61. Strickland, *History of the Chicago Urban League,* 34. See also *BA,* December 22, 1917; Urban League Annual Reports, box 1, folders 1–3, 67. Chicago Commission, "The Migration of Negroes from the South, 1916–1918," 44–45.

62. Weiss, *The National Urban League, 1910–1940,* 88–89.

NOTES TO CHAPTER 6

1. Here I refer to Gates's notion of "speakerly text," wherein written texts are related to oral discourse through the metaphoric and rhetorical use of signifying. See Gates, *The Signifying Monkey.*

2. Porter, "The Organized Educational Activities of Negro Literary Societies, 1828–1846," 555–576.

3. Yee, *Black Women Abolitionists,* 62. Such morality dovetailed with the club women's visions of mother and home life. As the character Iola Leroy in Harper's book exclaimed religiously in one of her papers delivered before a parlor group, "Prisons would not be as full if there were moral homes." See *Iola*

Leroy. Harper's novels were not the only ones to emphasize young women's moral character and respectability. See Johnson, *The Hazeley Family;* and Johnson, *Clarence and Corinne.*

4. Cited in Lerner, *Black Women in White America,* 438–439.

5. Sterling, *We Are Your Sisters,* 107–108.

6. Ibid., 110–111.

7. See Ripley et al., *Witness for Freedom,* which documents African American abolitionism and the antislavery movement.

8. Ripley et al., *Witness for Freedom.* See McDowell's astute essay on the novel *Iola Leroy,* in which she noted that public speaking is represented by men and that Iola's talk is shaped as "carefully reasoned oration" (97). McDowell, "'The Changing Same,'" 91–115.

9. Bode, *The American Lyceum,* 19.

10. Ibid., 22.

11. Richmond, *Chautauqua,* 26, 29. Katherine Tillman noted how elocution was one arena in which African American women excelled, citing the examples of Hallie Q. Brown, Henrietta Vinton Davis, and Ednorah Nahar. She also provided examples of notable African American female speakers, including Fannie Jackson Coppin, Ida B. Wells, Mrs. Rodgers Webb, and Frances Harper. See Tillman, "Afro-American Women and Their Work," 84–85.

12. Gates, *The Signifying Monkey,* 66. Huggins noted the diversity of Douglass's topics on the lecture circuit, which included "Hittites, Galileo, Scandinavian history, and sagas from Iceland." See Huggins, *Slave and Citizen,* 128.

13. Mead, *Yankee Eloquence in the Middle West,* 227.

14. Bode, *The American Lyceum,* 96–97.

15. Scott, *Natural Allies,* 118–120. For further history on the Chicago Woman's Club, see Hard, *The Women of Tomorrow,* chap. 5; Croly, *The History of the Woman's Club Movement.*

16. Woodson, *The History of the Negro Church,* 247.

17. Montgomery, *Under Their Own Vine and Fig Tree,* 300–303.

18. Woodson, *The History of the Negro Church,* 245–246. Loggins, in his book, featured writers of oratory, histories, and sociological treatises, many of whom were ministers. See *The Negro Author.* As in earlier anthologies, mostly male writers were featured.

19. Daniels, *In Freedom's Birthplace,* 203–204.

20. Higginbotham, *Righteous Discontent.*

21. Morrison, *Chautauqua,* 96.

22. Case and Case, *We Called It Culture,* 74.

23. Morrison, *Chautauqua,* 94; Richmond, *Chautauqua,* 26, 29, 65, 112.

24. Morrison, *Chautauqua,* 166.

25. See Pratt, "Chautauqua Summer Kindergarten," 72–77; "The First Summer School for Parents Held in Chautauqua, N.Y.," 1–8. Many of the Chicago kindergartners, such as Mary Louise Butler, also taught in the kindergarten department at Chautauqua, New York, during the summer. Richmond, *Chautauqua,* 114–116.

26. *BA,* June 9, 17, 1906.

27. Rev. Mary Lark Hill was known in Chicago as an evangelist, a composer of camp meeting songs, and a successful cafe owner. In 1905 she founded the Queen Esther Mission at 5040 State Street. The mission's Sunday services of preaching, platform meetings, and children's preaching were conducted by females only. In 1906 she became pastor of the Queen Esther Church, the first church of the Women's Evangelistic Union of America. See *BA,* October 31, 1903, June 17, 1905, December 1, 1906. For further information on women preachers, see Dodson, "Nineteenth-Century A.M.E. Preaching Women," 276–289; Lincoln and Mamiya, *The Black Church,* chap. 10; Krueger, *The Reader's Repentance.*

28. J. Washington, "What the Club Does for the Club-Woman," 222.

29. Gatewood, *Aristocrats of Color,* 241.

30. The same held true for church lyceums, where classical works of Mozart, Beethoven, or Mendelssohn were usually performed by soloists, whereas choruses, choirs, and quartets sang the more popular African American pieces, including hymns, spirituals, jubilee songs, and plantation melodies.

31. See Carson, *Settlement Folk,* particularly for the influence of Ruskin.

32. *BA,* November 11, 1905, March 10, 1906, January 10, 1914; *CD,* April 26, 1919.

33. Wood, *The Negro in Chicago,* 16.

34. For examples of literary study of Illinois clubs, including those in Chicago, see those listed under Illinois in Croly, *The History of the Woman's Club Movement,* 381–430. The Hull House Woman's Club occasionally discussed ethnic literature and issues. At one meeting Ida B. Wells spoke on "Social Prejudice"; at another meeting, under the theme of "Living Great Americans," Booker T. Washington's accomplishments were discussed alongside those of Theodore Roosevelt, Thomas Edison, and Jacob Riis. See Hull House Association Records, Hull-House Bulletins 3:5, 7:9–11.

35. Martin, *The Sound of Our Own Voices,* 108.

36. Croly, *The History of the Woman's Club Movement,* 410–413.

37. Ibid., 383–386, 415–416.

38. *BA,* March 25, 1911.

39. *BA,* January 10, 1914. For examples of Forston's poetry, see *BA,* August 1, 1914.

40. *CD,* May 20, 1911; *BA,* March 7, 1914; *CD,* November 18, 1916, January 27, 1917.

41. *CD,* November 18, 1916, September 1, 22, 1917, July 22, 1916.

42. *BA,* November 25, 1905.

43. *BA,* March 24, 10, February 3, 1906.

44. *CD,* April 28, 1917; *BA,* April 25, 1914; *CD,* May 31, 1913; *BA,* December 2, 1913; *CD,* November 29, 1913.

45. *BA,* November 11, 1905, January 20, 1906.

46. *CD,* November 29, 1913.

47. *BA,* January 20, 1906.

48. *BA,* May 5, 1906; *CD,* November 12, 1910, April 29, 1916; F. B. Williams, *The Colored Woman and Her Part in Race Regeneration,* 417.

49. *BA,* November 4, 1899.

50. *BA,* November 11, 1899.

51. *CD,* October 11, November 15, 1913; *BA,* December 1, 1900; *CD,* February 2, 1918. Two of Mrs. E. W. Wright's novels have recently been discovered and published. See Wright, *Black and White Tangled Threads; Kenneth.*

52. *BA,* January 8, 1916.

53. *CD,* January 27, 1917.

54. *CD,* June 28, 1913.

55. Matthews cited in Johnson, *Clarence and Corinne,* xvi.

56. Gatewood, *Aristocrats of Color,* 175–177.

57. *CD,* August 2, 1913.

58. *BA,* July 9, 1913.

59. *CD,* May 31, 1913.

60. *CD,* September 14, 1918.

61. *BA,* April 15, 1905.

62. *CD,* January 1, 1910.

63. *CD,* August 31, September 7, February 23, 1912; *BA,* April 26, 1913.

64. *CD,* January 23, 1915.

65. Holt, "Influence of Lyceums," *CD,* October 26, 1918. Nora D. Holt was a composer and music critic who wrote for the *Chicago Defender.*

66. *CD,* October 9, 1920. I was unable to locate any studies on youth lyceums or other church clubs for youth during this time period. Mays and Nicholson, in *The Negro's Church,* do give some attention to youth clubs in the 1930s, especially recreational clubs, in chapter 9. Also, Drake and Cayton examine church life in the African American communities of Chicago during the 1930s. See chapters 8 and 9, *Black Metropolis,* wherein great concern is expressed over the waning interest of youth in the church.

67. *CD,* June 2, 1917.

68. *CD,* November 9, 1918.

69. *BA,* February 17, 1905.

70. *CD,* March 9, 1918. The essay contests were not unlike those that Brady documented in Kansas during the 1920s. See Brady, "Organizing Afro-American Girls' Clubs in Kansas," 69–73. See also *CD,* March 18, 1905; *BA,* May 25, 1912.

71. *CD,* November 3, 1917, May 24, 1919.

72. *CD,* December 22, 1913. The essay contests were elaborate affairs and included the participation of more than forty women in committees on advertisements, decorations, music, and ushering. See *BA,* December 15, 1917.

73. *BA,* January 10, 1914.

74. Du Bois, *The Negro Church,* 85.

75. Woodson, *The History of the Negro Church,* 250.

NOTES TO CHAPTER 7

1. Burroughs cited in Gatewood, *Aristocrats of Color,* 245.
2. Tillman, "Afro-American Women and Their Work," 90.
3. Hunton, "The National Association of Colored Women," 418.
4. Gatewood, *Aristocrats of Color,* 211–212.
5. *BA,* April 29, 1905.
6. *BA,* February 29, 1908.
7. *BA,* April 29, 1905.
8. *BA,* May 13, 1905. For biographical information on Mrs. George Hall, see *BA,* May 20, 1905.
9. *BA,* May 13, 1905.
10. *BA,* May 5, 1905.
11. *BA,* June 23, 30, July 7, 21, 1905.
12. *BA,* January 8, 1909.
13. *BA,* June 13, 1907.
14. *CD,* November 1, 1913.
15. *CD,* October 8, 1910.
16. *CD,* March 4, 1910.
17. See Gatewood, *Aristocrats of Color,* chap. 7.
18. *CD,* February 23 1912; *BA,* June 6, 1908.
19. Tillman, "Afro-American Women and Their Work," 81–82; Tillman, "Paying Professions for Colored Girls," 118–119.
20. "Tillman, "Paying Professions for Colored Girls," 118–119.
21. Dunham, *A Touch of Innocence,* 129–132.
22. Vivian Harsh Collection, Illinois Writers Project, "The Negro in Illinois," box 25, folder 4; *CD,* May 4, 1918.
23. *BA,* December 27, 1902, December 30, 1905.
24. *CD,* March 3, 1917.
25. *CD,* March 3, 10, 1917.
26. *CD,* March 19, 1910.
27. *BA,* December 25, 1905.
28. *BA,* March 21, 1914. Banner estimated that by 1909 there were a number of manicuring parlors and well over sixty beauty shops along downtown State Street. By 1890 there were 9,000 female hairdressers nationally; by 1907 the number had leapt to more than 36,000. Banner, *American Beauty,* 215–216.
29. Vivian Harsh Collection, Illinois Writers Project, "The Negro in Illinois," box 25, folders 5, 6.
30. *CD,* October 14, 1919.
31. *BA,* May 14, 1911.
32. *BA,* May 4, 1918.
33. *CD,* October 26, 1918.
34. For further information on home dressmaking, see Fernandez, "Innovations for Home Dressmaking," 23–34.

35. Most of the members of the whist clubs resided in neighborhoods between 3100 and 3800 Streets, and between 4300 and 5300 Wabash. There were several youth whist clubs, including the Junior League Social Club, the Junior Half-Century Clubs, and the Junior Swastika Girls' Clubs.

36. *BA,* March 14, 1914.

37. *BA,* April 11, 1914.

38. *BA,* April 25, 1914.

39. *BA,* November 27, 1914.

40. *BA,* May 9, 1903.

41. *BA,* February 21, 1914.

42. *BA,* August 31, 1913.

43. *CD,* May 20, 1916.

44. *BA,* August 11, 1906.

45. *CD,* August 12, 1916.

46. *CD,* April 24, 1915.

47. *CD,* August 7, 1915.

48. *BA,* February 23, 1912.

49. *CD,* March 20, 1915.

50. *CD,* October 11, 1913.

51. *BA,* February 28, 1914.

52. *BA,* March 14, 1914.

53. *CD,* January 2, 1915.

54. *CD,* January 8, 1916, August 11, February 17, November 3, 24, 1917.

55. *CD,* June 8, 1918.

56. *CD,* January 27, 1917.

57. *CD,* February 2, 9, 1918.

58. *CD,* November 29, August 30, 1913.

59. *BA,* May 9, 1914.

60. Drake and Cayton, *Black Metropolis,* 688.

61. Ibid., 689–690.

62. Ibid., 693.

NOTES TO CONCLUSION

1. *Chicago Tribune,* March 3, 1994, sec. 1, p. 20.

2. Ibid.

3. Ibid., February 12, 1995, sec. 2, p. 4.

4. Ibid., May 7, 1995, sec. 2, p. 3; *CD,* November 8, 1993, p. 5.

5. Duneier, *Slim's Table.*

6. *Chicago Tribune,* August 13, 1995, sec. 2, pp. 1–3.

7. Ibid.

8. Ibid., December 19, 1994, sec. 1, p. 8.

BIBLIOGRAPHY

MANUSCRIPT COLLECTIONS

Chicago Historical Society, Chicago
  Chicago Woman's Club Records, 1894–1900
  Harris Gaines Collection
  Irene McCoy Gaines Collection
Evanston Historical Society, Evanston, Illinois
  Evanston Community Hospital File
  Iroquois League File
Harold Washington Library, Chicago
  Carter Woodson Regional Library, Vivian Harsh Collection. Illinois Writers Project,
    "The Negro in Illinois"
  Cook County Juvenile Court Annual Reports, 1901–1920
  Municipal Reference Collection
Joseph Regenstein Library, University of Chicago
  Julius Rosenwald Papers
  Ida B. Wells Papers
National Louis University, Evanston
  Elizabeth Harrison Papers
University of Illinois at Chicago
  Mary Bartelme Papers

Hull House Association Records
Illinois Children's Home and Aid Society Records
Jane Dent Home for Aged Colored People Papers
Juvenile Protective Association Papers
Phyllis Wheatley Association Papers
Urban League Annual Reports, 1917–1920

NEWSPAPERS AND JOURNALS

Broad Ax (Chicago)
Chicago Defender
Chicago Tribune
The Colored American Magazine
Co-operation Magazine
The Crisis
Half-Century Magazine
The Southern Workman
Voice of the Negro

PUBLISHED SOURCES

Abbott, Edith, and Sophonisba Breckinridge. *The Administration of the Aid-to-Mothers Law in Illinois.* Washington, D.C.: Government Printing Office, 1921. Reprint, New York: Arno Press and *New York Times,* 1972.

———. *The Tenements of Chicago, 1908–1935.* Chicago: University of Chicago Press. 1936. Reprint, New York: Arno Press, 1970 (page references are to the reprint edition).

———. *Truancy and Non-Attendance in the Chicago Schools.* Chicago: University of Chicago Press, 1917.

Abramovitz, Mimi. *Regulating the Lives of Women. Social Welfare Policy from Colonial Times to the Present.* Boston: South End Press, 1988.

Addams, Jane. *The Spirit of Youth and the City Streets.* 1909. Reprint, Urbana: University of Illinois Press, 1972.

———. *Twenty Years at Hull-House.* Urbana: University of Illinois Press, 1990.

Alexander, William T. *History of the Colored Race in America.* 1887. Reprint, New York: Negro University Press, 1968 (page references are to the reprint edition).

Anderson, James D. *The Education of Blacks in the South, 1860–1936.* Chapel Hill: University of North Carolina Press, 1988.

Aptheker, Bettina. *Woman's Legacy: Essays on Race, Sex, and Class in American History.* Amherst: University of Massachusetts Press, 1982.

Aptheker, Herbert, ed. "The National Association of Colored Women, 1904." In *A Documentary History of the Negro People in the United States.* Vol. 2. New York: Citadel Press, 1968.

Baker, Ray Stannard. *Following the Color Line. An Account of Negro Citizenship in the American Democracy.* New York: Doubleday, Page, 1908.

Banner, Lois. *American Beauty.* New York: Alfred A. Knopf, 1983.

Barnett, Evelyn. "Nannie Burroughs and the Education of Black Women." In *The Afro-American Woman: Struggles and Images,* edited by Sharon Harley and Rosalyn Terborg-Penn, 97–108. Port Washington, N.Y.: Kennikat Press, 1978.

Barrett, Jane Porter. "Social Settlement for Colored People." *Southern Workman* 41 (September 1912): 511–518.

Batterham, E. Rose. "Negro Girls and the Y.M.C.A." *The Southern Workman* 48 (1919): 437–441.

Bederman, Gail. " 'Civilization,' the Decine of Middle-Class Manliness, and Ida B. Wells's Antilynching Campaign (1892–94)." *Radical History Review* 52 (1991): 5–30.

Benson, Susan Porter. *Counter Cultures. Salewomen, Managers, and Customers in American Department Stores, 1890–1940.* Urbana: University of Illinois Press, 1988.

Blauvelt, Mary Taylor. "The Race Problem As Discussed by Negro Women." *American Journal of Sociology* 6 (1900–1901): 662–672.

Bode, Carl. *The American Lyceum.* Carbondale: Southern Illinois University Press, 1968.

Bogue, Mary F. *Administration of Mothers' Aid in Ten Localities.* Washington, D.C.: Department of Labor, Children's Bureau, 1928.

Boris, Eileen. "Reconstructing the 'Family': Women, Progressive Reform, and the Problem of Social Control." In *Gender, Class, Race, and Reform in the Progressive Era,* edited by Noralee Frankel and Nancy S. Dye, 73–86. Lexington: University Press of Kentucky, 1991.

Bowen, Louise de Koven. *The Colored People of Chicago.* Chicago: Juvenile Protective Association, 1913.

―――. *Our Most Popular Recreation Controlled by the Liquor Interests.* Chicago: Juvenile Protective Association, 1911.

―――. *The Public Dance Halls of Chicago.* Chicago: Juvenile Protective Association, 1917.

―――. *Safeguards for City Youth at Work and at Play.* New York: Macmillan, 1914.

Bowen, Mrs. Joseph T. (Louise de Koven). "The Early Days of the Juvenile Court." In *The Child, the Clinic, and the Court,* 298–309. New York: New Republic, 1925.

Brady, Marilyn Dell. "Organizing Afro-American Girls' Clubs in Kansas in the 1920s." *Frontier* 9, 2 (1987): 69–73.

Branham, Charles. "Black Chicago: Accommodationist Politics before the Great Migration." In *The Ethnic Frontier. Group Survival in Chicago and the Midwest,* edited by Melvin Holli and Peter d'A. Jones, 212–262. Grand Rapids: William B. Eerdmans, 1977.

Brawley, Benjamin. *Negro Builders and Heroes.* Chapel Hill: University of North Carolina Press, 1939.

————. *Women of Achievement*. Chicago: Women's Baptist Home Mission Society, 1919.

Breckinridge, Sophonisba P. "The Color Line in the Housing Problem." *Survey* 39 (February 1, 1913): 575–576.

Breckinridge, Sophonisba, and Edith Abbott. *The Delinquent Child and the Home.* New York: Charities Publication Committee, 1912.

Bremner, Robert. *Children and Youth in America.* Vol. 2. Cambridge: Harvard University Press, 1970–74.

Brown, Elsa Barkley. "Womanist Consciousness: Maggie Lena Walker and the Independent Order of Saint Luke." In *Unequal Sisters: A Multicultural Reader in U.S. Women's History,* edited by Ellen Carol DuBois and Vicki L. Ruiz, 208–223. New York: Routledge, 1990.

Brown, Hallie Q. *Homespun Heroines and Other Women of Distinction.* 1926. Reprint, New York: Oxford University Press, 1988 (page references are to the reprint edition).

Bruce, Mrs. Blanche K. "Colored Women's Clubs." *The Crisis* 10 (August 1915): 190.

Buechler, Steven M. *The Transformation of the Woman Suffrage Movement: The Case of Illinois, 1850–1920.* New Brunswick, N.J.: Rutgers University Press, 1986.

Burgess, Norma J., and Hayward Derrick Horton. "African American Women and Work: A Socio-Historical Perspective." *Journal of Family History* 18, 1 (1993): 53–63.

Burroughs, Nannie. "Black Women and Reform." *The Crisis* 10 (August 1915): 187.

————. "Industrial Education—Will It Solve the Negro Problem?" *The Colored American Magazine* (March 1904): 188–190.

————. *Ten Reason Why We Should Have a Trade School for Girls.* Washington, D.C., n.p., n.d.

Campbell, Karlyn Kohrs. *Women Public Speakers in the United States, 1800–1925. A Biocritical Sourcebook.* Westport, Conn.: Greenwood Press, 1993.

Carlson, Shirley J. "Black Ideals of Womanhood in the Late Victorian Era." *Journal of Negro History* 77 (Spring 1992): 61–73.

Carlton-LaNey, Iris. "The Career of Birdye Henrietta Haynes, A Pioneer Settlement House Worker." *Social Service Review* 68 (June 1994): 259–263.

Carson, Mina. *Settlement Folk. Social Thought and the American Settlement Movement, 1885–1930.* Chicago: University of Chicago Press, 1990.

Case, Victoria, and Robert O. Case. *We Called It Culture. The Story of Chautauqua.* Garden City, N.Y.: Doubleday, 1948.

Chestnutt, Charles W. "Women's Rights." *The Crisis* 10 (August 1915): 182–183.

Chicago Commission on Race Relations. "The Migration of Negroes from the South, 1916–1918." In *The Rise of the Ghetto,* edited by John H. Bracey, Jr., August Meier, and Elliott Rudwick, 44–56. Belmont, Calif.: Wadsworth, 1971.

————. *The Negro in Chicago. A Study of Race Relations and a Race Riot in 1919.* 1922. Reprint, New York: Arno Press and *New York Times,* 1968 (page references are to the reprint edition).

Chicago Northern District Association. *The Story of Seventy-Five Years of the Chicago and Northern District of Club Women, Inc., 1906–1981.* Chicago: Chicago Northern District Association, 1981.

Clarke, Walter. "Social Hygiene in Settlement Work." *Journal of Social Hygiene* 2 (July 1916): 383–434.

Clifford, Carrie. "Votes for Children." *The Crisis* 10 (August 1915): 185.

Collins, Patricia Hill. *Black Feminist Thought.* New York: Routledge, 1990.

Collins, Randall. *Three Sociological Traditions.* New York: Oxford University Press, 1985.

Comstock, Alzada. "Chicago Housing Conditions, 6: The Problem of the Negro." *American Journal of Sociology* 18 (September 1912): 241–257.

Cooper, Anna J. "The Colored Woman Should Not Be Ignored." In *Black Women in White America,* edited by Gerda Lerner, 572–576. New York: Vintage Books, 1972.

————. *A Voice from the South, by a Black Woman of the South.* Xenia, Ohio: Aldine Press, 1892.

Cott, Nancy F. *Bonds of Womanhood. "Woman's Sphere" in New England, 1780–1835.* New Haven, Conn.: Yale University Press, 1977.

Cripps, Thomas R. "The Reaction of the Negro to the Motion Picture *Birth of a Nation."* *The Historian* 25 (May 1963): 344–362.

Crocker, Ruth Hutchinson. *Social Work and Social Order. The Settlement Movement in Two Industrial Cities, 1889–1930.* Urbana: University of Illinois Press, 1992.

Croly, Jennie J. *The History of the Woman's Club Movement in America.* New York: Henry G. Allen, 1898.

Cromwell, Adelaide M. *The Other Brahmins. Boston's Black Upper Class, 1750–1950.* Fayetteville: University of Arkansas Press, 1994.

Crummell, Alexander, ed. "The Black Woman of the South: Her Neglects and Her Needs." In *Africa and America: Addresses and Discourses,* 61–82. 1891. Reprint, New York: Negro Universities Press, 1969.

Culp, D. W., ed. *Twentieth Century Negro Literature. A Cyclopedia of Thought. Vital Topics Relating to the American Negro by One Hundred of America's Greatest Negroes.* Naperville, Ill.: J. L. Nichols, 1902.

Daniel, Sadie Iola. *Women Builders.* Washington, D.C.: Associated Press, 1931.

Daniels, John. *In Freedom's Birthplace. A Study of Boston Negroes.* Boston: Houghton Mifflin, 1914.

Davis, Allen F. *Spearheads for Reform. The Social Settlements and the Progressive Movement, 1890–1914.* 2d ed. New Brunswick, N.J.: Rutgers University Press, 1984.

Davis, Allen F., and Mary McCree, eds. *Eighty Years at Hull-House.* Chicago: Quadrangle Books, 1969.

Davis, Angela Y. *Women, Race, and Class.* New York: Random House, 1981.

Davis, Elizabeth Lindsay. *Lifting As They Climb*. Boston: National League of Afro-American Women League, 1895.

Decosta-Willis, Miriam. *The Memphis Diary of Ida B. Wells*. Boston: Beacon Press, 1995.

Dempsey, Travis. *An Autobiography of Black Chicago*. Chicago: Urban Research Institute, 1981.

de Priest, Oscar. "Chicago and Woman's Suffrage." *The Crisis* 10 (August 1915): 179.

Dickson, Lynda F. "Toward a Broader Angle of Vision in Uncovering Women's History: Black Women's Clubs Revisited." In *Black Women in United States History: From Colonial Times through the Nineteenth Century,* edited by Darlene Clark Hine, Elsa Barkley Brown, Tiffany R. L. Patterson, and Lillian S. Williams. Vol. 9, 103–119. Brooklyn, N.Y.: Carlson, 1990.

Dill, Bonnie Thornton. "The Dialectics of Black Womanhood." *Signs* 4, 3 (1979): 543–555.

Diner, Steven J. "Chicago Social Workers and Blacks in the Progressive Era." *Social Service Review* 44 (December 1970): 393–410.

Dodson, Jualynee. "Nineteenth-Century A.M.E. Preaching Women." In *Women in the New Worlds,* edited by Hilah F. Thomas and Rosemary Skinner Keller, 276–289. Nashville, Tenn.: Abingdon, 1981.

Drake, St. Clair. *Churches and Voluntary Associations in the Chicago Negro Community.* Chicago: Work Projects Administration, 1940.

Drake, St. Clair, and Horace R. Cayton. *Black Metropolis. A Study in the Negro Life in a Northern City.* New York: Harcourt, Brace, 1945.

Dubin, Steven C. "The Moral Continuum of Deviancy Research: Chicago Sociologists and the Dance Hall." *Urban Life* 12 (April 1983): 75–94.

Du Bois, W. E. B. *The Black North in 1901. A Social Study.* New York: Arno Press and *New York Times,* 1969.

———. *Souls of Black Folk.* 1903. Reprint, New York: Penguin Books, 1989.

———. "Votes for Women." *The Crisis* 4 (September 1912): 234.

———, ed. *Efforts for Social Betterment among Negro Americans.* Atlanta: Atlanta University Press, 1909.

———, ed. *The Negro Church.* Atlanta: Atlanta University Press, 1903.

Duke, Charles S. *The Housing Situation and the Colored People of Chicago.* Chicago, 1919.

Dulaney, W. Marvin. *Black Police in America.* Bloomington: Indiana University Press, 1996.

Dunbar, Alice. "A Kindergarten Club." *The Southern Workman* 32 (1903): 386–390.

Duneier, Mitchell. *Slim's Table. Race, Respectability, and Masculinity.* Chicago: University of Chicago Press, 1992.

Dunham, Katherine. *A Touch of Innocence: Memoirs of Childhood.* Chicago: University of Chicago Press, 1959.

Duster, Alfreda M., ed. *Crusade for Justice. The Autobiography of Ida B. Wells.* Chicago: University of Chicago Press, 1970.

Emerson, Helena Titus. "Children of the Circle: The Work of the New York Free Kindergarten Association for Colored Children." *Charities* 15 (October 1905): 81–83.

Evans, Sara M. *Born for Liberty. A History of Women in America.* New York: Free Press, 1989.

———. "Women's History and Political Theory: Toward a Feminist Approach to Public Life." In *Visible Women. New Essays on American Activism,* edited by Nancy A. Hewitt and Suzanne Lebsock, 119–140. Urbana: University of Illinois Press, 1993.

Evans, William L. "The Negro in Chicago Industries." *Opportunity* (January 1923): 15–16.

Fernandez, Nancy. "Innovations for Home Dressmaking and the Popularization of Stylish Dress." *Journal of American Culture* 17 (Fall 1994): 23–34.

"The First Summer School for Parents Held in Chautauqua, N.Y." *Kindergarten Magazine* 12 (September 1899): 1–8.

Fisher, Miles Mark. "Negro Church in Illinois: A Fragmentary History with Emphasis on Chicago." *Illinois State Historical Society Journal* 56 (Fall 1963): 552–569.

Fitzpatrick, Ellen. *Endless Crusade. Women Social Scientists and Progressive Reform.* Oxford: Oxford University Press, 1990.

Flexnor, Eleanor. *Century of Struggle.* Rev. ed. Cambridge, Mass.: Harvard University Press, 1975.

Frazier, E. Franklin. "Chicago Black Belt: Residential Patterns and Social Class." In *The Rise of the Ghetto,* edited by John H. Bracey, Jr., August Meier, and Elliott Rudwick, 70–80. Belmont, Calif.: Wadsworth, 1971.

Freeman, Eunice P. "The Home-Making Arts." *The Colored American Magazine* 13 (December 1907): 427–428.

Friedman, Lawrence. *White Savage, Racial Fantasies in the Post-Bellum South.* Englewood Cliffs, N.J.: Prentice-Hall, 1970.

Fuell, Melissa. "The Value of Domestic Science." *The Colored American Magazine* 13 (September 1901): 429–430.

Gaines, Kevin K. *Uplifting the Race. Black Leadership, Politics, and Culture in the Twentieth Century.* Chapel Hill: University of North Carolina Press, 1996.

Gates, Henry Louis. *The Signifying Monkey. A Theory of Afro-American Criticism.* New York: Oxford University Press. 1988.

———, ed. *Reading Black, Reading Feminist.* New York: Meridian, 1990.

Gatewood, Willard B. *Aristocrats of Color: The Black Elite, 1880–1920.* Bloomington: Indiana University Press, 1990.

Gerth, H. H., and C. Wright Mills. *From Max Weber: Essays in Sociology.* New York: Oxford University Press, 1946.

Gibbs, Ione. "Woman's Part in the Uplift of the Negro Race." *The Colored American Magazine* 3 (March 1907): 264–267.

Giddings, Paula. *When and Where I Enter. The Impact of Black Women on Race and Sex in America.* New York: William Morrow, 1984.

Gilkes, Cheryl Townsend. " 'Holding Back the Ocean with a Broom':

Black Women and Community Work." In *The Black Woman,* edited by La Frances Rodgers-Rose, 217–231. Beverly Hills, Calif.: Sage Publications, 1980.

———. "Liberated to Work Like Dogs! Labeling Black Women and Their Work." In *The Experience and Meaning of Work. Women's Lives,* edited by Hildreth Y. Grossmen and Nia Lane Chester, 165–188. Hillsdale, N.J.: Lawrence Erlbaum Associates, 1990.

Gittens, Joan. *Poor Relations. The Children of the State of Illinois, 1818–1990.* Urbana: University of Illinois Press, 1994.

Goodwin, Joanne. "An Experiment in Paid Motherhood: The Implementation of Mothers' Pensions in Early Twentieth-Century Chicago." *Gender and History* 4 (Autumn 1992): 323–343.

Gordon, Linda. "Black and White Visions of Welfare: Women's Welfare Activism, 1890–1945." *Journal of American History* 78 (February 1991): 559–590.

———. *Pitied but Not Entitled. Single Mothers and the History of Welfare.* New York: Free Press, 1994.

Graves, Mrs. A. "Motherhood." *The Colored American Magazine* 14 (September 1908): 395–396.

Grimke, Francis. "The Logic of Woman Suffrage." *The Crisis* 10 (August 1915): 178–179.

Grossman, James R. *Land of Hope: Chicago, Black Southerners, and the Great Migration.* Chicago: University of Chicago Press, 1989.

Guy-Sheftall, Beverly. *Daughters of Sorrow. Attitudes toward Black Women, 1880–1920.* Vol 11 of *Black Women in United States History: From Colonial Times through the Nineteenth Century,* edited by Darlene Clark Hine, Elsa Barkley Brown, Tiffany R. L. Patterson, and Lillian S. Williams. Brooklyn, N.Y.: Carlson, 1990.

Hard, William. *The Women of Tomorrow.* New York: Doubleday, Page, 1913.

Harley, Sharon. "Beyond the Classroom: Organizational Lives of Black Female Educators in the District of Columbia, 1890–1930." Vol. 2 of *Black Women in United States History: From Colonial Times through the Nineteenth Century,* edited by Darlene Clark Hine, Elsa Barkley Brown, Tiffany R. L. Patterson, and Lillian S. Williams, 475–486. Brooklyn, N.Y.: Carlson, 1990.

———. "For the Good of Family and Race: Gender, Work, and Domestic Roles in the Black Community, 1880–1930." In *Black Women in America. Social Science Perspectives,* edited by Micheline R. Malson, Elisabeth Mudimbe-Bry, Jean F. O. Barr, and Mary Wyer, 159–172. Chicago: University of Chicago Press, 1988.

———. "When Your Work Is Not Who You Are: The Development of a Working-Class Consciousness among Afro-American Women." In *Gender, Class, Race, and Reform in the Progressive Era,* edited by Noralee Frankel and Nancy S. Dye, 42–55. Lexington: University Press of Kentucky, 1991.

Harley, Sharon, and Rosalyn Terborg-Penn, eds. *The Afro-American Woman. Struggles and Images.* Port Washington, N.Y.: Kennikat Press, 1978.

Harper, Frances E. W. *Iola Leroy, or Shadows Uplifted*. New York: Oxford University Press, 1988.

Harrison, Alferdteen, ed. *Black Exodus. The Great Migration from the American South*. Jackson: University Press of Mississippi, 1991.

Harrison, Elizabeth. *A Study of Child-Nature from the Kindergarten Standpoint*. Chicago: Chicago Kindergarten College, 1890.

Haynes, Elizabeth Ross. "Negroes in Domestic Service in the United States." *Journal of Negro History* 8 (October 1923): 384–442.

Head, Elizabeth. *Chicago Social Settlements*. Chicago: Social Settlement Committee, Chicago Woman's Club, 1902.

Hendricks, Wanda A. "Vote for the Advantage of Ourselves and Our Race." *Illinois Historical Journal* 87 (Autumn 1994): 171–184.

Hewitt, Nancy A. "Beyond the Search for Sisterhood: American Women's History in the 1980s." *Social History* 10 (March 1985): 299–321.

Higginbotham, Evelyn Brooks. "Beyond the Sound of Silence: Afro-American Women in History." *Gender and History* 1, 1 (1989): 50–67.

———. *Righteous Discontent. The Women's Movement in the Black Baptist Church, 1880–1920*. Cambridge, Mass.: Harvard University Press, 1993.

Hine, Darlene Clark. *Hine Sight. Black Women and the Re-Construction of American History*. Brooklyn, N.Y.: Carlson, 1994.

———. "Rape and the Inner Lives of Black Women in the Middle West: Preliminary Thoughts on the Culture of Disemblance." *Signs* 14, 4 (1989): 912–920.

Hine, Darlene Clark, Elsa Barkley Brown, Tiffany R. L. Patterson, and Lillian S. Williams, eds. *Black Women in United States History: From Colonial Times to the Present*. 16 vols. Brooklyn, N.Y.: Carlson, 1990.

"Home for Aged Colored People." *Co-operation Magazine* 1 (December 1901): 5–6.

hooks, bell. *Ain't I a Woman. Black Women and Feminism*. Boston: South End Press, 1981.

———. *Black Looks. Race and Representation*. Boston: South End Press, 1992.

Hopkins, Pauline. "Famous Women of the Negro Race." *The Colored American Magazine* 4 (August 1912): 273–277.

Huggins, Nathan Irvin. "Afro-Americans." In *Ethnic Leadership in America*, edited by John Higham, 91–118. Baltimore: Johns Hopkins University Press, 1978.

———. *Slave and Citizen. The Life of Frederick Douglass*. Boston: Little, Brown, 1980.

Hunton, Addie W. "The National Association of Colored Women: Its Real Significance." *The Colored American Magazine* 14 (1908): 417–424.

———. "Women's Clubs: Caring for Children." *The Crisis* 2 (May 1911): 78–79.

Intercollegiate Wonder Book. Vols. 1, 2. Washington, D.C.: Intercollegiate Club of Chicago, 1927.

Jackson, Philip. "Black Charity in Progressive Era Chicago." *Social Service Review* 52 (September 1978): 400–417.

Jeter, Helen Rankin. *The Chicago Juvenile Court.* Chicago: University of Chicago Libraries, 1922.

Johnson, Amelia E. *Clarence and Corinne, or God's Way.* Oxford: Oxford University Press, 1988.

———. *The Hazeley Family.* Philadelphia: American Baptist Publication Society, 1894.

Jones, Anna H. "The American Colored Woman." *Voice of the Negro* 2 (October 1905): 692–694.

———. "A Century's Progress for the American Colored Woman." *Voice of the Negro* 2 (September 1905): 631–633.

———. "Woman Suffrage and Social Reform." *The Crisis* 10 (August 1915): 190.

Jones, Beverly Washington. "Mary Church Terrell and the National Association of Colored Women, 1896–1901." *Journal of Negro History* 67 (Spring 1982): 20–33.

———. *Quest for Equality. The Life and Writings of Mary Eliza Church Terrell, 1863–1954.* Vol. 13 of *Black Women in American History: From Colonial Times through the Nineteenth Century,* edited by Darlene Clark Hine, Elsa Barkley Brown, Tiffany R. L. Patterson, and Lillian S. Williams. Brooklyn, N.Y.: Carlson, 1990.

Jones, Jacqueline. *Labor of Love, Labor of Sorrow.* New York: Vintage Books, 1985.

Jones, Peter d'A., and Melvin G. Holli, eds. *Ethnic Chicago.* Grand Rapids: William B. Eerdmans, 1981.

Jordan, Winthrop D. *White over Black. American Attitudes toward the Negro, 1550–1812.* New York: W. W. Norton, 1977.

Kendrick, Ruby M. " 'They Also Serve': The National Association of Colored Women, Inc., 1895–1954." Vol. 3 of *Black Women in United States History: From Colonial Times through the Nineteenth Century,* edited by Darlene Clark Hine, Elsa Barkley Brown, Tiffany R. L. Patterson, and Lillian S. Williams, 817–825. Brooklyn, N.Y.: Carlson, 1990.

Kerber, Linda. *Women of the Republic: Intellect and Ideology in Revolutionary America.* Chapel Hill: University of North Carolina Press, 1980.

Kletzing, Henry F., and William H. Crogman. *Progress of a Race, or The Remarkable Advancement of the Afro-American.* New York: Negro Universities Press, 1897.

Knupfer, Anne M. "If You Can't Push, Pull, If You Can't Pull, Please Get Out of the Way." *Journal of Negro History,* in press.

———. " 'Toward a Tenderer Humanity and a Nobler Womanhood': African American Women's Clubs in Chicago, 1890 to 1920." *Journal of Women's History* (Fall 1995): 58–76.

Kraditor, Aileen S. *The Ideas of the Woman Suffrage Movement, 1890–1920*. New York: Columbia University Press, 1965.

Kronus, Sidney. *The Black Middle Class*. Columbus: Charles E. Merrill, 1971.

Krueger, Christine L. *The Reader's Repentance. Women Preachers, Women Writers, and Nineteenth-Century Social Discourse*. Chicago: University of Chicago Press, 1992.

Kunzel, Regina G. *Fallen Women, Problem Girls*. New Haven, Conn.: Yale University Press, 1993.

Kusmer, Kenneth L. *A Ghetto Takes Shape. Black Cleveland, 1870–1930*. Urbana: University of Illinois Press, 1976.

Ladd-Taylor, Mollie. *Mother-Work. Women, Child Welfare, and the State, 1890–1930*. Urbana: University of Illinois Press, 1994.

Lammermeier, Paul J. "Cincinnati's Black Community: The Origins of a Ghetto, 1870–1880." In *The Rise of the Ghetto*, edited by John H. Bracey, Jr., August Meier, and Elliott Rudwick, 24–28. Belmont, Calif.: Wadsworth, 1971.

Landry, Bart. *The New Black Middle Class*. Berkeley: University of California Press, 1987.

Lasch-Quinn, Elisabeth. *Black Neighbors. Race and the Limits of Reform in the American Settlement House Movement, 1890–1945*. Chapel Hill: University of North Carolina Press, 1993.

Leff, Mark. "Consensus for Reform: The Mothers'-Pension Movement in the Progressive Era." *Social Service Review* 47 (1973): 397–417.

Lerner, Gerda. "Early Community Work of Black Club Women." *Journal of Negro History* 59 (April 1974): 158–167.

———, ed. *Black Women in White America*. New York: Vintage Books, 1972. Reprint, 1992.

Lewis, Morris. "The Old Folks' Home of Chicago." *The Colored American Magazine* 2 (March 1901): 329–335.

Lincoln, C. Eric, and Lawrence H. Mamiya. *The Black Church in the African American Experience*. Durham, N.C.: Duke University Press, 1990.

Lissack, Rivka Shpak. *Pluralism & Progressives. Hull House and the New Immigrants, 1890–1919*. Chicago: University of Chicago Press, 1989.

Logan, Adella Hunt. "Colored Women as Voters." *The Crisis* 4 (September 1912): 242.

———. "Woman Suffrage." *The Colored American Magazine* 9 (September 1905): 488.

Loggins, Vernon. *The Negro Author. His Development in America to 1900*. Port Washington, N.Y.: Kennikat Press, 1959.

Lou, Herbert. *Juvenile Courts in the United States*. Chapel Hill: University of North Carolina Press, 1927.

"Louise Juvenile Home Opening." *Co-operation Magazine* 40 (October 5, 1907): 339.

Lowenberg, Bert James, and Ruth Bogin, eds. *Black Women in Nineteenth-Century American Life: Their Words, Their Thoughts, Their Feelings.* University Park: Pennsylvania State University Press, 1976.

Lubove, Roy. *The Professional Altruist.* Cambridge, Mass.: Harvard University Press, 1965.

Luker, Ralph E. "Missions, Institutional Churches, and Settlement Houses: The Black Experience, 1885–1910." *Journal of Negro History* 44 (Summer/Fall 1984): 101–113.

Majors, Monroe A. *Noted Negro Women. Their Triumphs and Activities.* 1893. Reprint, Freeport, N.Y.: Books for Libraries Press, 1971 (page references are to the reprint edition).

Marks, Carole. "The Social and Economic Life of Southern Blacks during the Migration." In *Black Exodus. The Great Migration from the American South,* edited by Alferdteen Harrison, 36–50. Jackson: University Press of Mississippi, 1991.

Martin, Penney. *The Sound of Our Own Voices. Women's Study Clubs, 1860–1910.* Boston: Beacon Press, 1987.

Mason, Bettie. "The Suffragette." *Half-Century Magazine* (November 1916): 6.

Massa, Ann. "Black Women in the 'White City.' " *Phylon* 26 (Winter 1965): 354–361.

Massey, Douglas S., and Nancy A. Denton. *American Apartheid: Segregation and the Making of the Underclass.* Cambridge, Mass.: Harvard University Press, 1993.

Mays, Benjamin E., and Joseph W. Nicholson. *The Negro's Church.* New York: Institute of Social and Religious Research, 1933.

McDowell, Deborah E. " 'The Changing Same': Generational Connections and Black Women Novelists." In *Reading Black, Reading Feminist,* edited by Henry Louis Gates, 91–115. New York: Meridian, 1990.

Mead, David. *Yankee Eloquence in the Middle West: The Ohio Lyceum, 1850–1870.* East Lansing: Michigan State College Press, 1951.

Meier, August, and Elliott Rudwick. *From Plantation to Ghetto.* Rev. ed. New York: Hill and Wang, 1966.

Meyerowitz, Joanne J. *Women Adrift. Independent Wage Earners in Chicago, 1880–1930.* Chicago: University of Chicago Press, 1988.

Mjagkij, Nina. *Light in the Darkness. African Americans and the YMCA, 1852–1946.* Lexington: University Press of Kentucky, 1994.

Montgomery, William. *Under Their Own Vine and Fig Tree. The African-American Church in the South 1865–1900.* Baton Rouge: Louisiana State University Press, 1993.

Morrison, Theodore. *Chautauqua: A Center for Education, Religion, and Arts in America.* Chicago: University of Chicago Press, 1974.

Mossell, N. F. *The Work of the Afro-American Woman.* 1894. Reprint, Freeport, N.Y.: Books for Libraries Press, 1971 (page references are to the reprint edition).

Neil, Henry. *Our Little Men and Women. Boy Scouts and Girls Open-Air Clubs.* Chicago: Bible House, 1912.

Neverdon-Morton, Cynthia. *Afro-American Women of the South and the Advancement of the Race, 1895–1925.* Knoxville: University of Tennessee Press, 1985.

Newby, I. A. *Jim Crow's Defense: Anti-Negro Thought in America, 1900–1930.* Baton Rouge: Louisiana University Press, 1965.

Nichols, J. L., and William H. Crogman. *Progress of a Race, or the Remarkable Advancement of the American Negro.* Naperville, Ill.: J. L. Nichols, 1920. Reprint, New York: Arno Press and *New York Times,* 1969 (page references are to the reprint edition).

Noble, Jeanne, ed.. *Beautiful, Also, Are the Souls of My Black Sisters. A History of the Black Woman in America.* Englewood Cliffs, N.J.: Prentice-Hall, 1978.

O'Donnell, Sandra. "The Care of Dependent African-American Children in Chicago: The Struggle between Self-Help and Professionalism." *Journal of Social History* 27 (Summer 1994): 763–776.

Osofsky, Gilbert. *Harlem. The Making of a Ghetto: Negro New York, 1890–1930.* New York: Harper and Row, 1966.

Perkins, Linda M. "The Impact of the 'Cult of True Womanhood' on the Education of Black Women." *Journal of Social Issues* 39 (March 1983): 17–28.

Phelps, Howard A. "Negro Life in Chicago." *Half Century Magazine* 6 (May 1919): 12–14.

Philpott, Thomas. *The Slum and the Ghetto. Immigrants, Blacks, and Reformers in Chicago, 1880–1930.* Belmont, Calif.: Wadsworth, 1991.

Platt, Anthony. *The Child Savers. The Invention of Delinquency.* Chicago: University of Chicago Press, 1969.

Porter, Dorothy. "The Organized Educational Activities of Negro Literary Societies, 1828–1846." *Journal of Negro Education* 5 (October 1936): 555–576.

Powers, Jane Bernard. *The 'Girl Question' in Education. Vocational Education for Young Women in the Progressive Era.* London: Falmer Press, 1992.

Pratt, Alice Day. "Chautauqua Summer Kindergarten." *Kindergarten Magazine* 11 (July 1899): 72–77.

Proceedings of the Conference on the Care of Dependent Children. Washington, D.C.: Government Printing Office, 1909.

Richings, G. F. *Evidence of Progress among Colored People.* 1900. Reprint, Chicago: Afro-American Press, 1969 (page references are to the reprint edition).

Richmond, Rebecca. *Chautauqua: An American Place.* New York: Duell, Sloan, and Pearce, 1943.

Ripley, C. Peter, Roy E. Finkenbine, Michael F. Embree, and Donald Yacovone, eds. *Witness for Freedom. African American Voices on Race, Slavery, and Emancipation.* Chapel Hill: University of North Carolina Press, 1993.

Rouse, Jacqueline A. "Atlanta's African-American Women's Attack on Segregation, 1900–1920." In *Gender, Class, Race, and Reform in the Progressive Era,* edited by Noralee Frankel and Nancy S. Dye, 511–518. Lexington: University Press of Kentucky, 1991.

Ryan, Mary. *Womanhood in America: From Colonial Times to the Present.* New York: New Viewpoints, 1975.

Salem, Dorothy. *To Better Our World. Black Women in Organized Reform, 1890–1920.* Vol. 14 of *Black Women in United States History,* ed. Darlene Clark Hine, Elsa Barkley Brown, Tiffany R. L. Patterson, and Lillian S. Williams. Brooklyn, N.Y.: Carlson, 1990.

Scheiner, Seth M. *Negro Mecca. A History of the Negro in New York City, 1865–1920.* New York: New York University Press, 1965.

Schlossman, Steven L. *Love & the American Delinquent.* Chicago: University of Chicago Press, 1977.

Scott, Anne Firor. *Natural Allies. Women's Associations in American History.* Urbana: University of Illinois Press, 1992.

Shaw, Stephanie J. *What a Woman Ought to Be and to Do: Black Professional Women Workers during the Jim Crow Era.* Chicago: University of Chicago Press, 1996.

Sklar, Kathern Kish. "Hull House in the 1890s: A Community of Women Reformers." *Signs* 10, 4 (1985): 658–677.

Skocpol, Theda. *Protecting Soldiers and Mothers: The Political Origins of Social Policy in the United States.* Cambridge, Mass.: Harvard University Press, 1992.

Smith, Amanda. *An Autobiography of Mrs. Amanda Smith, the Colored Evangelist.* Chicago: Meyer and Brother, 1893.

Smith, Susan Lynn. *"Sick and Tired of Being Sick and Tired": Black Women and the National Negro Health Movement, 1915–1950.* Philadelphia: University of Pennsylvania Press, 1995.

Smith-Rosenberg, Carroll. "The Female World of Love and Ritual: Relations between Women in Nineteenth-Century America." *Signs* 1, 3 (1975): 1–29.

Solomon, Barbara. *In the Company of Educated Women.* New Haven, Conn.: Yale University Press, 1985.

"Some Chicagoans of Note." *The Crisis* 10 (September 1915): 234–242.

Spear, Allan H. *Black Chicago. The Making of a Negro Ghetto, 1890–1920.* Chicago: University of Chicago Press, 1967.

———. "The Rise of the Chicago Black Belt." In *The Rise of the Ghetto,* edited by John H. Bracey, Jr., August Meier, and Elliott Rudwick, 57–69. Belmont, Calif.: Wadsworth, 1971.

Steady, Filomina Chioma, ed. *The Black Woman Cross Culturally.* Cambridge: Schenkman, 1981.

Stehno, Sandra M. "Public Responsibility for Dependent Black Children: The Advocacy of Edith Abbott and Sophonisba Breckinridge." *Social Services Review* 62 (September 1988): 485–503.

Stephens, Judith L. "Anti-Lynching Plays by African American Women: Race, Gender, and Social Protest in American Drama." *African American Review* 26 (Summer 1992): 329–339.

Sterling, Dorothy, ed. *We Are Your Sisters. Black Women in the Nineteenth Century.* New York: W. W. Norton, 1984.

Stovall, Mary E. "The *Chicago Defender* in the Progressive Era." *Illinois Historical Journal* 83 (Autumn 1990): 159–172.

Strickland, Arvarh E. *History of the Chicago Urban League.* Urbana: University of Illinois Press, 1966.

Tate, Claudia, ed. *The Works of Katherine Davis Chapman Tillman.* New York: Oxford University Press, 1991.

Terborg-Penn, Rosalyn. "African-American Women's Networks in the Anti-Lynching Crusade." In *Gender, Class, Race, and Reform in the Progressive Era,* edited by Noralee Frankel and Nancy S. Dye, 148–161. Lexington: University Press of Kentucky, 1991.

———. "Discrimination against Afro-American Women in the Woman's Movement, 1830–1920." In *The Black Woman Cross Culturally,* edited by Filomina Chioma Steady, 301–316. Cambridge: Schenkman, 1981.

———. "The Historical Treatment of Afro-Americans in the Women's Movement, 1900–1920: A Bibliographical Essay." *A Current Bibliography on African Affairs* 7 (1974): 245–259.

Terrell, Mary Church. "The Progress of Colored Women." *Voice of the Negro* 1 (July 1904): 291–294.

Thomas, Hilah F., and Rosemary Skinner Keller. *Women in the New Worlds.* Nashville: Abingdon, 1981.

Thompson, Mildred I. *Ida B. Wells-Barnett: An Exploratory Study of an American-Black Woman, 1893–1930.* Vol. 15 of *Black Women in United States History,* edited by Darlene Clark Hine, Elsa Barkley Brown, Tiffany R. L. Patterson, and Lillian S. Williams. Brooklyn, N.Y.: Carlson, 1990.

Thornbrough, Emma Lou. "The History of Black Women in Indiana." In *Black Women in United States History: From Colonial Times through the Nineteenth Century,* edited by Darlene Clark Hine, Elsa Barkley Brown, Tiffany R. L. Patterson, and Lillian S. Williams. Vol. 10, 645–658. Brooklyn, N.Y.: Carlson, 1990.

Thorne, Barrie, and Marilyn Yalom, eds. *Rethinking the Family. Some Feminist Questions.* New York: Longman, 1982.

Thorne, Jack. *A Plea for Social Justice for the Negro Woman.* New York: Lincoln Press Association, 1912.

Thrasher, Max. *Tuskegee: Its Story and Its Work.* Boston: Small, Maynard, 1901.

Tillman, Katherine Davis Chapman. "Afro-American Women and Their Work." In *The Works of Katherine Davis Chapman Tillman,* edited by Claudia Tate, 70–92. New York: Oxford University Press, 1991.

———. "Paying Professions for Colored Girls." In *The Works of Katherine Davis Chapman Tillman,* edited by Claudia Tate, 116–121. New York: Oxford University Press, 1991.

Trolander, Judith. *Professionalism and Social Change. From the Settlment House to the Neighborhood Centers, 1886 to Present.* New York: Columbia University Press, 1987.

Tucker, David M. "Miss Ida B. Wells and Memphis Lynching." *Phylon* 32 (Summer 1971): 112–122.

Tuttle, William M. "Contested Neighborhoods and Racial Violence: Prelude to the Chicago Riot of 1919." *Journal of Negro History* 55 (October 1970): 266–288.

————. *Race Riot: Chicago in the Red Summer of 1919*. New York: Atheneum, 1970.

Vandewalker, Nina C. *The Kindergarten in American Education*. New York: Macmillan, 1923.

Wald, Sadie. "Chicago House Conditions." *Charities and the Commons* 13 (December 30, 1905): 455–461.

Waring, Mary Fitzbutler. "Training and the Ballot." *The Crisis* 10 (August 1915): 185–186.

Washington, Josephine. "What the Club Does for the Club-Woman." *The Colored American Magazine* 7 (March 1907): 222–223.

Washington, Lucius William. *The Chicago Negro Business Men and Women and Where They Are Located*. Chicago: Chicago Association of Commerce, 1912.

Weber, Max. *Sociological Writings*. New York: Continuum, 1994.

Weiss, Nancy J. *The National Urban League, 1910–1940*. New York: Oxford University Press, 1974.

Wells-Barnett, Ida B. "Let the Afro-American Depend but on Himself." In *Black Women in White America,* edited by Gerda Lerner, 537–539. New York: Vintage Books, 1972.

————. *On Lynchings, Southern Horrors. Red Record Mob Ride in New Orleans*. New York: Arno Press, 1969.

Welter, Barbara. "The Cult of True Womanhood: 1820–1860." *American Quarterly* 18 (Summer 1966): 151–174.

————. *Dimity Convictions. The American Woman in the Nineteenth Century*. Athens: Ohio University Press, 1976.

Wesley, Charles Harris. *History of the National Association of Colored Women's Clubs. A Legacy of Service*. Washington, D.C.: National Association of Colored Women's Clubs, 1984.

Wheeler, A. Mitchell. "Conflict in the Illinois Woman Suffrage Movement of 1913." *Journal of the Illinois State Historical Society* 76 (Summer 1983): 95–114.

White, Deborah Gray. *Ar'n't I a Woman? Female Slaves in the Plantation South*. New York: W. W. Norton, 1985.

————. "The Cost of Club Work, the Price of Feminism." In *Visible Women: New Essays on American Activism,* edited by Nancy A. Hewitt and Suzanne Lebsock, 247–269. Urbana: University of Illinois Press, 1993.

Williams, Fannie Barrier. "The Accusations Are False." In *Black Women in White America,* edited by Gerda Lerner, 164–166. New York: Vintage Books, 1972.

————. "The Club Movement among the Colored Women." *The Voice of the Negro* 3 (March 1904): 99–102.

————. "The Colored Girl." *Voice of the Negro* 2 (June 1905): 400–403.

————. *The Colored Woman and Her Part in Race Regeneration.* 1900. Reprint, Miami: Mnemosyne, 1969 (page references are to the reprint edition).

————. "Colored Women of Chicago." *The Southern Workman* 43 (March 1914): 564–566.

————. "An Extension of Conference Spirit." *Voice of the Negro* 1 (July 1904): 300–303.

————. "The Frederick Douglass Centre." *Voice of the Negro* 1 (December 1904): 602–603.

————. "Industrial Education—Will It Solve the Negro Problem?" *The Colored American Magazine* 7 (July 1904): 491–495.

————. "The New Black Woman." In *Black Women in White America,* edited by Gerda Lerner, 575–576. New York: Vintage Books, 1972.

————. "Social Bonds in the 'Black Belt' of Chicago." *Charities* 15 (October 1905): 40–44.

————. "The Woman's Part in a Man's Business." *Voice of the Negro* 1 (July 1904): 543–547.

Williams, Katherine E. "The Alpha Suffrage Club." *Half-Century Magazine* (September 1916): 12.

Wilson, Jeremiah Moses. "Domestic Feminism, Conservatism, Sex Roles, and Black Women's Clubs, 1893–1896." *Journal of Social and Behavioral Science* 24 (1987): 166–177.

Wilson, William Julius. *The Declining Significance of Race.* 2d ed. Chicago: University of Chicago Press, 1980.

Wood, Junius. *The Negro in Chicago.* Chicago: Chicago Daily News, 1916.

Woods, Robert A., and Albert J. Kennedy, eds. *Handbook of Settlements.* New York: Charities Publication Committee, 1911.

Woodson, Carter G. *The History of the Negro Church.* 2d ed. Washington, D.C.: Associated Publishers, 1945.

Wright, R. R. "Social Work of the Negro Church." *Annals of the American Academy* 30 (November 1907): 81–93.

Wright. R. R. Jr. "The Negro in Times of Industrial Unrest." *Charities* 15 (October 1905): 69–73.

Wright, Zara. *Black and White Tangled Threads.* 1920. Reprint, New York: AMS Press, 1975.

Yates, Josephine Silone. "Kindergartens and Mothers' Clubs." *The Colored American Magazine* 8 (1905): 304–311.

————. "The National Association of Colored Women." *Voice of the Negro* 1 (July 1904): 283–287.

Yee, Shirley J. *Black Women Abolitionists. A Study in Activism, 1828–1860.* Knoxville: University of Tennessee Press, 1992.

Youcha, Geraldine. *Minding the Children. Child Care in America from Colonial Times to the Present.* New York: Scribner's, 1995.

Zaretsky, Eli. "The Place of the Family in the Origins of the Welfare State." In

Rethinking the Family. Some Feminist Questions, edited by Barrie Thorne and Marilyn Yalom, 188–244. New York: Longman, 1982.

Zorbaugh, Harvey W. *The Gold Coast and the Slum.* Chicago: University of Chicago Press, 1929.

UNPUBLISHED SOURCES

Crawley, Charlotte Asby. "Dependent Negro Children in Chicago in 1926." Master's thesis, University of Chicago, 1927.

Hendricks, Wanda A. "The Politics of Race: Black Women in Illinois, 1890–1920." Ph.D. diss., Purdue University, 1990.

Leonard, Kevin Barry. "Paternalism and the Rise of a Black Community in Evanston, Illinois: 1870–1930." Master's thesis, Northwestern University, 1982.

McClellan, Larry, and Dave Bartlett. *The Final Ministry of Amanda Berry Smith. An Orphanage in Harvey, Illinois.* Paper presented at the fourth annual conference on Rhetoric and the Historical Imagination, Normal, Ill., December 10, 1994.

Smith, Susan Lynn. "The Black Women's Club Movement: Self-Improvement and Sisterhood, 1890–1915." Master's thesis, University of Wisconsin, 1986.

Townes, Emilie Maureen. "The Social and Moral Perspective of Ida B. Wells-Barnett as Resources for a Contemporary Afro-Feminist Christian Social Ethic." Ph.D. diss., Northwestern University, 1989.

INDEX

Social class, 4, 38, 45; and church membership, 31, 33, 95–96, 97; and club membership, 21–22, 24, 34–36, 98–99, 100, 105, 116, 123–28, 130–32, 132–33, 138; and residential segregation, 2, 3, 30–31, 32–33, 39–41, 135, 166 n. 11
Social hygiene, 180 n. 40
St. Thomas Episcopal Church, 31, 33
Suffrage clubs, 51–56
Suffrage, female, 7, 25, 45, 46–56, 109–10, 112, 170 n. 15; Second Ward, 14; African American and white clubs, 46–47, 170 n. 26, 171 n. 39. *See also* National Association of Colored Women

Taylor, Julius, 36, 50, 81, 86, 102, 126
Taylor, Mrs. Julius, 36, 155
Tenements, conditions of, 27, 40, 49
Terrell, Mary Church, 13, 19, 21
Theater productions, 55, 82, 87, 102, 103, 118
Tillman, Katherine Davis, 123, 163 n. 44, 182 n. 11
Trinity Mission, 43, 81, 96, 143
Twentieth Century Penny Club, 62–63

University of Chicago Settlement, 94
University Society, 95, 115–16, 131

Vice areas, 32, 41–42, 70, 71, 98, 164–65 n. 63
Volunteer Workers' Club, 69, 73–74, 75, 86, 127, 130, 132

Waring, Mary, 25, 49, 130, 155
Washington, Booker T., 11, 39, 62; and his industrial education model, 16–17, 20, 111, 112
Weber, Max, 4
Wells, Ida B., 33, 36, 120, 136, 137, 156; and club involvement, 59–60, 62, 77–78, 114, 117, 126, 130; and the Negro Fellowship League, 44, 45, 57–58, 97–98, 107; and the suffrage clubs, 52–54
Wells-Barnett, Ida B. *See* Wells, Ida B.
Wendell Phillips High School, 59–60, 120
Wendell Phillips Settlement, 43–44, 91, 95, 98, 99, 105, 143, 179 n. 23
West Side Woman's Club, 55, 78–79, 80, 95, 127
Whist clubs, 10, 124, 130–32, 186 n. 35
White women's clubs, 13; cooperation with African American clubs, 13, 51, 54, 55, 64, 99, 101, 115, 171 n. 39; discrimination against African American women, 13, 23, 51, 80, 163–64 n. 52; differences between African American and, 23–24, 138, 170 n. 26; General Federation of Women's Clubs, 51
Williams, Fannie Barrier, 114, 137, 156; on African American womanhood, 15, 16, 18, 100, 119; and club activities, 24, 36, 51, 117, 130; on club life, 10, 23, 24, 44; on the poor, 34, 41; and social class, 33, 35, 37, 39
Williams, Laing, 33, 34, 39, 50
Wilmette, 167 n. 19
Women's clubs, African American: listing of, 139–43
Woodlawn, 33, 135
Woolley, Celia Parker, 44, 51, 60, 74, 116, 126. *See also* Frederick Douglass Center

Yates, Josephine Silone, 15, 179
YMCA, African American, 36, 43, 74, 100
Youth clubs, 91, 98, 101–4, 107, 180 n. 43
YWCA, African American, 24, 37, 43, 48, 69, 70, 78, 81